Water under the Bridges

Newcastle's Twentieth Century

'What is the city but the people?'

William Shakespeare, *Coriolanus*, act 3 sc.1

Tyneside photographer Jimmy Forsyth records demolition men at the old and new Scotswood Bridges, 1967.

Water under the Bridges

Newcastle's Twentieth Century

Introduced by Professor Norman McCord

edited by Anna Flowers and Vanessa Histon

Tyne Bridge Publishing

Tyne Bridge Publishing is the Publications Section of Newcastle Libraries & Information Service.

Tyne Bridge Publishing gratefully acknowledge the support of the following Directorates of Newcastle City Council for their generous support in the production of this book:

City Works

Community & Housing

Education & Libraries

Social Services

We would also like to thank all the contributors to *Water Under the Bridges* for their unfailing hard work, enthusiasm and patience, particularly Professor Norman McCord for his supportive advice.

Many thanks, for their contributions of photographs, to Jimmy Forsyth; Mike Figgis; Tony Hillman; City Repro; Gateshead Council; Newcastle Chronicle & Journal Ltd.; Stagecoach; University of Northumbria; West Newcastle Local Studies.

Photographs not otherwise attributed are copyright of Newcastle Libraries and Information Service or held by them.

O.S. Landranger 88 map on page 16 is ©Crown Copyright. All rights reserved. Newcastle City Council. LA 07644 99/01.

Cover photograph: Dr Lynn F. Pearson

Back cover photograph: West Newcastle Local Studies

Cover design by Anthony Flowers

©Tyne Bridge Publishing
City of Newcastle upon Tyne
Education & Libraries Directorate
Newcastle Libraries & Information Service, 1999

ISBN: 1 85795 140 9

Printed by Elanders Hindson, North Tyneside

Contents

Foreword by Tony Flynn, Leader of Newcastle City Council

IT GIVES ME GREAT PLEASURE to introduce the series of essays contained in *Water Under the Bridges: Newcastle's Twentieth Century*. The timing of this publication is particularly appropriate, poised as we are at the birth of a new millennium. Here we have not only an opportunity to reflect on the history and achievements of our city, but a time to pause and consider our hopes for the future.

As a regional capital Newcastle upon Tyne has had particular significance in the shaping of the current social and political landscape, and will doubtless play a role in its future. The changes that both the city and the region have experienced within the last 100 years have been phenomenal. Over the next 100 years the acceleration of events will no doubt surpass even our wildest expectations.

The entertaining essays which follow have been written by specialists in their respective fields, from journalists to historians and university lecturers and they explore a variety of themes illustrating some significant aspects of Newcastle's 20th century. I am sure readers will find them as enjoyable and informative as I have.

In the beginning ... Newcastle from Byker Bridge c.1901.

A Backward Glance

Professor Norman McCord

IN THE FOLLOWING CHAPTERS, WHICH FORM THE CORE OF THIS BOOK, a group of local writers addresses a number of different aspects of the experience of the city of Newcastle upon Tyne during the 20th century. It could be argued that the pace of change in human affairs has accelerated ever since the first primitive communities came into existence. Certainly there can be no doubt that the 20th century has seen increasingly rapid transformations and the experience of this city is no exception.

At the beginning of the 20th century, Newcastle upon Tyne was the centre of a generally prosperous region which had seen tremendous and unprecedented growth in the previous few generations. The second half of the 19th century had seen some of the most remarkable changes in human history, including a ten-fold increase in international trade between 1850 and 1914. In the economically advanced regions there were dramatic, unprecedented and unforseeable increases in the size and distribution of population. Newcastle, and the surrounding region, had taken a prominent and well-recognised part in the shaping of these changes. In the great Age of Coal, Iron and Steam, the North East's inter-connected industrial elements of coal-mining, iron and steel making, engineering and shipbuilding had made a significant contribution to the shaping of the modern world.

Associated with these developments, the region of which Newcastle was the centre had developed a wide range of other activities. As population and prosperity increased, an ever-widening network of supporting enterprises was necessary in order to house, feed, clothe, educate, entertain, and transport the swollen numbers. At the beginning of this century Newcastle's retailing facilities already would have astonished the inhabitants of earlier periods. The goods available were now drawn from all over the world and sold in a variety of outlets ranging from the great department stores, such as Bainbridge and Fenwick, to the city's markets and the innumerable corner shops scattered throughout the growing urban area. Newcastle served as the commercial hub of one of Britain's most distinctive growth regions. The city was a great port, a centre of important industrial enterprises and the headquarters of the banking, insurance and trading activities which sustained the region's industrial base.

The standard of living for the majority of the population was higher than ever before. Basic schooling was freely available to all and caught all but a small minority of children. There remained great and obvious inequalities. Conspicuous displays of wealth abounded and co-existed with appalling poverty, much of it concentrated in what were still some of the worst slums in Britain, though the overwhelming majority of the population existed at various levels between these two extremes. The organisation of society was already much more complex than the situation in earlier periods. Occupations were more diverse and a growing service sector added further complexities to older patterns.

The North East towns generally came out badly from the league tables of social conditions which multiplied as late Victorian and Edwardian Britain increasingly investigated its own condition. Newcastle saw a great deal of drunkenness, and violent crime was a frequent occurrence. In the early 20th century prostitution was so well established that the city's police orders included stipulations, inherited from earlier versions, that officers should not interfere with prostitutes unless they were responsible for causing disturbances. Suffragettes sometimes resorted to outrageous tactics to draw attention to their cause. Industrial disputes were sometimes marked by violent confrontations.

Yet, as the present century opened, optimism seemed justified. Despite the enormous increases in population in the recent past, such aspects as health and housing were showing distinct signs of improvement. Although hindsight enables us to appreciate that the booming economy rested on a dangerously narrow base, this was not generally appreciated at the time. Demand for the basic products of the region's heavy industry remained generally buoyant in the early 20th century. Within the existing patterns of production, some far-sighted entrepreneurs already grasped at the need for further diversification. Armstrong directors began to move into motor-car and even aircraft production. In general, however, there was little appreciation that the prosperity, which had grown so astronomically in the recent past, might not be secure.

In a variety of ways, World War I was a watershed. The massive bloodshed and destruction shattered much of the easy optimism which had flourished in pre-war days. More than 830 old boys of Rutherford School enlisted in the armed forces; over 150 of them were killed. The figures for Dame Allan's School were 625 serving and 84 killed. The local impact of the swollen casualty lists was often emphasised by the local basis of much of the recruiting campaigns; heavy losses in one battle on the Western Front could be disproportionately felt by local communities which had sent numerous recruits to an individual regiment or battalion. It was generally believed that those who were killed or wounded in the war had suffered for a worthy cause, fighting for freedom and democracy against brutality and aggression. Throughout the inter-war years November 11th meant more to British society than 1st May or any other commemorative event.

To an extent which was slow to become appreciated, the post-1918 world had shifted irremediably. It was widely assumed, and sustained by a short post-war boom in local industries, that things would soon return to normal, while the needs of war-related production had reinforced the region's dependence upon a restricted range of heavy industry. The great majority of the women who had held men's jobs during the war gave way to returning servicemen, with varying degrees of willingness, and a fair amount of social pressure being exerted. In fact conditions had turned drastically against the region for which Newcastle was the centre. The naval shipbuilding race of the pre-war years had been replaced by an era in which fleets were drastically reduced. North East industries had depended heavily on overseas markets, many of which had been lost or reduced by wartime conditions. The spiral of interdependent prosperity which had tied the major industrial sectors of the region together was now replaced by an equally effective downward spiral, in which reduced demand for one product brought a domino effect on all. Coal-mining, iron and steel, engineering and shipbuilding had prospered together and now they were doomed to suffer together. Drop in demand for coal meant less demand for iron and steel, for engineering, for coal-carrying ships. Decline in shipbuilding orders brought decline in iron and steel, engineering and coal-mining. The North East contained a disproportionately large share of the industries which were particularly hard-hit by the inter-war depression years, a disproportionately small share of the newer industries which weathered the storm more successfully. The tragedy of the inter-war depression years, especially in the early 1930s, was heightened by the way in which many of the workers involved had, in immediately preceding generations, been seen – and had seen themselves – as an élite work force at the spearhead of the world's economic progress. As unemployment grew and became more prolonged, thousands of families, only recently well-paid and highly regarded in their own circles, now found themselves poor, dependent on meagre public assistance which, though probably more substantial than in any earlier period, still contrasted starkly with standards of living which had been experienced in the recent past.

Yet even here there are qualifications which have to be made. The impact of the depression was far from uniform. Throughout the inter-war years the majority of the local work force remained in employment, at a time when world prices for many staples were dropping significantly. Gosforth and Jesmond in the early 1930s were in many ways different in character from Byker and Scotswood (just as Whitley Bay was different from North Shields and even Hebburn different from Jarrow). Newcastle itself enjoyed some protection from the worst impact of the depression because of its role as a centre of administration, retail services, entertainment, banking, insurance – sectors which did not suffer the worst consequences of depression and unemployment. Unlike neighbouring communities such as Gateshead, Newcastle's role as regional capital provided the city with a variety of buildings of relatively high rateable value, which meant that local government revenue held up better than in communities dominated by thousands of terrace houses of low rating valuation.

The most important qualification, however, relates to the distinctly mixed nature of the district's inter-war experiences. The inter-war depression and unemployment burned so deeply into the North East's consciousness that it is not always remembered that the years 1918-1939 saw the greatest improvement in social conditions which the region had ever experienced. The 1921 census computed that a third of Newcastle's population was living in overcrowded housing. During the 1920s, 5,549

A meeting of unemployed men in the Bigg Market, 7 April 1930.

new houses were built in the city, with a leap to 22,160 during the 1930s, at a time when the increase in the city's population had slowed drastically. In 1927 an appeal raised £143,000 for improvements to Newcastle's Royal Victoria Infirmary. Newcastle General Hospital treated 3,048 patients in 1930, 6,695 in 1936. The Princess Mary Maternity Hospital had 16 beds in 1920, 86 at the beginning of World War II. In 1920, infant mortality in Newcastle was 101 per 1,000 (some other Tyneside towns were appreciably worse) as against a national average of 73; in 1938 the Newcastle figure was 66, still above the national average but showing a significant improvement. In 1920 whooping cough killed 45 in Newcastle, three in 1938. For the first time, the inter-war years saw sustained efforts to tackle the region's appalling slums, even if much remained to be done in later years.

The trough of the great inter-war depression lasted for only a few years. In 1935, the Newcastle postal area handled 11.8 million more letters than in 1934, and 2.5 million more telephone calls; wireless licences were up by 10,500. In 1936 there were further signs of improvement. By 1939, the effects of re-armament on the region's basic industries had promoted an extensive recovery, and unemployment levels had shrunk, with significant effects on the local standard of living. It remained true that the basic economic problems of the region had not been eradicated to any great extent; the dependence on the older and precarious basic industries remained great. Indeed the re-armament programme, a boon in other respects, confirmed this dangerous dependence. In 1943 coal, iron and steel, engineering and shipbuilding provided 40 per cent of all employment in the North East, and jobs indirectly depending on these sectors were another substantial proportion.

By 1940, the region's unemployment problem had effectively disappeared, for the time being, and the demands of war production were in the forefront of local activity. During the war there was only limited capital expenditure on modernising industrial equipment, and most of the extra demands of the war effort were met by working existing plant more intensively and increasing the relevant labour supply. At Elswick the Vickers Armstrong factory in 1940 held naval contracts worth £12 million, and a total of defence contracts of more than £20 million. The plant was worked to the maximum possible, and from 1943 the manufacture of Centurion tanks was a main preoccupation (and indeed kept the works busy for a total of 16 years).

Again there was a substantial volume of losses on active service for North East communities, although the impact was not as serious as in 1914-18. All three services provided their contributions to the casualty lists, and a region like North East England, with its maritime traditions, suffered then, as in 1914-18, from the tragic loss of merchant seamen which the war at sea entailed. Civilian casualties had been slight in World War I, but in 1939-45 German bombing meant that the civilian population was much more exposed to enemy action. The destruction of Newcastle's principal goods station in 1941 was the enemy's most conspicuous success here. Towns lower down the Tyne suffered more than Newcastle itself from the attacks; the borough of Tynemouth, for example, saw 329 bombing incidents between June 1940 and March 1943. The war years saw a significant display of national unity and fortitude.

The improvement in social conditions which had marked the inter-war years, managed to continue during the war. The pressures of war brought about reorganisation in social services and medical facilities, precursors of the post-1945 National Health Service. In 1938, 100 Tyneside children under 15 had died from tuberculosis; the 1947 figure was 85. Continued improvement in post-war years saw this drop to 18 in 1951, four in 1954. In 1930 there had been a total of 822 TB deaths on Tyneside; in 1986 there were 13. In 1930, two-thirds of all deaths on Tyneside were of those under 65; by 1986 the proportion was under one-quarter.

During the war the building of new houses was effectively halted, but building resumed on a large scale in post-war years. Within 20 years Newcastle's housing stock had been increased by more than a third, with much of the old slum property disappearing.

Newcastle Chronicle & Journal Ltd.

Guildford Place, Heaton, after bombing raid of the night of 25 April 1941. There were heavy casualties.

All was not unmixed gain, however. Large groups were removed from structurally decayed but coherent communities in older areas and decanted into new estates built on the periphery of the urban areas. In Newcastle's Newbiggin Hall Estate, for instance, an extensive area of new housing to the North West of the city was populated by families moved from old-established communities. No doubt the housing was usually a big improvement, but at first social amenities on the new estates were limited, and little thought had been given to the effect on limited incomes of the extra costs involved when families were removed to areas without easy access to city centre facilities. Some of the new post-war housing proved unsatisfactory; for instance, Newcastle's Noble Street flats of 1958 had been demolished by 1977. Generally, however, by 1981 in terms of over-crowding and poor housing quality, Newcastle, and Tyneside more generally, was at least up to national average. Other building sectors saw similar progress. When the Eldon Square Shopping Centre opened in the 1970s it was the biggest project of the kind in Europe, and subsequently it has proved capable of fighting off even the formidable competition provided by Gateshead's Metro Centre.

There were some significant differences between Newcastle society in the second half of the century and that of 1900. The temperance movement was a shadow of its vigorous existence in 1900. Support for organised religion dropped considerably (although for some worship of Newcastle United provided an acceptable substitute faith). Drunkenness still existed, but the 477 convictions for drunkenness in Newcastle in 1947 would have astonished a late Victorian chief constable by its moderation. Other murkier aspects of life continued. Prostitution was by no means dead, though the wartime years had probably marked a peak here. In 1953, Newcastle clinics reported 2,587 new cases of venereal dis-

Newcastle and its bridges at mid-century, c.1956. The West Road ribbons away through densely packed terraces and industry still flourishes beside the Tyne. There are no tower blocks yet.

ease. The continuance of this social problem, despite advances in medical techniques, was variously attributed to greater promiscuity and to the survival of significant inhibitions in sexual matters; conceivably it reflected both.

In the 1960s a charismatic leader of the city council, T. Dan Smith, made Newcastle famous as a centre of modernisation by municipal initiative, but in the next decade he went to prison because of his involvement in a web of corrupt practices centred on the architect John Poulson.

Educational provision improved markedly in the decades after 1945, with enormous investment of public funds in the state education system. In the later 1990s, Newcastle spends annually something over £150 million on this sector. At the time of writing, it could be fairly stated that there is no consensus of opinion as to how far this enormous expenditure has been proportionately rewarded in terms of educational and cultural improvement in cities like Newcastle. An official Newcastle report of 1955 noted, perhaps with some surprise, that: 'Young people seem able … to create for themselves a society which is colourful, healthy, satisfying and harmless but lacks much contact or concern with some of the traditional virtues and values, particularly those which are roughly called "spiritual"'.

When peace was restored in 1945, the fundamental weaknesses of the North East's old industrial structure re-emerged. Coal-mining, once the principal agent in promoting the region's economic expansion, suffered particularly badly. During the 1950s alone, 22,000 mining jobs were lost on the Great Northern Coalfield. In the mid-1980s, mining employed only two per cent of the Tyneside work force. Before the end of the century, this once-proud industry was effectively eliminated from the regional scene. The shrinkage of the old industrial base has not been an even progress, but fluctuated markedly within its general downward trend. For example, 1978-81 were bad years, during which Tyneside lost 11 per cent of total employment; another six per cent went in 1981-4. In January 1988, Tyneside's official unemployment rate was 15.4 per cent, as against a national figure of 9.6 per cent, but in one particularly depressed area of west Newcastle, the local figure in April 1987 was 39.4 per cent; at the same time Gosforth returned seven per cent.

There was a major shift in the structure of local employment. At the end of the 20th century, Newcastle's biggest employers are not great industrial enterprises, but include the social services complex at Longbenton, employing about 8,000, and the city's two universities. Work in the service sector, administration, education, entertainment and similar fields, provided 59 per cent of all Tyneside employment in 1978, 63 per cent in 1981. Not surprisingly, the regional centre of Newcastle has benefited from the growth in service employment.

During World War II there had emerged a substantial consensus that when peace came there would be no return to what was seen as the appalling conditions which hard-hit regions had experienced during the worst of the inter-war depression. Wartime governments had amassed a great variety of special powers and established higher levels of taxation. For the past half-century successive administrations have tried with varying degrees of energy and success to tackle the fundamental economic and social problems of regions like the North East. A wide variety of devices has been resorted to in order to try to provide a prosperous and balanced regional economy. The agencies involved have included the European Community, national and local government, semi-official bodies such as the Tyne and Wear Development Corporation, and private industry.

Some of the recent economic developments have been on a considerable scale. The offshore oil and gas industries have provided one growth area here. In 1999, those industries are served by more than 300 companies on Tyneside, directly providing more than 20,000 jobs – about the same level provided by Armstrong's before World War I. Newcastle, in such elements as Walker Riverside, profits directly from this sector as well as reaping a variety of indirect benefits from the investment and income provided.

The turnover at Newcastle Airport tripled between 1988 and 1993, with a quadrupling of profits, and further increases are reflected in major extensions to the facilities there. The Newcastle Business Park, largely based on information technology enterprises, produced more than 4,000 jobs by the mid-1990s. British Airways considered 13 other possible sites before deciding to site its £36 million investment in flight path computing in the Business Park. The Insurance and Financial Services headquarters of the Automobile Association employs 1,200 people there. In recent years, enormous resources have been devoted to such schemes as the rehabilitation of Newcastle's quayside area, but it will take time to see how far the results in practice correspond to the magnitude of the investment and efforts made here. The first fruits are undoubtedly impressive.

The jury must still be out as to how successful in the long run these formidable exertions will be. There must remain some doubts as to the inherent viability of some of the enterprises brought into existence by the provision of substantial external subsidies, and such local episodes as the unhappy story of the vast Siemens project in North Tyneside can be worrying. Nevertheless, in view of many recent signs of growth and expansion, there is room for optimism as to the economic future of Newcastle and the region for which it is the centre.

There can be no doubt that overall those living in Newcastle, as elsewhere, as the new century dawns, enjoy a standard of living much better than has ever been known at any earlier point in the city's long history. Life expectancy has seen a great extension during this century, and the twin processes of increased wealth and continual improvement in medical science have brought unprecedented improvements in the health of the people. The great majority of households now regard colour television, video recorders, microwave ovens, washing machines, holidays abroad, as normal accompaniments to everyday living, without perhaps much reflection on how lucky we are to have them. Retail services have attained a range and a degree of sophistication far outstripping those available in any earlier period. In many ways there is more freedom and toleration for the individual than at any earlier date and the overwhelming majority of the city's inhabitants enjoy sufficient resources to enable them to take advantage of this freedom.

All is not unmitigated gain however. Poverty, deprivation and suffering are still to be found, though not on anything like the scale known a few generations ago. In earlier periods, even in the earlier 20th century, the inhabitants of the city were in considerable measure more subject to communal and family discipline, living in close-knit local communities which could usually apply effective sanctions in the face of what was seen as anti-social behaviour. Much of this has now gone, and doubts remain as to how far self-discipline and individual responsibility are proving effective in replacing these earlier communal forces of social cohesion. No doubt such communal pressures have in the past appeared cruel and oppressive in some aspects, but their weakening has allowed occasional elements of individual irresponsibility to reveal themselves. Anyone who knows the Newcastle of 1999 will not need to be told that the widespread acquisition of comforts and freedom have coincided with increases in graffiti, litter and worse forms of senseless vandalism. It is for instance sad that many older people in the city are worried at the prospect of being out late in the city centre, even if their fears are often exaggerated. No doubt the lively social scene, which has given the city a national, or even international, reputation as a centre for recreation of various kinds, does not always exhibit itself in seemly fashion. The security cameras which survey much of the city centre are eloquent witnesses to some of the limitations in the achievements of modern British society.

The technological progress which they represent also points to one of the remarkable paradoxes evident in our society. Newcastle, at the end of the 20th century, exhibits a degree of individual freedom and opportunity, toleration and prosperity, greater than anything which has gone before. At the same time, the city's inhabitants are dependent upon a complex and sophisticated network of services and facilities provided by people whom they do not know, to feed them, house them, clothe them, entertain them, transport them and cater for an immense variety of other needs. This paradox means that the extent to which individual self-discipline can, within this increasingly inter-dependent fabric,

City Repro

And at the end of the century ...

take the place of earlier communal cohesive influences must be one of the crucial determinants of this society's future.

Overall, though, anyone who will soberly compare the condition of the people in Newcastle at the beginning and end of the 20th century, will surely conclude that, despite two world wars and a major international economic depression, life in the North East's regional capital has shown a general improvement far surpassing the achievements of any previous century. We need not expect to have attained perfection, but only wilful blindness will deny the significant progress in many spheres which the 20th century has brought. The chapters which follow explore in more detail a variety of themes within this complex process of development.

∿ Professor Norman McCord is Emeritus Professor of Social History at the University of Newcastle upon Tyne. His published works include: *North East England: The Region's Development 1760-1969*, 1979; *British History 1815-1906*, 1991; *North East History from the Air*, 1991; (With Richard Thompson) *The Northern Counties from AD 1000*, 1998.

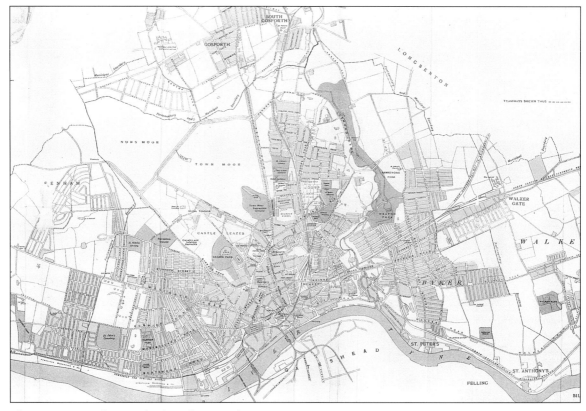

Above: An extract from Reid's Plan of Newcastle upon Tyne, 1919.

Below: An extract (reduced) from O.S. Landranger 88 Tyneside and Durham Area, 1998.

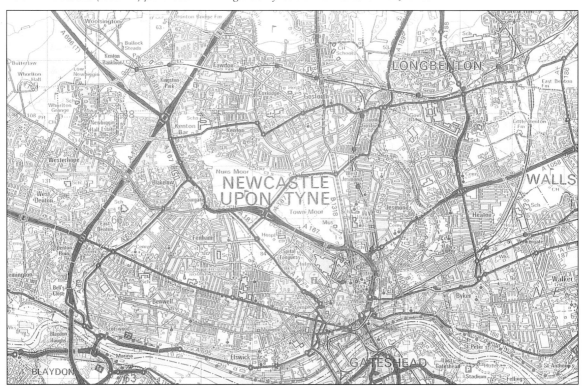

Cityscape

Dr Michael Barke and Professor R.J. Buswell

As with any large city, the story of Newcastle's growth in the 20th century is not just one of simple physical expansion. Just how that growth took place tells an interesting tale about changes in the way a city like Newcastle works, and the economic and social forces which cause those changes.

A comparison of Reid's Plan of Newcastle, 1919, and the 1998 O.S. Landranger Map of Newcastle upon Tyne, provides a 'snapshot' picture of the nature of such transformation. The visual images from these two periods stand in stark contrast. It is clear that, up to the beginning of the 20th century, the most important aspects of physical expansion were dictated by the River Tyne and the major roads that mainly follow the river to east and west, linking the city to other important centres – the Coast and Tyne Valley, Hexham and on to Carlisle. For most of the 20th century, although these routes remain important for growth and development, there has been massive increase in development in the areas lying between them. This was made possible by the invention of the internal combustion engine, and the flexibility it brought to both public and then private transport. It has also been accomplished through the agency of 'planning' – a much maligned aspect of the welfare state in post-war Britain. Without controls on land-use and transportation, without public policies for upgrading towns and cities, and conservation, largely introduced after the Second World War, Newcastle – and most other British cities – would have succumbed to relentless and distant sprawl, and the heart of the city left to stagnate. Only at the very end of the 20th century has the protective circle of the green-belt come under pressure. The commuting patterns, the popularity of city centre shopping, and the lively night life, are all witnesses to the way in which a Victorian city has been able to remodel itself to survive. Newcastle has remained a relatively compact, accessible – and increasingly sustainable – city over the last century. It has also, almost uniquely, managed to preserve a huge area of open space – the Town Moor – within one mile of the main business centre.

However, the plans of Newcastle at the beginning and end of the 20th century do indicate some fundamental changes in the 'texture' of the urban fabric over its course. The 1919 plan shows a town centre which still demonstrates traces of its medieval past with some narrow, irregular streets and many closes and alleyways. Superimposed upon this, of course, is the early 19th century 'New Town' of developer Richard Grainger with its more regular layout. Large amounts of industrial land alongside the river, with associated railway lines and sidings, give a further distinctive and powerful feel to the cityscape. But perhaps what catches the eye more than anything are the linear, geometric and highly regulated areas of housing – the long rows of dwellings of uniform size and standard which, regardless of the social class of their inhabitants, gave the built-up area a monotonous and standardised feel.

By the end of the 20th century living and working have become more mixed. It is with the broad out-lines of how this more varied cityscape developed that this chapter is concerned, in particular where and how people lived, where they worked and where they shopped.

Homes and Gardens

At the turn of the 19th and 20th centuries a number of movements came together to produce chang-ing attitudes to city living. At a national level, the combined effects of the growing Town Planning movement, the Garden City movement, and the example of a limited number of pioneer model hous-ing developments, created a climate of opinion which changed the way houses and housing were designed. Essentially 'anti-urban' in origin, these influences opened the way for a more 'romantic' view of the house, with the design of dwellings reflecting strong rural images – such as the country cottage. These influences were felt in Newcastle as several campaigns to develop the Walker area on Garden City (or, more accurately, Garden Suburb) lines demonstrate. Although the small development at Walkerville was the only pre-World War I success, the form of housing in the inter-war period in Newcastle, in both the private and public sectors, was powerfully influenced by these earlier ideas and ideals. Indeed, mainly because of a generous level of government help, the public sector initially set very high minimum standards which the private sector was virtually forced to match.

One of the earliest estates to be built by the Council was Pendower in the west of the city where the dwellings would be '… so designed and grouped as to be sequestered among the natural world, and the reproduction of an old English village.' Instead of the typical terraced housing density of 50 to the acre, Pendower and several similar estates, for example in High Heaton and Fenham, were built with around 12 to 14 houses to the acre. By 1930 the city council had built over 5,500 dwellings, about one third located in the exten-sive development of Walker in the east of the city. In the same period, the private sector had built just under 3,000 homes but 50 per cent of these had some form of state assistance.

Part of the High Heaton estate under construction in the 1920s. The design and layout of such housing was influenced by the Garden City movement. The emphasis on 'cottage' style can be seen in the use of gables, the design of the windows, and the high chimney-stacks.

Although influenced by the same ideals, and similar in many ways, there gradually began to emerge some telling differences between the two types of housing development. Development for private owners grew more important in the 1930s as circumstances combined to make house purchase relatively easier for those in regular employment. In the same decade, and somewhat ironically, economic difficulties were frequently cited as the reason for lowering the standard of public sector housing. Owner-occupiers increasingly sought to make sure that their homes 'looked' privately owned, but uniformity was the keynote on council estates. This was in part due to the economies of scale demanded in such things as the decoration of front doors, windows and gates.

Changes in family structure were a fundamental cause of changes in housing design. Households were significantly smaller than in the 19th century and the employment of servants had become much less common. At the same time more domestic technology was available to assist in running the home and 'convenience' for the housewife became the watchword. The middle-class owner-occupied home of the inter-war period became ever more powerfully influenced by rural, traditional images. This was epitomised by mock Tudor designs, the use of half timbering, herring-bone brickwork, leaded lights, ingle-nooks, tile-hung bays and porches, and gabled roofs, often with dormer windows.

Where new homes, both council and private, were built, depended largely on the nature and attitude of landowners. Although they realised that significant profit could be made by selling plots of land for public sector housing, many held out for higher prices and delayed the programme significantly. To the east, Newcastle merged with the formerly separate administrative area of Walker but the extensive area of council housing in this district is explained by the fact that Newcastle Council already owned a substantial amount of land there. Elsewhere, especially when the market for owner occupation started to expand in the 1930s, landowners increasingly differentiated between public and private in their allocation of sites for development. For example, the auction in 1920 of the Blackett-Ord estate in Newcastle's west end reserved 'superior land' north of the West Road for private sector development whilst the 'inferior land' on more difficult, steeply sloping sites was sold for council housing.

In the 1930s there was a marked shift in council housing policy, away from satisfying general needs and in favour of building replacements for households displaced by slum demolition. This housing was considerably different in character from the more usual developments. Less space was made available, so it often took the form of flats rather than conventional two-storey dwellings. Inadvertently, this change in policy also brought about two classes of council estate, with very different levels of popularity with tenants, which was to be a lasting legacy and problem in terms of later housing management. Much of this housing was built on small sites in inner areas where land had become available through slum clearance.

Environmental Health

Buckingham Street slum clearance area in 1937 with slum property on the right and replacement council housing on the left. Note the contrast in design and space standards with the High Heaton estate and the 'modernist' influence in the use of metal window frames.

The acute housing shortage after World War II lead to the introduction of temporary 'pre-fabs' which were constructed in a factory, brought to a site and erected on concrete slabs. Originally intended to last only 10 years, these South Gosforth prefabs are still popular with their residents.

World War II was a considerable watershed, in housing no less than in many other spheres, and from the 1940s onwards there were some fundamental changes in the character of home building. In the immediate post-war period, in contrast to the ideas of most of the inter-war years, there was a more determined effort on the part of national policy makers to come to terms with how city-dwellers lived. 'Rational' planning was to be the watchword. As far as house design was concerned, the semi-detached predominated to start with, but its essential style was different to that of the 1930s. Rather like the situation after World War I, there was an initial short-lived coming together of public and private sectors in terms of style, although of course the public sector built more houses. Metal window frames, the use of concrete, shallower pitched roofs, large picture windows, much plainer interior fixtures, and front doors partially or sometimes fully glazed, were all key features of this period. Many of these features may be seen in the 'pre-fabs' of the 1940s which, although intended to be only temporary dwellings, actually became very popular as permanent residences. Externally, simpler façades, often more 'Georgian' in style, became much more common and there was more uniformity between houses even in private developments.

Growth at this time was dictated by where the local authority owned or could obtain land, but acquisition did not guarantee development as some sites were 'sterilised' for a number of years owing to their possible value for coal mining and also because of drainage problems. In 1954, however, the highest number of dwellings built so far – 1,824 – was achieved. The main areas of expansion were in the outlying estates of Blakelaw, Longbenton, Montagu, Slatyford Lane and West Denton.

A further phase of development began in the mid to late 1950s and was marked by an increasing contrast between the private and public sectors, with the character of new developments being more socially distinctive. Although Newcastle lagged behind the national private housing boom of the mid 1950s it eventually came to share in it to some extent and, in relative terms, the city experienced a marked growth in home-ownership. The favourite style was still semi-detached, mock Georgian and its variants although layouts increasingly began to reflect new necessities, especially those relating to the motor car. It was in this period that many Newcastle families sought to buy their own homes for the first time, and the new estates reflected many of their social aspirations and pretensions, gently satirised in the character of Thelma in the long-running television series *The Likely Lads*. As well as a considerable increase in quantity, council housing also changed in quality with the dramatic emphasis on slum clearance. This period saw the end of many of the characteristic long terraced rows of mid to late 19th century flats and houses in Elswick, Benwell and Byker. The switch marked the brief triumph of industrialised building systems. Although 'high rise' development in Newcastle was limited compared to many cities, large numbers of three- and five-storey flats and maisonettes were built. These have, arguably, proved more of a problem than

The innovative Byker Wall is silhouetted against the city skyline in 1977.

many high rise blocks. The first slum clearance plan in 1953 scheduled 4,500 dwellings for demolition and a review of 1963 scheduled a further 5,820 (plus 3,580 to be demolished to make way for city centre improvement). Most of this bulldozing and redevelopment was in Elswick and Benwell in the west end and, of course, Byker in the east end, but there was still some council house building going on on the outskirts, for example at North Kenton and Newbiggin Hall. However, these developments also reflected new, less generous, space standards with the design of the North Kenton estate being changed at the insistence of central government to include a higher density of houses.

The late 1960s and 1970s saw a third phase of post-war housing development with a shift of emphasis to prolonging the life of older properties through improvement grants and renovation in General Improvement Areas (GIAs) and Housing Action Areas (HAAs). Newcastle lagged behind much of the rest of the country, largely because of the delays building up from the previous phase of policy – slum clearance. The city had attempted one of the most ambitious schemes of community-led renovation subsequent to slum clearance in the form of the Byker redevelopment. Its story is well known and does not need to be repeated, but this and other schemes took a long time to complete – much longer than originally intended and led to delays in the next phase of policy. Slum clearance schemes were still taking place in the late 1970s when they had all but come to an end in other parts of the country. Nevertheless, GIAs and HAAs were declared in Lemington, Scotswood, Benwell, Elswick, Arthur's Hill, Wingrove, Sandyford and Heaton (areas which otherwise would have seen much demolition) and in a number of these areas the Newcastle experience was more positive than in many other parts of the country. Mere declaration of GIA or HAA status did not guarantee that renovation would take place, for example because of the difficulty of persuading private landlords that it was worth their while. However, in Newcastle significant intervention by the council ensured that many houses within

City Repro

The St Thomas's Improvement Area, originally scheduled for demolition but reprieved when national policy swung in favour of prolonging the life of older houses. Built in the 1830s, the area is among the oldest and most handsome architecture remaining in the city centre.

these areas, including some on local authority estates, were modernised. Sometimes property was sold for owner-occupation and sometimes Housing Associations became involved. One very positive outcome from this renovation policy was the 'demonstration effect' of the successful renewal of the oldest domestic property left in the city centre, for example in the St Thomas's area which had been scheduled for demolition. The success of this scheme had an important impact on the return of residential living to central Newcastle.

The final phase of housing development has lasted from the late 1970s to the century's end, and although characterised by some as representing the triumph of the private sector, it has, in reality, seen important partnerships emerging between key players. While suburban areas have grown, albeit slowly, and sometimes changed their character through, for example, the sale of former council houses to sitting tenants, the location of much new development shows an important switch back to the inner areas of the city. Although developing so-called 'brown field' sites is currently a feature of national and local policy, 'in-fill' developments of various kinds had been happening for some time. For instance, a number of mature residential areas, containing large detached houses on large plots have experienced a 'second cycle' of residential development with additional dwellings being built on former gardens or, in some cases, complete redevelopment at higher densities. Such developments have begun to change the face of some suburbs. Significant residential development has taken place, however, as sites have become available through industrial decline or dereliction. Much of this development has been in special zones such as those under the control of the Urban Development Corporation. The design of dwellings has been strongly influenced by post-modern trends in architecture with extensive 'borrowing' from the styles of the past, the use of more decorative details (although sometimes carried out in a rather penny-pinching manner) and more colourful materials and painted external wood. In part, the search for more, smaller, urban sites is a product of social change with the important trend to smaller but more distinctive households – households which have specific but not necessarily long-term requirements from a residential area. Perhaps the main characteristic of contemporary housing developments is how they reflect the break up of traditional society, with distinctive groups based on age, ethnicity, incomes, life styles and even sexual orientation expressing their residential preferences with other groups being 'left behind' as a residual population.

Going to work

A striking feature of Reid's Plan of 1919 is the importance of industry. However, from being a major manufacturing centre of the UK at the start of the century, Newcastle has declined to a point where fewer than one in eight workers in the city are employed in factories – and this is typical of most British towns and cities. The relentless decline, apart from the wartime increases, was especially acute in the two depressions of the late 1920s to early 1930s and the 1980s. Nineteen per cent of factory jobs were lost between 1979 and 1981 alone. Some of the decline may be blamed on location, on both a local and national scale, but most of it was the result of long-term lack of demand. In other words, Newcastle was unable to sell its goods either in this country or abroad. It is also true to say that the type of manufacturing carried out in Newcastle did not respond quickly enough to changing market demands and competition, resulting in permanent losses of jobs and firms. The city pioneered the production of armaments, naval and commercial shipbuilding, electrical engineering and marine engineering but was slow to develop new products and processes. Despite some world-class examples of innovation, the manufacturing sector in this century has generally been characterised by low levels of research and development. For too long manufacturers persisted with the staples of ships, tanks, mining equipment, heavy generators, switchgear and marine engines, and emerging markets for new products went undeveloped. Although the changing pattern of industry on Tyneside has shown elements of decentralisation, it is dominated by absolute decline, especially in the riverside area. A classic example is the demise of Vickers (Armstrong's) from its heyday in the Edwardian era, when it employed 20,000 workers making anything from railway engines, ships, even motor cars, to a general engineering works that could not find new products (Vickers), to the sad rump of a relocated factory making tanks in lower Scotswood. The ten hectare industrial site in Elswick was bulldozed to the ground in 1989 and in its

Armstrong's Works in Elswick in 1900. The most potent physical symbol of Tyneside's heavy industrial past and one with a massive impact on the cityscape.

place rose the Newcastle Business Park, a location for office-based services rather than manufacturing industry.

Unlike some other British cities, Newcastle's industrial structure has been dominated by a small number of large firms through most of the century – Armstrongs, Parsons, Hawthorn Leslie, Mitchells. There have been, and remain, too few small and medium-sized enterprises, making this sector vulnerable to changing demand. This characteristic continued to the very end of the century on Tyneside, if not in Newcastle itself, with the collapse or contraction of large, and often multinational firms such as Siemens or Rolls Royce. The process of merger, acquisition and take-over with accompanying rationalisation has frequently been observed in Newcastle this century – Andrews Liver Salts taken over by the US company Sterling Chemicals, Parsons taken over by Siemens (1997), Armstrongs merged with the Manchester-based firm of Vickers in 1927 – but rarely has it been able to safeguard either plants or jobs for long. In this Newcastle is not unique. It is far from alone amongst Britain's industrial areas in exhibiting a de-industrialisation that began irreversibly in mid 1960s.

If Newcastle's economy seemed to be dominated by its manufacturing industry before World War I, at that time the majority of people actually worked in the service sector. As in most late Victorian cities, a substantial number of workers were employed in insurance (Newcastle specialised in marine and engine insurance), in the legal profession, in property, in banking and in retailing. In most cases the city acted as the regional centre for services that were closely linked to the industrial base of the area. By the 1930s the offices that housed these activities, especially those associated with shipping, were in the Quayside area, but the major concentration had developed in the New Town – in Grey Street, Grainger Street and Market Street – where they had replaced some of the retailing activity that had developed in the mid to late 19th century. This geographical pattern persisted until the shipping, engineering and coal trades declined in the 1950s and 1960s. Whilst some finance and banking activities have remained at prestigious addresses such as Grey Street, many of the new and expanding services such as the building societies that were re-invigorated by the Finance Act of 1986, sought new locations out of the town centre. Northern Rock set the trend by moving to Gosforth in 1966 and later

Malcolm Maybury

The site of Armstrong's Works today. Offices replace factories. Landscaped gardens replace railway sidings and scrapyards. However, local unemployment is unacceptably high.

acquired enough land to expand in situ when it became a bank with a national presence in 1996.

Both land-use planning policies and national urban development policies affected the location of services. In the case of higher and further education, for example, the city's post-war plans encouraged the development and expansion of Newcastle University to the north of Percy Street and the Haymarket after it became independent of Durham University in 1963. During the T. Dan Smith and Wilfred Burns era the city enacted the first large scale Compulsory Purchase Order on 10.8 hectares of land around the eastern end of Northumberland Road, St Mary's Place and Sandyford Lane to create a site for what was to become Newcastle Polytechnic in 1969, later the University of Northumbria (1992). These two Universities today employ over 6,000 people, educate 35,000 students and have an annual turnover in excess of £200 million. Although they have suburban outposts it is interesting to note that both institutions have focused their development on inner city sites with good access to the central business district and to city transport as envisaged in the 1963 Plan Review.

The other policy 'force' that has kept so much office-based activity in the core of the city has been the various urban renewal or regeneration policies coming from central government since the 1980s. These include Enterprise Zones (1982), the Urban Development Corporation (1988-1998), Single Regeneration Budgets (1994) and the use of National Lottery funding. Most of them have had a property focus with a major role for the private sector and later partnerships with a wide range of stakeholders. The development of the Quayside, under the auspices of the Tyne and Wear Development Corporation, revived an important historical area whose economic raison d'être had slipped away after the 1960s, with offices, hotels, restaurants and law courts. Another example would be the revitalisation of Grainger Town to provide hotels, modern hi-tech office space and cultural facilities in one of Britain's most important planned neo-Classical Victorian townscapes. The state has also played a major part in the development of the health and social security services in Newcastle. Large scale social welfare reforms and policies, introduced by the Labour Government elected in 1945, resulted in Beveridge's plans for pensions and benefits being administered from what was to become Europe's largest single office complex, established in Longbenton in 1948. The National Health Service's foundation at about the same time saw the development of the city's major hospitals – the Royal Victoria Infirmary, the General and the Freeman. The two National Health Service Trusts now employ more than 7,000 people in the city; the Department of Social Security and its agencies employ about 12,000.

Going shopping

Planning was to play an important role in the development of retailing in the city after the passing of the Town and Country Planning Act in 1947 but significant developments had taken place long before this. Newcastle was a leader in the development of the department store in the UK in the late 19th century. Messrs Bainbridge and Fenwick had set up their large, imposing stores in the 1860s and 1880s respectively and both have retained city centre locations. Later, the Newcastle Co-operative Society opened its magnificent art deco store in Newgate Street in 1931-32. Unable to command these central locations, other department stores opened at less significant sites, such as Parrish's in Shields Road.

The massive scale of the Eldon Square shopping centre is evident from this March 1976 view. Whatever opinion one holds on the impact of planning in Newcastle there can be no doubt that the Eldon Square development allowed Newcastle's city centre to withstand the competition from 'out-of-town' shopping attractions.

Until World War II much retailing was local in ownership and small in scale. High quality goods were sold in the New Town with district centres such as Shields Road, the West Road and Gosforth High Street serving more local needs with a wide range of everyday goods. In the two decades either side of World War II branches of national chains in food, clothing and general retailing, including Woolworths, Burtons and Boots the Chemist established themselves in Northumberland Street, Blackett Street and New Bridge Street despite the fact that until 1973 the A1 sliced through through a city centre that was constantly disfigured and polluted by lorries, buses and cars.

The focus of shopping between the beginning and middle of this century gradually shifted further north. This movement was encouraged by the proposals of the 1963 and 1973 Plan Reviews. The latter introduced a late 20th century element into the Newcastle townscape – the shopping mall – first in the Newgate Centre in 1969 and later in the large scale development of Eldon Square. These necessitated the demolition of large areas of shops, markets, cinemas and residences to accommodate a series of indoor streets and a controlled environment, attractive to some, but for the most part blank and characterless externally. If aesthetically off-putting to many, Eldon Square shopping centre has been a great success in terms of retail sales and turnover, popularity, and employment opportunities, particularly after it was extended to include in effect other major shopping zones such as Northumberland Street, Monument Mall, the Green Market and Eldon Gardens. The recent (1998) pedestrianisation of Northumberland Street and of the upper parts of Grainger Street, Blackett Street and Grey Street (around Grey's Monument) is creating a more relaxed, traffic free environment for shoppers at the end of the century. Newcastle city centre's shopping space has expanded considerably since the 1920s and has mostly managed to survive the competitive threat posed by the out-of-town Metro Centre originally established in the Enterprise Zone of Gateshead. Indeed, the recent massive expansion of Marks and Spencer, the refurbishment of Fenwick's and the redevelopment of the old Bainbridge site demonstrate considerable confidence in the retail future of the city centre.

City and Region

Compared to North American cities, British urban areas have been remarkable in keeping a significant proportion of their social and economic activities within a short distance of their original centres. In the case of Newcastle upon Tyne, the population has only risen from 267,000 in 1911 to 280,000 in 1991. Even though the city's boundaries were substantially expanded in 1974 a large proportion of the resident and working population of the city still lives within ten miles of Grey's Monument. Much manufacturing industry has disappeared but it has died in situ rather than being relocated. The growth

City Repro

Newcastle in 1990.

Malcolm Maybury

Quayside redevelopment. Modern flatted housing in the foreground with new offices and the Lawcourts to the rear. A completely new landscape for the river frontage.

of housing, offices, shops, entertainment and leisure, and public services has largely taken place in this same area. This is not to deny that suburban expansion has taken place, but the retention of shops and offices and the growth of other activities such as leisure-based industries, health and higher education has been remarkable and helps to define the city's character. The Quayside lost its shipping and small scale industries but is now a growth centre of hotels and restaurants; large areas of redundant industrial and transport land have been recycled into office complexes and residential developments. Richard Grainger's commercial New Town is being revivified for a range of new uses but within historically important buildings and historic townscape. As we have seen, there is an increasing resident population in the central business district as developers are prepared to build on small and awkward sites and convert the upper storeys of old buildings into apartments and flats.

The incorporation of new administrative areas in 1904, 1935 and 1974 enabled the suburban fringes to be managed as part of the greater city. The Edwardian and Georgian estates of the early part of this century such as Fenham, Kenton and Walker have been complemented by new developments in Gosforth, Dinnington and Newburn. Just as significantly, this process must be seen as part of the development of Tyneside as a whole which began at the turn of the century with the electrification of local rail networks and the building of arterial roads. Throughout this century Newcastle has become ever more dominant as the centre of the wider geographical region. Against this background of a suburbanising population, of de-industrialisation, of pressure at the city's edge, of changing but generally declining employment, it is largely planning and firmly directed urban policies – mostly centrally devised but locally administered – which have ensured Newcastle's position as a national city – and as the North East's regional capital.

∼ Dr Michael Barke is Reader in Human Geography and Professor R.J. Buswell is Head of the School of Behavioural and Environmental Sciences, University of Northumbria at Newcastle. They are editors of *Newcastle's Changing Map*, Newcastle City Libraries, 1993.

From Ships to Shops

Ken Smith

IN 1900 NEWCASTLE WAS A CITY OF HEAVY INDUSTRY at the heart of a region of heavy industry. Coal, steel, ships, locomotives, armaments and engines poured forth from this great regional capital to markets worldwide. Newcastle was the hub of intense activity, energy and endeavour. Its industries provided employment for a hard-working people. However, the city in the early 1900s was not merely a manufacturing centre, it was also a bustling port. The Quayside accommodated vessels of many descriptions. Cargoes of food, livestock and numerous other products were unloaded at the wharves on a daily basis. A large number of the ships ran between British and Continental ports and it was possible to travel as a passenger on steamers from the Quayside to destinations which included London, Aberdeen, Rotterdam, Antwerp, Oslo and Bergen.

As well as being a significant port linked to the North Sea by the watery highway of the Tyne, the city's river frontage was a place where ships were born and started out on their often adventurous

Newcastle Quayside bustles with activity c.1900.

A ship is born. The launch of the battlecruiser HMS Invincible at Armstrong Whitworth's Elswick Shipyard, Newcastle, on 13 April 1907. A crowd of 12,000 people turned out to watch the new ship enter the Tyne.

careers. Newcastle's riverside in 1900 featured three major shipyards. Using present day boundaries, furthest east, at Low Walker, was the Neptune Yard of John Wigham Richardson, founded in 1860.

The Neptune Yard was to gain a fine reputation for building cableships, the first, the *Colonia*, being delivered in 1902. Twenty-four of these vessels, built to lay and repair telegraph and telephone cables, were eventually constructed. By 1900, the yard had launched many queens of the ocean, among them the pioneering *Hornby Grange*, one of the world's first large refrigerated cargo ships, completed in 1890. Also of great credit to the yard was the elegant Spanish passenger liner and troopship, the *Alfonso XII*, delivered in 1888.

Wigham Richardson's merged in 1903 with C.S. Swan & Hunter, of the Wallsend Shipyard, to form Swan Hunter and Wigham Richardson Ltd. The amalgamation enabled the firms to combine their resources to bid for the prestigious *Mauretania* passenger ship contract. This 'marriage' between the Neptune and Wallsend yards was to prove highly successful.

Slightly further to the west of Neptune was the Low Walker Shipyard of Armstrong Whitworth, the great shipbuilding and armaments company which played a leading role in the economy of the city in the early 20th century. This shipyard had been founded by Charles Mitchell, a hard-working man of great talent who had eventually merged his business with Armstrong's. By 1900 the Low Walker yard had pioneered the construction of many of the world's early oil tankers, reducing the fire risks associated with this type of ship. Its first tanker, the *Massis*, was completed in 1881. Built for service in the Caspian Sea oil trade, she was followed by the *Poseidon* and *Armeniak*. The pioneering *Gluckauf*, regarded by many as the prototype of the modern day oil tanker, was launched at the yard in 1886 for German owners. In this ship the shell plating constituted an integral part of the oil tanks. Another example of Low Walker's craftsmanship and design skills was the British tanker *Silverlip*, launched in 1902. Armstrong Whitworth's Low Walker yard was also known for its construction of icebreakers. A number of these ships were delivered to Russia, Finland and Canada. The icebreaking train ferry *Baikal*, built for service on Lake Baikal in the middle of Siberia, was an extraordinary achievement by the workforce and management. The vessel was first constructed at the yard and then dismantled. The ship was then transported to Siberia in thousands of parts and reconstructed on the shores of the lake under the guidance of a team of men from Low Walker. Other notable icebreakers from the yard included the *Yermack*, launched in 1898 for the Russian government and which served in the Baltic Sea and Arctic Ocean. Also constructed for Russia were the icebreakers *Alexander Nevski* (later *Lenin*) and *Sviatogor* (later *Krasin*), both completed in 1917.

A little further to the west, at Walker, lay the land which was to become the site of Armstrong Whitworth's Walker Naval Yard. This famous shipbuilding base began production in 1912-1913. Its first vessel was the battleship HMS *Malaya*, which entered service during World War I, fought at Jutland in 1916 and survived to serve Britain during World War II.

The Walker Naval Yard produced many significant ships, including the world's first passenger liner to be driven by diesel motor engines, the *Gripsholm*, delivered to the Swedish American Line in 1925, and the battleship HMS *King George V*, which played a major role in the sinking of the *Bismarck* during World War II. The yard also launched destroyers, the cruiser HMS *Sheffield* and the aircraft carrier HMS *Victorious*, all of which served in the conflict. After the war, the output of the Walker slipways included prestigious passenger ships such as the *Ocean Monarch*, launched in 1950, Canadian Pacific's *Empress of England*, completed in 1957, and the *Empress of Canada*, completed in 1961.

Furthest west of Newcastle's shipyards was the Elswick Yard of Armstrong Whitworth, 11 miles from the mouth of the Tyne. Founded in 1884 by William Armstrong, later to become Lord Armstrong, by 1900 the yard was one of the world's most important builders of warships. Elswick had already launched a considerable number of ships for the Japanese, Chinese, Brazilian, Argentine and Chilean navies as well as for Britain. During the Russo-Japanese War, Elswick cruisers helped Admiral Togo's fleet to decisively defeat the Russians at the Battle of Tsushima in 1905. Indeed, cruisers were a speciality of the Elswick slipways.

The year 1900 saw the Elswick Yard launch the cruiser *Iwate* for Japan and the coastal defence battleships *Norge* and *Eidsvold* for Norway. The yard went on to build such vessels as the battlecruiser HMS *Invincible*, the battleships HMS *Canada*, HMS *Agincourt* and HMS *Superb* and the cruisers HMS *Hampshire* and HMS *Birmingham*. All these British warships fought at the Battle of Jutland in 1916. Tragically, the *Invincible* was sunk with great loss of life. World War I also saw the yard construct nine submarines. The last ship from Elswick was the aircraft carrier HMS *Eagle*, completed in 1924. Afterwards the yard was closed and all Armstrong Whitworth shipbuilding on the Tyne was switched to the Walker Naval Yard.

But the construction of ships was only one of several heavy industries which provided employment in Newcastle. The Elswick Shipyard was a part of the great Elswick Works of Armstrong Whitworth, which were the centre of a world famous armaments and engineering business. Founded by William Armstrong in 1847, the most important products in the early years of the works included Armstrong's hydraulic cranes. Later the great industrialist and inventor moved into the field of armaments, making Elswick one of the largest gun-manufacturing complexes in the world.

The Elswick Works had its own blast furnaces for the production of the iron and steel used in building its numerous products. By 1900 it was turning out hundreds of tons of high-quality steel every week. Using steel from its mills, Elswick produced many of the guns and their mountings for battleships which served during World War I. The company also opened an adjoining works at Scotswood to house its shell-filling and fuse-making departments. Many women were employed in the fuse factory during the war years 1914-18.

The addition of the Scotswood site meant that the company's various departments now stretched along the Tyne's banks for three quarters of a mile. By 1900 the firm employed around 20,000 people, many of them living close to the works in the city's West End. By 1913 the figure had risen to 25,000 and by the end of World War I 78,000 people worked for the company. Armstrong Whitworth was thus by far the largest employer in Newcastle and the whole of Tyneside.

Ships, guns and shells may have been the most important products of the company, but the year 1913 saw the firm begin the manufacture of aircraft. A factory was set up in an old skating rink on the

Workers leaving night shift at Elswick Works Shipyard c.1920. They are walking up Water Street towards Scotswood Road.

edge of the Dukes Moor in Grandstand Road, Gosforth, which turned out BE2a, BE2b, BE2c, FK3 and FK8 aircraft for the war effort. The FK8 proved to be one of the most successful and versatile biplanes during the conflict. The firm of Angus Sanderson, which had a factory in the city's St Thomas's Street, also produced FK8s.

The advent of the fighting tank proved to be a milestone development for Armstrong Whitworth. It manufactured the guns for the first tanks which went into action on the Somme in 1916. The following year over 100 Mark IV tanks were produced by the firm. The Mark IV was successfully deployed at the Battle of Cambrai in November 1917. The company went on to become a major tank manufacturer. But even before World War I this huge business empire had turned its attention to vehicle production. As early as 1902 Elswick had made a batch of motor-driven vehicles – a small van which ran on paraffin. By 1906 full-scale production of motor cars had begun, a factory for this purpose being opened at the Scotswood Works. Cars, as well as vans, continued to be made until the outbreak of hostilities in 1914. With the coming of peace in 1918 the market for armaments took a major downturn. The Elswick and Scotswood works had to find other orders. They began building railway locomotives, internal combustion engines, pneumatic tools and other civilian products.

At the end of 1927 most of the business interests of Armstrong Whitworth were merged with those of Vickers, with the resulting new company adopting the name Vickers-Armstrong. Re-armament in the 1930s and the outbreak of World War II in 1939 again saw the Elswick Works busy with military orders. Its output included Infantry (Valentine) Tanks, Light Tanks and Cruiser Tanks.

At the dawn of the 20th century, Newcastle was also the site of other engineering businesses of great national and international importance. One of the most significant of these was the Forth Street works of Robert Stephenson & Co, which during the 19th century had built many of the world's first railway locomotives. This business had been founded in 1825 by Robert Stephenson and his father George, the two men who pioneered the development of the railways. Indeed, many of the engines for the first public railway in the world, the Stockton & Darlington, had been constructed at Forth Street. In 1829 the works also produced the famous improved locomotive *Rocket*, delivered to the Liverpool & Manchester Railway. But Stephenson's did not confine itself to locomotive construction for markets worldwide. Under the talented direction of Robert the firm also built major bridges, boilers, and marine and stationary engines.

By 1900 Robert Stephenson had been dead for over 30 years, but the Forth Street works had continued to boom, manufacturing a wide range of railway engines. However, orders for locomotives were so numerous and many of the engines were now so large that the Forth Street premises were becoming too small. Accordingly, Stephenson's built a new works at Darlington in 1901-02 and most of the old works in Newcastle was sold to the neighbouring company of Hawthorn Leslie at Forth Banks.

The history of Hawthorn Leslie can be traced back to 1817 when Robert Hawthorn set up a business as a millwright in Forth Banks. Robert, who was joined by his brother William, later began building locomotives and marine engines as well as undertaking general engineering work. In 1872 R&W Hawthorn, as the firm was known, opened a marine engine building works at St Peter's in the East End of Newcastle. The St Peter's Works supplied many of the engines for ships built by Andrew Leslie's yard at Hebburn and it was not surprising that the two firms merged in 1885 to become Hawthorn Leslie & Co. Hawthorn Leslie's St Peter's Works began building Parsons turbine engines for ships in 1904 and received many orders during World War I. After the war the firm built some of the earliest diesel locomotives in a joint venture with English Electric. Then, in 1937, came an important development when the locomotive department of Hawthorn Leslie merged with Stephenson's to become Robert Stephenson & Hawthorns Ltd. While Darlington concentrated mainly on large locomotives, Forth Banks manufactured small ones, gaining a good reputation for industrial railway engines.

The St Peter's Works continued to build engines for ships under the banner of Hawthorn Leslie. Following World War II its workforce was engaged on turning out marine diesel and turbine engines for vessels built to replace those lost during the conflict. In the 1950s they were producing 12 diesel engines and four sets of turbines a year. Engines were produced for Hawthorn Leslie ships launched at Hebburn on the Tyne until 1960 and also for vessels built in Sunderland, Middlesbrough, Norway, and Germany.

The firms of Stephenson and Hawthorn Leslie were not the only engineering concerns which won the city world renown and acclaim for craftsmanship and technical knowhow. The brilliant engineer Sir Charles Parsons will always be associated with Newcastle. He set up his famous Heaton Works in 1889 to develop and manufacture his extraordinary invention, an efficient and practical steam turbine engine. The works staff initially numbered only 48, but from such a small beginning grew a venture which was to loom large in global importance. The turbines for Parsons' experimental vessel *Turbinia* were manufactured at Heaton, demonstrating to the world that this precision machinery was far superior to the reciprocating engine in terms of seagoing travel.

The Prince of Wales, later Edward VIII, on the right, visits Sir Charles Parson's Heaton Works in 1923. Sir Charles is centre.

Although the turbine was to be used to drive ships at fast speeds upon the oceans of the world, its greatest importance has been in the electricity industry. The turbine has enabled electricity to be generated cheaply and efficiently and in so doing has proved of incalculable value to the world. Parsons' Heaton Works in the east of Newcastle pioneered the production of turbo-generators for power stations throughout the globe. In 1901 the city of Elberfeld in Germany ordered two turbine units of 1,000 kilowatts from the company. Two years later Parsons supplied turbo-generators to the Neptune Bank Power Station, Wallsend.

The machinery grew ever larger and more powerful. In 1912 the Heaton Works built turbine machinery for the Fisk Street Power Station in Chicago. The Chicago staff were so impressed with their turbo-generator that they nicknamed it 'Old Reliability'. Indeed, the American owners were as delighted as their workers. Accordingly, in 1923 Parsons received a further order, this time for a 50,000 kilowatt turbo-generator to be supplied to the Crawford Avenue Power Station in Chicago. In 1937 a 50,000 kilowatt machinery order was received from the Bunnerong Power Station in Sydney, Australia.

The distinguished engineer also had a keen interest in optics, telescopes and binoculars. In 1925 Parsons took over a company of astronomical instrument makers, Sir Howard Grubb & Sons Ltd., which had been in danger of closing. The new company, Sir Howard Grubb, Parsons & Co, operated a major telescope works at Walkergate, not far from the Heaton Works. Parsons' production during World War II included tank, field gun and aircraft components as well as searchlights.

But ships and machinery needed metal and Newcastle played its part in supplying this vital material in the shape of steel. The steelworks of John Spencer at Newburn provided work for around 2,000 people and made steel plates for the illustrious Tyne-built passenger liner *Mauretania*, whose huge turbine engines were built by the Wallsend Slipway and Engineering Co Ltd. to the designs of Sir Charles Parsons. The Newburn steelworks closed in 1926, but it reopened again in 1928 and during World War II made gun barrels and springs.

In the early years of the 20th century the city's oldest heavy industry, coal mining, still flourished alongside the shipbuilding, engineering and steel concerns. Indeed, mining can been seen as the mother of all these enterprises. In 1900 coals still came from Newcastle, literally. Collieries within the city at that time (using present day boundaries) included Walker, Throckley Isabella, Coxlodge, Montague Caroline, Montague View, Elswick, North Elswick, Delaval Benwell, Benwell, Dinnington, Walbottle and North Walbottle. The Montague View colliery disaster at Scotswood in 1925 brought home to people the dangers which still faced pitmen, despite advances in safety. An inrush of water led to the deaths of 38 miners, including boys. Many of them are buried in Elswick Cemetery.

A spin-off from coal was the city's brick and tile industry. Fireclay was plentiful in the ground under sections of the coal measures. Pits and brickworks were therefore often operated together. Also won from the ground by hard

Tyne & Wear Archives

The funeral procession for the victims of the Montague View Pit disaster of 1925 winds through Scotswood.

Kenton Quarry, c.1900.

Lemington Glass Works, 1920s.

Demolition at Carr's Timber Yard, 1931.

toil was stone. Quarrying was an important Newcastle activity in the districts away from the city centre. For example, Kenton Quarry was well known for supplying grindstones to countries throughout the world. In addition, sandstone from Kenton was used in major buildings, including such Newcastle landmarks at St Thomas's Church. Brunton Quarry at Gosforth also turned out grindstones and stone for the construction industry. Rock hewn and blasted from the terra firma of Kenton and Brunton found its way to markets throughout Britain and beyond.

The busy and energetic capital of the North East did not confine itself solely to the heaviest industries. Glass-making, tanning and leather, flour milling, lead, brewing and electricity supply were among a large number of other enterprises for which the city was well known in the early 1900s. The Lemington Glass Works had been opened in the 18th century. Taken over by GEC in 1906, it began concentrating on the production of bulbs and tubes for electric lighting. By the late 1930s the works was turning out cathode ray tube bulbs for the earliest television sets. The last remaining cone of the now closed glassworks is still a prominent landmark. Nearby, at Scotswood, the works of Adamsez Ltd began producing porcelain sanitary-ware for toilets and bathrooms from 1903-04. Adamsez also operated its own fireclay mine a short distance to the north of its three-part works site on the banks of the Tyne. Edward and James Richardson's Leather Works at Elswick was another important employer in the west of the city. Its workforce made a wide variety of products, including shoe, chrome and sealskin leather, as well as belting and high-quality book-binding leather. Elswick also featured a major Lead Works, complete with a 174 ft shot tower.

The most successful representative of the pottery industry in Newcastle was the firm of C.T. Maling & Sons, which in 1900 had two potteries operating in the east of the city. These were the Ford A pottery at Ford

Street, Byker, in the Lower Ouseburn valley and the Ford B in Walker Road, St Lawrence. The majority of the workers were women and the total number of people employed in 1900 was more than 1,000. Maling porcelain, now sought after by collectors, included commemorative items, mugs, cups, jugs and plates. Jam and marmalade pots were one of the most important products for many years, being manufactured mainly at the Ford A pottery. In 1928-29 Maling began making items for the Rington's tea company, which were then sold to customers together with the tea. Porcelain produced for Rington's included teapots, tea caddies, vases, jugs and coffee pots.

Flour-milling was another prominent activity of the North East's regional capital. In 1896 the firm of Spillers took over the Phoenix Mill in The Close. Spillers' Tyne Mill at the extreme eastern end of the Quayside was opened in 1938 to replace the Phoenix.

The city was at the forefront in the development of electricity supply. In 1889 the Forth Banks power station of the Newcastle and District Electric Lighting Company became the first public electricity station in the world to use a turbo-generator. That same year saw the formation of the Newcastle Electric Supply Company which went on to open a power station at Pandon Dene to supply the east of the city. This plant was superseded by the Neptune Bank station at Wallsend in 1901. It was the first station in Britain to produce three phase electricity for industrial use.

Newcastle Breweries can trace its origins to the 1770s when the Gateshead businessman John Barras began operating a small, family-run brewery on the south bank of the Tyne. The business proved so successful that in 1884 John Barras Junior moved the operation to the present Tyne Brewery site in the centre of Newcastle. In 1890 the enterprise underwent further expansion when John Barras & Co amalgamated with four other North East brewers to form The Newcastle Breweries Ltd. The year 1900 saw the brewery continuing to enjoy success and two milestones in its history occurred after World War I with the launch of new beers destined to achieve great fame. These were Newcastle Brown Ale, launched in 1927, and Newcastle Exhibition, which made its debut in 1928, the year the Tyne Bridge was opened. The popularity of these beers further boosted the company's prosperity. The famous blue star trademark also appeared during the late 1920s. With its attractive design featuring a skyline of

A 1929 advertisement celebrates Newcastle Breweries' success at the 1928 Brewers' Exhibition.

A bustling scene outside Bainbridge & Co. on Market Street c.1912.

Newcastle's familiar landmarks the Castle Keep and the newly opened Tyne Bridge (1928), the logo soon came to be regarded as a symbol of Tyneside and the city in particular.

The second half of the 19th century saw the rise of Newcastle as a major shopping centre. In 1841 E.M. Bainbridge had opened a shop in Market Street and he went on to become one of the pioneers of the department store. Indeed, Newcastle can be said to have played a major role in the development of modern shopping. John J. Fenwick opened his store in Northumberland Street in 1882, later moving to other premises in the street. He even sent his two sons to Paris to learn the ways of the large continental department stores. Both Bainbridge and Fenwick encouraged people to come in and walk around their shops without any obligation to buy. People began to realise that they would not be unduly bothered by shop assistants and this was one factor in the success of the two businesses.

The city in the early 1900s also featured a host of miscellaneous businesses, some of them catering for a now forgotten market. The Newcastle Trades Directory of 1900 makes fascinating and sometimes amusing reading. Among the miscellaneous trades listed are billiard table manufacturers (Burroughes & Watts Ltd, 4 Northumberland Street); banjo maker (J. Clamp, 22 Simpson Street); feather dresser (Miss J. Tucker, 106 Hartington Street); feather dyer (W. Taylor, 1 Ashfield Terrace East and 1 St Mary's Place); and straw bonnet cleaner (Mrs J. Ripsher, 47 Elswick Row). The list also included pit clothing manufacturers (Dodds & Co, 7 Charlotte Square); whip maker (R. Tiffin, 1 Grainger Street); tallow chandler (M. Marshall, 22 Low Friar Street); slag crusher (E. Squire, St Nicholas Chambers, The Side); raquet maker (E. George, College Street); ship telegraph manufacturers (Chadburn & Son, 83 Quayside); lightning conductor erectors (F. Reid, Ferens & Co, 13 & 14 Railway Arches, Westgate Road); alkali manufacturers (United Alkali Co Ltd., Pandon Buildings, City Road); hat and cap manufacturers (Anderson & Miller, 14 Hood Street); and barrow proprietor (J. Fawcett, 17 Bell's Court, Pilgrim Street).

Today, a century on, much of the city's heavy industry has vanished along with the straw bonnet cleaner and feather dresser. The mines have closed, leaving little trace of their once flourishing existence. Some ceased production early in the century. Walker Colliery, for example, closed in 1918 at the end of World War I. The last mine to shut down was Brenkley Drift, in the far north of the present day city area, in 1985, shortly after the end of the miners' strike.

The Low Walker, Walker Naval and Elswick shipyards have also disappeared into history. The final ship to be built in Newcastle, the Type-22 frigate HMS *Chatham*, was launched at the Neptune Yard in 1988. Neptune (now operated by A&P Tyne) is the only shipyard remaining in the city. However, it no longer builds ships but instead carries out repair, refitting and conversion work. The steel mills have gone too, and the engineering sector has greatly contracted. The world renowned companies of Armstrong Whitworth, Stephenson, and Hawthorn Leslie have all vanished from the Newcastle scene.

However, heavy industry is still represented by such leading businesses as Vickers Defence Systems, a division of Vickers PLC, which produces tanks at its Armstrong Works, Scotswood, and Siemens Power Generation Ltd, which in 1997 bought the former Parsons' Heaton Works business. Vickers currently makes Challenger 2 Main Battle Tanks for the British Army at the Armstrong Works (site of the former Armstrong Whitworth Scotswood works) and in 1998 was employing 620 people there. The factory was opened in 1982, replacing the Elswick Works which closed in that year. Siemens Power Generation was employing around 890 in 1998 at the Heaton Works, and is continuing the turbine business pioneered by Parsons on the same site. It supplies a range of products from small steam turbines to large power stations and related services. Recent contracts have included the upgrading of steam turbines for the Alcan aluminium plant at Lynemouth in Northumberland.

Business parks have sprung up on the banks of the Tyne where two of the city's shipyards once stood. The land occupied by the Elswick Yard and Works is now the site of the Newcastle Business Park, home to many modern enterprises. Streets in the park are named after Armstrong's warships, providing a nostalgic link with the past. The former Walker Naval Yard site is also part of a new business park. Its streets also recall its former maritime connections.

Heavy industry has shrunk to a fraction of its former importance, but today, at the close of the 20th century, Newcastle has become the North East's premier shopping city. The original Mr Bainbridge and Mr Fenwick would, no doubt, have approved of this development. The city has also achieved a pre-eminent position in the leisure market. Its pubs, bars, nightclubs, discos and restaurants are a magnet for lively revellers from throughout Tyneside and beyond. Indeed, it is regarded as one of the world's top 'party' cities and this reputation is due in large part to its vibrant atmosphere and warm, friendly people. Newcastle Breweries still flourishes as it did in the early years of the century. In 1960 it merged with Scottish Brewers, makers of McEwan's and Youngers' beers, the resulting company becoming known as Scottish & Newcastle. In 1988 an attempt was made by Australian brewers Elders IXL to take over S&N but the bid was successfully defeated after a vigorous campaign, ending in 1989. Six years later S&N acquired Courage Ltd. and this led to the formation of Scottish Courage Ltd., the new beer business of S&N. Newcastle Breweries' most famous brand, Newcastle Brown Ale, is the biggest selling bottled beer in Britain and will always be strongly associated with the city. It has enjoyed great success in the export market, being now available in 45 countries.

High fashion in Eldon Square in 1976. The 'space-age' coffee shop still thrives.

With its origins in the 19th century, the steady development of Newcastle as a major retail centre is a success story of improvement and innovation. The showpiece Eldon Square shopping centre, which provides employment for 6,000 people, was opened in March 1976, with 17 stores and the new Greenmarket. This first phase was followed six months later by the opening of a second wave of shops, which included two new stores for Boots and Bainbridge (John Lewis Partnership). Both are among the largest of their companies' outlets. Integrated into Eldon Square is Newcastle's famous Fenwick department store as well as a Marks & Spencer's store, which is one of the most successful branches outside London. In November 1976 the Eldon Square Recreation Centre opened and it remains the largest indoor recreation centre in a shopping complex in Europe. Eldon Square has successfully fought back against its major rival, the MetroCentre at Gateshead, opened in 1987. At first, as the challenge of the MetroCentre asserted itself, the 'footfall' at Eldon Square fell by about 10 per cent, but within two years the 'footfall' returned to its previous level. This highly successful Newcastle shopping complex continues to flourish and is maintaining its market share.

Surveying the last 100 years of industry in Newcastle, one is struck by the sheer hard work and energy which the spirited people of the city have shown in turning out high-quality products for the world and in so doing making a major contribution to the British economy. The peacetime output of the city's shipyards, factories and mines has been of inestimable benefit to mankind. Coal, ships, locomotives, engines and many other products from Newcastle have made an enormous contribution to modern civilisation. Without the skill, labour and vigour of the Geordie working people Britain's efforts to overcome its foes and avoid defeat in the two world wars would have been seriously weakened. The people of Newcastle still display that quality of spirited endeavour which their forbears so ably demonstrated. As the city stands poised on the edge of the 21st century, its people remain its most priceless asset.

꙳ Ken Smith is a sub-editor on *The Journal*, Newcastle. He is author of *Turbinia*, 1996, *Mauretania*, 1997, *Tyne to Titanic*, 1998; co-author with Ian Rae of *Swans of the Tyne*, 1994 and *Built With Pride*, 1995; and co-author with Dick Keys of *Down Elswick Slipways*, 1996, *From Walker to the World*, 1997, and *Black Diamonds by Sea*, 1998, all published by Newcastle Libraries & Information Service.

Feeding the People

Dr Brian Bennison

THIS CHAPTER CONSIDERS HOW THE ORDINARY FOLK OF NEWCASTLE – members of what might once have been termed 'wage-earning households' – have shopped for food and fed themselves over the last 100 years. When the century opened the average Newcastle family allocated around two-thirds of its income to buying food and drink, including 32 lbs of bread and flour each week. Developments in world trade, improved transportation and refrigeration meant agricultural products from around the globe were appearing on stalls and shop counters on Tyneside. But a 1904 report on the spending of 1,944 'workmen's families' revealed an emphasis on basic provisions and stodgy, uninspiring meals.

The rising popularity of jams, treacles and syrups was testimony to their ability to add colour, sweetness and taste to the otherwise monotonous staples of bread, porridge and puddings. One Edwardian schoolboy in Newcastle remembered puddings 'made solid to fill up empty stomachs … almost the texture of lead'. One, made from tapioca, 'had the appearance and consistency of gela-tinised grape shot', but if plates were not cleared the child would be admonished with the expression

West Newcastle Local Studies

Gibson's fruit shop, 286 Scotswood Road, c.1925. Fruit became more common in the inter-war years.

A small local bakery c.1910.

'BBB than GFS', an abbreviated form of 'better belly burst than good food spoil'. In many homes meals of 'jam and bread' were regularly served, and as households hit upon hard times their food intake gradually reduced to a diet founded unremittingly on bread or grain. In his book, *Kiddar's Luck*, Jack Common recounts his mother's experience of trying to manage when the breadwinner had lost his job. As money became more scarce, there was 'less and less to eat, until mebbe there was only rice left, and it was rice every day, boiled rice, no milk, not much sugar. Eh, when I hear now how the poor Indians live I'm sorry for them, 'cos I know what it is'.

Relatively small amounts of what we now regard as the healthier foods, were consumed. Fruit on sale at the Sunday Quayside market in 1900 was described as 'wonderfully cheap', with barrow-loads of plums at 2lbs for a penny, pears and green grapes at a penny a half pound, plus bananas, apples, oranges, and tinned pineapples sold by the slice. But in general little fruit was eaten. The consumption of fresh milk was also limited, reflecting both its cost and suspicions about its quality. The notion of milk-drinking as a safe and nutritious activity did not apply at the beginning of the century: Newcastle's public analyst reported that tuberculosis matter was 'exceptionally active' in milk, dairies were often 'sanitarily defective' and gum, dextrine and starch were sometimes 'fraudulently mixed with inferior milk'.

With little opportunity in overcrowded Newcastle to keep hens, grow vegetables or poach, families looked to shops, markets and handcarts for their food. There was an extensive network of small shops across the city, ensuring provisions were available within yards of most homes and where the housewife with limited funds and storage facilities could make frequent purchases of small quantities. In 1900 the Grainger or 'Meat and Provision Market' was open until 11.30 PM on Saturdays, 10 PM on Fridays and 8 PM on other weekdays. A feature of one section, the Butcher Market, was the Saturday night scramble for meat when traders unable to keep their meat fresh over weekends sold it off very cheaply to 'swarms of boarding house keepers and bargain hunters, occasionally causing disorder'.

A directory for 1901 lists over 600 grocers, tea, flour and provision merchants in Newcastle, including such familiar names as the London & Newcastle Tea Company, Home & Colonial, Lipton's and, most conspicuously, the Newcastle upon Tyne Co-operative Society which had opened its first grocery store in 1861 and by 1900 had added another dozen. There were also a number of locally-based, independent owners with two or three grocery shops, often sited close together in the same district. But this still left a big proportion, perhaps three-quarters of all food sales, in the hands of single shopkeepers. The fundamental feature of the grocery trade remained the basic corner shop, or converted front parlour, offering long opening hours and the possibility of 'tick'. And the shopkeeper was not necessarily male; directories indicate that two-fifths of Newcastle's 'one-man' grocery stores were run by women.

But wherever people bought their food, it was served in domestic quantities by a shopkeeper or assistant who weighed out small amounts scooped from sacks or boxes, cut from blocks, or run off from barrels.

The city had over 300 butchers' shops and stalls in 1901, the vast majority single outlet, sole-proprietorships. Local meat came via the city's 124 licensed slaughterhouses of varying standards. Inspectors reported some as 'foul and dirty' and several slaughterhouses in Walker were wooden buildings without proper water supplies or drainage. But meat from abroad was growing in importance: in 1902 imports into the Tyne included 8,000 tons of bacon and pork (mainly from Denmark), and 3,000 tons each of beef and mutton from South America. Nevertheless, some butchers sought the patronage of those in higher income groups by concentrating on the more expensive home-produced meat. James Dickinson of Byker sold only 'meat carefully selected from the best home markets … no foreign or inferior descriptions being, under any circumstances, purveyed'. The type of meat products families were able to enjoy obviously depended on income levels, with the poorest households limited to cheap cuts and offal. Nothing was wasted and that natural by-product of cooking meat – the resultant 'drip' – would make subsequent reappearances to complement the innumerable slices of bread eaten. The staff of life itself was made in over seventy retail bakehouses, although the quantities of flour purchased by families also suggests a high incidence of home-baking.

At the turn-of-the-century Newcastle's 50 fishmongers were matched by the same number of fried fish shops, but by 1911 there were 140 of the latter. There were obvious attractions in visiting the cooked meat stalls, pie shops and fish fryers; they offered an alternative to meals prepared at home which were restricted by cooking facilities. If Jack Common's mother was in funds he was 'given a jug and sent off to the corner shop to get two penny pies and a penn'orth of peas' or told to 'run along to the fish-and chip saloon for a penny one and a ha'porth twice'. When there was no spare cash the family would make do with roast potatoes or an onion cut up in vinegar.

By 1914 the 'co-op store' held a prominent position in the heart of foodbuying Newcastle folk, although not as dominantly as might be supposed. The Newcastle Co-operative Society had 27,000

D. Proctor

Eastman's Ltd, one of a chain of family butchers, including three in Shields Road, around the turn of the century.

Beaumont Street Co-op, a typical branch, around the turn of the century.

members, but the development of other multiples and the continued survival of so many independent shops suggest that many co-operative members were patronising rival traders and not taking full advantage of the 2s 6d in the £1 dividend. The co-op was however the leading food retailer, with nineteen strategically placed grocery shops, seventeen greengrocery shops, 17 butchers and nine chilled meat departments. In 1914 food sales accounted for over three quarters of the Newcastle Co-operative Society's revenue.

When war was declared in 1914 the Government at first relied upon requests for voluntary self-restraint and the observance of 'meatless days', before eventually enforcing rationing. It began with sugar and then extended to butter and margarine, jam, tea, bacon and meat. Bread escaped the ration, although regulations about flour mixes created 'war bread' of a 'dirty-grey colour'. Meat rationing was compensated for by the arrival of abundant supplies of bacon – unkindly described by one source as 'fatty, unpleasant stuff' – from the United States. Housewives improvised with what was available and local newspapers printed recipes for such things as 'pig's head and potato pie'. New substitute foods were invented: the authorities came up with recipes for such delicacies as haricot-bean fritters, barley rissoles and savoury oatmeal pudding.

Despite the war, families were no worse fed and calorie consumption was much the same when the conflict ended as when it began. What had changed was the diet itself: a lot less meat, sugar and butter, but more flour, potatoes, bacon and margarine. It was those on higher incomes who most felt the gastronomic impact of rationing. State distribution of meat, for example, saw prime home-killed joints finding their way to poorer families for the first time. As price controls made the best cuts accessible to housewives in all parts of the city, some disgruntled consumers in Gosforth had to make do with their proportion of inferior frozen meat.

With the Armistice came the first slight relief on the food front as pre-war flour reappeared, but rationing continued for some time on such items as meat, sugar and butter. In these immediate post-war years there was no shortage of food in the sense that people went hungry, but the levels of wages and relief determined the extent to which families fell back on the cheapest forms of energy. As the 1920s came to a close unemployment hit hard and reduced many households to a grim, basic diet: a survey amongst North East households found a concentration on a handful of low-cost foods, the commonest being home-baked bread, suet puddings, stew and dumplings and some vegetable dishes such as pan haggerty. Meat was a once-a-week luxury and fresh milk rarely bought.

By the early 1930s unemployed households had little room for manoeuvre when managing the domestic budget. An enquiry amongst 230 Newcastle families concluded that 'after the deduction of the cost of rent, heat, light, insurance and clothing, the majority were left with inadequate resources for the purchase of food'. For them, bread formed the main food for breakfast, tea and supper, and for part of the week was the chief component of the mid-day meal. Even some of those equipped with gas ovens made bread but saved on fuel bills by taking it along to a local bakery to have it baked at a charge of 2d per half-stone of flour. The question of poverty and

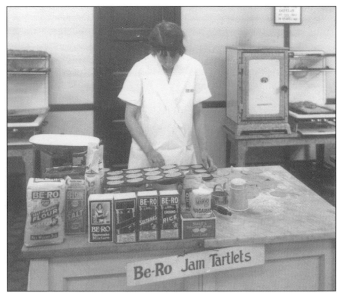

Demonstrating flour power at the 1929 North East Coast Exhibition.

malnutrition had been the focus of much debate between the wars: one 1936 report estimated that half the population had an inadequate diet and surveys in depressed areas revealed that energy intakes were back to nineteenth century levels. In one Tyneside unemployment blackspot almost one-third of the population was found to be undernourished.

In the inter-war period the number of grocers in Newcastle fell dramatically, the reduction in individual outlets coinciding with an increased concentration of ownership. In 1939 about two-fifths of shops were owned by multiples, some of them locally-based chains which had grown in recent decades. Inevitably, it was the Newcastle Co-operative Society which had most branches with 47 stores, followed by the Hadrian Supply Co with 22, Laws Stores with 20, the London & Newcastle Tea Company with 16, Moores Stores with 13 and Duncan's with eight.

Fruiterer's shops grew in number and by 1939 there were 27 belonging to the Newcastle Co-operative Society and eight branches of Bookless & Co. But fresh fruit, apart from apples, remained largely alien to the eating habits of the urban poor. Indeed, long after World War II the presence of fruit on the sideboard of a working-class household in which no member was ill was seen as a sign of affectation and aspirations towards poshness. Vegetables, other than potatoes, were not widely used other than to bulk up stews. Bought by price in two-penny bags, a request for 'two penn'orth of potstuff' was often heard in shops and markets.

Butchers' shops increased, but by 1939 the trader who sold only meat had effectively disappeared. The independent butcher survived but now stocked many processed products such as cooked meats, pies and sausages, and other food items like poultry, eggs, tinned soups and vegetables. The trend was towards the creation of multiple chains: as World War II began Newcastle had 33 butchers' shops belonging to the Newcastle Cooperative Society and five to the Walker Co-operative Society. One national firm, Dewhurst's, had six branches in the city and one local chain, R A Dodds, had nine outlets. The continued demand for butchery products was to some extent a consequence of the housewife's increased ability to prepare meals with even the cheapest and inferior cuts: by 1939 it was thought that three-quarters of local families had gas cookers.

Inter-war changes in retailing reflected the expansion of food manufacturing and the development of new processes. The variety of lines stocked by shops blossomed, as did the adoption of packaging, branding and advertising. Customers now looked for a greater choice of goods, prepackaged in smaller quantities, and handweighing in shops gave way to packing in warehouses. In the 1920s Duncan's, for example, developed a complex in South Shields which had the latest machinery for packing tea, cereals and flour; ham-cooking plants and smokehouses; and a printworks to produce paper bags, labels, coupons and posters. The firm's shops were standardised in red and black and managers instructed on windowdressing. Duncan's own brands – Tyne Towns and ARV (standing for all round value) – were vigorously promoted. A wave of standardisation enveloped grocery retailing, but Tyneside clung to some parochial preferences; one national chain was forced to concede that North East views on the 'cut and cure of bacon' and the 'degree of salt and colour in butter' were much more entrenched than in other parts of the kingdom.

One retailing success story in inter-war Britain was the development of the milk trade through home delivery by roundsmen; a pattern followed to a limited extent in the case of soft drinks and tea. Since 1907 Rington's had distributed its products directly to the housewife's door by horse-drawn cart and despite a few motorised vans being introduced in the 1920s, it was not until 1954 that there was complete mechanisation of the sales fleet.

World War II brought drastic changes in food supplies as imports were cut by half and home production of high energy foods stepped up. Rationing and food control were introduced. Housewives had to feed their families with reduced supplies of meat, eggs, fruit, sugar and fats, find ways of utilising increased supplies of potatoes and grains, and work with unfamiliar ingredients such as dried eggs and powdered milk. What the family ate was therefore largely determined by the authorities: rationing based on individual allowances – beginning in 1940 with butter, sugar and bacon – was extended and varied according to supplies; points systems covered other items such as tinned fruits and tinned fish; some foodstuffs were free from rationing but in very short supply; and comprehensive price controls were introduced. There were suspicions, particularly in the early days, about the fairness of the system. In 1941 the Newcastle Journal reported allegations of ample supplies of scarce food in restaurants whilst, according to Cllr Mrs Gibbons, 'housewives had trouble getting eatables for their husbands' bait'. In the same month the Crazy Gang's Nervo & Knox were cautioned about the wasteful use of flour in a slapstick pie-making routine at the Newcastle Empire.

The Ministry of Food was eager to inform the public of alternative recipes, substitute foods and different cooking methods. For example, previously unknown breeds of fish went on sale accompanied by doggerel from the Ministry arguing that if fishermen were courageous enough to risk death to catch it, the rest of the population should be bold enough to eat it. Whalemeat became the most celebrated example, partly because of the ease with which it could be inserted into a Vera Lynn parody.

During the war Tynesiders were probably better, if less interestingly, fed than in the 1930s. The resourceful housewife acted upon official advice about the healthiness of split peas and sago, saved butter papers to grease pie dishes, substituted beetroot for sultanas in steamed puddings, opened up tea packets to find the last few grains and obeyed the rule of 'none for the pot'. Catering establishments in Newcastle offered 'Woolton Menus': the chef at the Conservative Club in Pilgrim Street was proud of his mock haggis made with chicken livers. Newcastle millers, Hindhaugh's, published two-penny wartime cookery books showing how to make the most of rations to produce 'dainty, inexpensive, highly nutritious dishes'.

These two shops are at the corner of Westmorland Road and Elswick East Terrace. The date is 1936. A butcher boy's delivery bicycle is parked outside the butchery department.

As war progressed and customary products disappeared from shelves, shopping became more about queuing and much less about choice. The range of goods on offer narrowed considerably and the variety within each category fell markedly: local biscuit-makers Wright's, for example, were making only a dozen types of biscuit in 1942 compared with almost 70 kinds when war broke out. Many pre-war brands of foodstuffs continued to be available during the war, although in some cases this was a result of their long shelf-life and the absence of sell-by-dates. The story is told of an excited shopper spotting a favourite brand of porridge oats in 1943, taking it home and discovering a competition on the packet with a 1937 closing date.

Not all wartime food was bought in and allotments and gardens contributed to the food supply. 'Dig for Victory Weeks' – with exhibitions in the Northumberland Road Baths Hall, complete with cookery demonstrations, films and brains trusts – offered guidance on all aspects of vegetable gardening 'from seed to saucepan'. In 1941 part of the school playing fields in Gosforth were ploughed and the school canteen declared self-sufficient in potatoes and swedes. In the same year, Newcastle's Town Moor & Parks Committee were appraised of a growing wave of onion thefts from the open spaces the city had given over to cultivation. Of course, a family's ability to supplement its diet with 'free food'

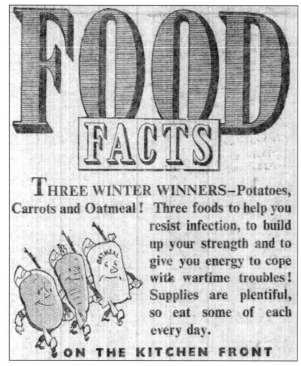

Wartime information from The Journal.

depended on access to land and there was less opportunity to 'dig for victory' in terraced streets. On the whole, the possession of a garden and the potential for enjoying 'free food' was a suburban phenomenon denied to the poorer citizens.

Thirteen months after war was declared an estimated 85,000 of Newcastle's residents regularly ate in places other then their own homes. For many people the main meal of a weekday was eaten in communal facilities, at school or at work. Lord Woolton's 1940 appeal for communal kitchens and feeding centres, offering the public a balanced meal at minimum cost, met with an immediate response in Newcastle where 14 were launched. Newcastle's first British Restaurant was opened in October 1941 at the Grand Assembly Rooms, Barras Bridge, where a three course meal plus a cup of tea could be had for a shilling. In its first two weeks the restaurant served 7,626 soups, 9432 main courses, 8,156 sweets and 6,032 cups of tea. For industrial and office workers, canteens were provided and during the six years of war the number of such facilities increased twelvefold. School dinners were the mainstay for most children: in 1945 Newcastle Education Committee was preparing 8,000 meals per day in its district kitchens.

World War II ended, and, as supplies gradually increased and rationing was phased out, people took advantage of the chance to sample again some of the foodstuffs denied them during the war and also turn their backs on some less appealing ones. National Food Surveys showed the adjustments being made to working-class diets in the immediate post-war years: for example, the reappearance on the market of many fruits saw consumption of fresh and tinned fruit rise significantly and people bought increasing amounts of jam. Conversely, the enforced reliance on vegetables in wartime, especially root crops, met with a swift reaction as post-war demand dropped. Another noticeable change in shopping habits was the two-thirds fall in flour bought between 1939 and 1949, although the North East's consumption was double the national average, indicating a continuance of the region's tradition of home-baking. It was still the case that the only literature found in many Newcastle homes, apart from a bible and rent book, was a volume of Be-Ro recipes.

The decade after 1939 had left the number of Co-operative Society outlets and branches of multiples almost constant, but the number of independent retailers down by one-third. This fall in independent grocers was really a move away from small shopkeepers triggered by wartime arrangements for rationing: housewives registered with those shops thought likely to stock a greater range of commodities and give a better chance of securing those non-rationed goods in short-supply. In 1950 around four-fifths of all food shops were independent but they were experiencing a rapidly failing share of the total food trade and by the late 1980s accounted for less than one fifth.

In 1955 that enduring symbol of convenience, refrigeration and self-service – the fish finger – arrived in Newcastle. In the ten years that followed the region experienced a huge increase in the consumption of convenience foods: for example, a trebling of frozen pea sales and staggering rises in the consumption of dehydrated soups and fruit juices. Other trends reflected a changing North

C. Fraser

Crowds gather at the opening of the Coxlodge Co-op in the 1950s.

East diet and the development of new products: poultry consumption rose sixfold between 1956 and 1965, the amount of instant coffee drank doubled in a little over four years from 1960 and whilst the consumption of potatoes fell, the amount of crisps eaten quadrupled. Bread sales fell, but the decline was confined to the uncut white loaf. Regional tastes died hard, however, and compared with rest of country the North East spent more on flour, biscuits, bacon, fish and chips, lard, potatoes, sweets and chocolate; but less on breakfast cereals, wet fish, fresh milk and fruit.

Between 1960 and 1980 the number of grocery shops in Britain more than halved, but the number of supermarkets rose almost twentyfold. The introduction of self-service had given the multiples a marked advantage over corner shops and, especially after the abolition of resale price maintenance in 1964, they could pursue a policy of 'piling high and selling cheap'. In 1960 the Newcastle Co-operative Society embarked upon a programme of re-equipping its shops with self-service facilities and the grocery department at North Kenton was the flagship of the society's 'modernisation and expansion scheme in the suburbs'. A few years later the society took delivery of two 'co-opmobiles', complete with checkout counters, air conditioning and refrigeration. These self-service shops on wheels toured outlying estates carrying four tons of merchandise.

Supermarkets were springing up across Newcastle. In 1961 'TV quiz king', Hughie Green, opened a Moores' supermarket in Newgate St which was heralded as the 'store in every woman's dreams'. To celebrate the occasion 250 cans of chopped pork were given away and a monster egg and pork pie, sixty feet long and weighing 56 lbs, was presented to Dr Barnardo's. In 1962, some 90 years after a young

A new tenant admires a gas cooker in 1962. One by-product of city re-housing schemes was that housewives now had access to the latest purpose-built kitchens.

Bishop Auckland counter assistant, Walter de Lancey Willson, started up on his own account, Walter Willson's opened their first self-service store.

With rehousing schemes came the creation of local shopping precincts to cater for the new residential areas such as that built at Denton Park and described at the time as 'a splendid example of the changing ideas in modern retailing'. Others, like Cruddas Park and Benwell, replaced the long ribbons of shops which disappeared from Scotswood Road and Elswick Road. At the Church Walk development in Walker, actress Margot Bryant (*Coronation Street*'s Minnie Caldwell) launched a Presto's supermarket. Its special opening offers included a free 1lb of lard with every packet of bacon bought. Brough's new supermarket in Gosforth promised coffee morning enthusiasts 246 varieties of biscuit and the suburb's more sophisticated cooks some 'luxury overseas products' such as artichokes, mangoes and courgettes.

Take-over and amalgamation saw the grocery trade dominated by a handful of national chains and the creation of much larger shops. As the range of goods magnified and the space required escalated, supermarkets migrated to low cost, out-of-town locations and food shopping moved towards a weekly, one-stop trip by car. As if to emphasise the fact that shopping had become an alternative leisure activity in its own right, Asda, in 1990, opened a store north of Gosforth on land previously occupied by a rugby stadium and dog-track; just as, 27 years earlier, the old Regal cinema in Two Ball Lonnen had become a supermarket. Meanwhile, large mixed-retailers in the centre of Newcastle – Woolworth's, British Home Stores and Bainbridge's ceased selling food.

The size of the new, edge-of-town stores partly reflects the magnitude of their food stockholding and the transformation in demand brought about by consumers' desires for both greater variety and greater convenience. There has been something of a revolution in dietary habits: families no longer stick to the long-established formula of 'meat and two veg', but seek healthier, more cosmopolitan foods. In the early 1970s Newcastle housewives were phoning the Post Office's 'dial-a-recipe' service much more than others and a newspaper was reporting that, as a result of the affluent society, tripe was no longer one of Tyneside's favourite foods. One of the more noticeable developments has been the vigour with which supermarkets have latched on to the provision of fresh fruit and vegetables, and in doing do have undermined the virtual monopoly once enjoyed by street markets and conventional greengrocers.

The message about healthy eating took longer to digest on Tyneside than in other parts of the country: when the Royal Turk's Head Hotel introduced Continental-style breakfasts the management observed many people treating them as a starter and following up with the full English version. In the late 1980s a local café owner admitted that despite adding salads and healthier foods to the menu, it was 'the old fatty favourites which really sell'. Nevertheless, distinct trends of healthier eating are plainly seen in consumption statistics. For example, in 1990 regional sales of packet sugar and lard were only one-third of what they were in 1971. In the four decades after 1950 the consumption of potatoes and bread more than halved, whilst the intake of breakfast cereals more than trebled and the amount of fruit juice drank increased almost thirty-fold. By the mid-1990s only one-third of northerners took sugar in tea or coffee, over one-quarter ate wholemeal bread and two-fifths ate high fibre cereal. Over half ate fruit at least five days per week and in 1996 the banana overtook the apple as the fresh fruit most eaten.

Newcastle, as elsewhere, has been lapped by a second wave of convenience foods. Earlier versions – such as powdered mashed potato, packet soups and tinned spaghetti – have given way to chilled foods, prepared vegetables and ready-made salads; all an indication that the archetypal image of the Geordie housewife slaving over a heavy stew-pot on a hot stove has finally been put to rest. Working women, labour saving equipment and modern lifestyles that prevent common, fixed mealtimes now require food that can be prepared quickly and easily. The same factors explain the degree to which meals and snacks are bought away from home. The last quarter of the 20th century will be seen as the time when the takeaway took off.

The concentration of ownership and the consolidation of outlets not only compressed food shopping onto fewer sites, but have erased from the city's fascia boards identities long associated with food buying in Newcastle. There are no longer any shops bearing the names of Brough's, Hadrian, Maypole, London & Newcastle, Thompson's Red Stamp Stores, Home & Colonial, Law's, Lipton's, Amos Hinton and Fine Fare. However, one famous name – Marks & Spencer – has bucked the inner-city trend by exploiting an expanding market amongst the busy, well-to-do adherents of all that is pre-washed, ready-to-eat or microwavable. At the other end of the spectrum, amongst the poorer communities, two newer names – Kwik Save and Netto – trade on the basis of a no-frills provision of more essential items; a technique first pioneered by Brough's in 1894.

But size is not everything: supermarkets do not have it all their own way. The corner shop of old may have been eclipsed but the last 15 years have seen its modern equivalent – the convenience store and the petrol station – emerge as the local's local shop. Surveys indicate that Tynesiders spend more than the national average in such 'corner shops'. For most citizens such establishments only serve to remedy a memory lapse when shopping elsewhere or to meet an emergency, and their purchases run to little more than the odd pint of milk, a snack and some paracetamol. But it is estimated that one in three people in the region avoid weekly shopping expeditions and buy small amounts of food everyday. For a minority, therefore, the nearest convenience store meets most of their needs.

As the Millennium approaches, less than one-fifth of North East household expenditure goes on food. That food now comes in a variety and form unimaginable 100 years earlier and is purchased in radically different circumstances. The domestic storage and preparation of foodstuffs has been transformed: as the century closes, 70 per cent of the region's households have microwave ovens, 84 per cent have deep freezes and almost all have refrigerators. The 20th century has seen remarkable changes in the way families are fed. But in 1999 feeding the family at home is only half the story: figures now show that 50 per cent of all food is consumed outside one's abode. Families still sit down together to eat, but some of those meals are likely to be cooked by professionals in restaurants or enjoyed at a fast food chain such as MacDonald's.

⌒ Dr Brian Bennison lectures in Economics at the University of Northumbria and is the author of *Brewers and Bottlers of Newcastle upon Tyne*, 1995, *A History of Newcastle's Public Houses: Volume 1: Heady Days*, 1996, *Volume 2: Heavy Nights*, 1997, *Volume 3: Lost Weekends*, 1998, all published by Newcastle Libraries & Information Service.

A high fat diet is promoted by this branch of the Hadrian Supply Company in 1937.

Getting About

Noel Hanson

PEOPLE HAVE ALWAYS MADE ROADS – from haphazard tracks and lanes to modern motorways. The Great North Road and the West Road are local sections of ancient roadways, and many of our city streets still follow paths formed hundreds of years ago. However, the 20th century's transport revolution changed the cityscape of Newcastle dramatically including the construction of the motorway through the city centre.

The roads of the 20th century have utilised a variety of surfaces, reflecting the traffic which has used them. For horse traffic of the earlier years, most surfaces were constructed of stone setts or cobbled; another common material was wood block paving. On tram routes, the section of road between the rails and for 18 inches (450mm) on each side was paved, as the tramway undertaking was obliged by law to maintain this area of the roadway. Occasionally, special or experimental surfaces were laid, for example in Market Street in the city centre, where for many years the road was surfaced with rubber blocks. The intention was to reduce noise and increase grip. Unfortunately, when the roadway was wet, the street became very slippery and dangerous. In later years, asphalt or tarmac became almost universal for both main and side roads, although concrete was frequently used during the 1920s and 1930s – for example on the Newcastle-Tynemouth Coast Road and on some suburban streets.

The city's road network constantly developed and improved throughout the century, either through the alteration of existing roads or the building of new ones, and bridges are an essential part of the road network.

Looking across the almost completed Tyne Bridge 22 May 1928. Deck laying is in progress. The finished steel deck would be covered in concrete and woodblock paving.

A scene at Cochrane Park at the opening of the Coast Road, 1927.

The Tyne Bridge was opened in 1928 as an important improvement to the A1 trunk road, eliminating the steep climbs to and from river level that a trip across the Swing Bridge required, and the delays consequent on that bridge opening for river traffic – as much as 30 times a day in the 1920s. The Tyne Bridge also relieved the load on the narrow road deck of the High Level Bridge. At the same time existing roads were being improved. During the Twenties, the West Road (or West Turnpike as it was frequently referred to then) was greatly widened westwards from the Wingrove area. Additionally, the very steep gradient of Denton Bank (or Benwell Hill, to give it its earlier name) was eased by cutting off the top of the hill west of the Fox & Hounds public house.

The late 1920s and early 1930s were of course the time of the Great Depression, and various measures were taken to try to improve the economic situation on Tyneside. The Tyne Bridge, bringing extra trade to the city, has already been mentioned, and a further measure was the construction of the Coast Road from Chillingham Road Ends in Newcastle to Billy Mill in Tynemouth. This was intended to give more direct communication between Newcastle and the coast – previously, it had always been necessary to use what we now call 'The Old Coast Road' via Benton and Shiremoor, or the congested riverside route via Wallsend and North Shields. The new Coast Road cut straight as a die eastwards with its glaring white concrete surface: 'an arterial motor road' to use the phraseology of the time. With great foresight, the road, although built as single carriageway, was made wide enough to be converted to dual carriageway if required. The original road was opened with ceremony in 1927.

There were many other improvements to the city's road network over the years of this century. For instance, vastly increasing road traffic in the 1950s and 1960s led to the widening of the Coast Road to dual carriageway, with underpasses, in 1967. The narrow and inadequate Scotswood suspension bridge (which dated from 1831) was replaced in 1967 by the present bow-arched steel bridge and approaches. The 1963 City Development Plan envisaged a network of urban motorways and dual carriageways threading through the city, entailing much demolition of property to accommodate them. The improvement of the Coast Road, mentioned above, was part of this Plan, but the most obvious result is the East Central Motorway, skirting the city centre from the Tyne Bridge to just north of Barras Bridge. This opened in 1975, and is now greatly overloaded with traffic for much of the day, as other routes through the city centre have been made tortuous or closed to traffic completely. The majority of the 1963 plan was never implemented.

The Central Motorway East, 1975, looking up the Great North Road.

The Tyne Bridge has been congested for many years, and in an attempt to redistribute traffic, the new Redheugh Bridge was opened in 1983 on the western edge of the central area, replacing an earlier structure. This bridge is the highest above river level of the city centre bridges. The West Central Boulevard is designed to link Redheugh Bridge with Barras Bridge, and is seen as an environ-

The Cradlewell Bypass takes shape alongside the old Benton Bank.

mentally friendly road, in contrast to the planned West Central Motorway of the 1963 Plan, which would have had a similar impact to that of the East Central. The Newcastle Western Bypass was planned before World War II, but did not fully open for traffic until 1991. It now carries the A1 trunk road round the city. Such was the delay in building it that it is not really a 'bypass', but a western ring route, being well within the built up area of the western suburbs. It links, via a new high level Blaydon Bridge, with the Gateshead Western Bypass, opened in the early 1970s.

Other measures to try to alleviate ever increasing road traffic congestion have been taken. One such improvement is the Cradlewell Bypass on Jesmond Road, which, after years of controversy, finally opened in 1996, giving relief to the shopping area at the Minories, easing the gradient of Benton Bank, and greatly improving the environment on the southern fringe of Jesmond Dene.

The trams

Horse tramways were first introduced to Newcastle in 1879, but the beginning of the 20th century coincided with the upsurge of electrification of urban tramways throughout the British Isles. Newcastle's tramways were bought by the City Council ('municipalised') and electrified in 1901. Tracks had to be re-laid to carry the heavier electric trams, and extended. A power station was built, a depot, and the electrical feeder network was installed. A hundred new tramcars were delivered. Construction of the new tracks started in April 1900, and the first electric tram ran in December 1901, by which date some 14.75 miles of track were ready – a great effort had been made! The power station, to generate electricity to run the trams, was located at the Manors, just off City Road. The undertaking's Head Office was also situated here. A large depot to house the trams was built at Byker, and horse tram depots at Haymarket, in the City centre, and Gosforth, in the northern suburbs, were altered for the electric cars. In 1904, a new depot was opened at Wingrove, in the west end of the City, to house cars for routes serving the western suburbs. Passenger numbers increased so much that by 1903 there were 169 trams in service. Some of these trams ran until the final closure of the system in 1950, so the Newcastle ratepayers certainly had their money's worth out of them!

The main core of the system was completed by 1904, and included connections with the Tyneside Tramways & Tramroads Company at Wallsend Boundary on Shields Road, Carrville boundary at Neptune Bank, and Henry Street, Gosforth. Electric trams now ran through Elswick and Benwell (Scotswood Road, Westmorland Road and Elswick Road routes), up Westgate Road to Wingrove and Benwell Grove areas (Westgate Road route), up Stanhope Street through Arthur's Hill, and meandered through Spital Tongues via Claremont Road. Newcastle trams ran up the Great North Road to Gosforth, and traversed Osborne Road in leafy Jesmond. They also provided transport for Heaton and Byker, along Shields Road, Heaton Road and Chillingham Road. Additionally, trams ran down Raby Street in Byker, connect-

Tram rails are laid on Pilgrim Street in 1901.

ing with the busy City Road/Walker Road service along the riverside, as did the Welbeck Road route in Walker.

Electric trams revolutionised urban street transport; they provided a much more frequent and reliable service than the horse trams, more cheaply and cleanly. Working on this success, the Corporation (as the City Council was known then) pressed on with further route extensions. The final section of Scotswood Road to Scotswood Bridge was opened in 1906, the Fenham service in 1907, the Shieldfield-Sandy-

Munitions workers crush-load coupled trams on Scotswood Road in 1917.

ford route in 1912, and (after reconstruction of Benton Bank) the extension of the Jesmond Road route to connect with the Heaton routes in 1913. The final prewar extension was of the Scotswood route out to Newburn in 1913. Further tramcars entered service to supply this constant extension of the system, many built by the coachbuilders at Byker Depot. The result was that, by the outbreak of the Great War in 1914, there were about 200 trams in the fleet.

At this time, the tramway undertaking served the then built-up area of the city, and provided transport in adjoining areas (such as Newburn, Gosforth and Wallsend) with cheap fares and a frequent service. In some cases, the trams promoted the development of certain areas – the Benwell Grove area in the west end, and the Benton Road estates in the north eastern suburbs.

The coming of World War I in 1914 put a stop to the development of the City's tramways, as there were greater priorities for both men and materials. The Scotswood routes and the Walker routes carried vast numbers of workers to the munitions factories and the shipyards respectively. Shortages of men to crew the trams meant that a number of trams were coupled together in pairs, driven by one man. Additionally, women were employed as conductresses. The big open-top double-bogie trams played an invaluable part – they could, reputedly, carry 200 passengers each, crush-loaded.

After Peace was declared in 1919, the tramways in Newcastle continued to forge ahead, under the able guidance of the long-serving General Manager, Mr Ernest Hatton. In the 1920s, further extensions took place, new trams were placed into service, and older ones modernised. Newcastle expanded westwards, both council and private housing estates being built in Benwell, Denton and

The opening of Gosforth Park Light Railway, Gosforth Park Grandstand Tramway Station, 1924.

Fenham, though there was development in High Heaton and Benton too. To serve these new suburbs, the tram routes were extended: the Fenham route to Slatyford and Westerhope; the Westgate route to the Fox & Hounds, and the Elswick Road route to Delaval Road, during the period 1922 to 1925. On the other side of the City, the Benton route had been extended to Forest Hall in 1921, and from Four Lane Ends to West Moor in the same year.

The most spectacular extension took place in 1924 when the Gosforth Park Light Railway opened with an official ceremony. Trams were run through the park, connecting the Great North Road and West Moor routes along the path of a private right-of-way. There was a tram station at the racecourse grandstand, to serve the racegoers.

Two more significant links were opened in 1923 and 1928, when rails were laid across the road deck of the High Level Bridge and across the new Tyne Bridge respectively, thus connecting the Newcastle system with that of the Gateshead & District Tramways Company. This enabled joint through services to be worked and was of great benefit to the travelling public. The Tyne Bridge extension was the last to be made to the Newcastle tramways.

To work these new routes, many of the older trams were rebuilt as totally enclosed cars – gone were the open platforms or top decks; and a new class of trams also entered service. They were enclosed cars with front exits, and many of the other trams were rebuilt with front exits also. The tram fleet reached its maximum of around 300 at this time.

However, this period saw trams begin to fall from favour with both the general public and transport operators. The public regarded trams as 'old-fashioned' and the cause of traffic congestion to the rapidly increasing numbers of motor vehicles. The Corporation saw their passengers being stolen by newly established motor bus companies, whilst they were still left with tracks and overhead wires to maintain, and to agonise over whether to build costly extensions to serve new housing estates, or run their own motor buses more cheaply. After 1930, the City's transport undertaking began to develop 'motor omnibus' services into new housing estates rather than build new tramways.

In 1935, the electric trolleybus made its debut in Newcastle, and many east-west tram routes were converted to trolleybus operation. By 1939, the number of tramcars had shrunk to 200 and only 30 miles of route were covered. Trams still provided the main form of transport on the Gateshead joint routes, as conversion of these routes would require the Gateshead company to agree to change to trolleybuses. Trams did soldier on through another world war, again carrying large numbers of passengers to work and play – factories were going full blast on Scotswood Road, and crowds went to the cinema and dance halls in the evenings in the days before television. The 'Holidays at Home' scheme also meant that extra loads were placed on the urban transport services.

After the return of peace in 1945, Newcastle Transport, under a new general manager, resumed its tram abandonment policy. Both track and the trams themselves were worn out by the war. The Throckley route was converted to diesel buses in 1946, and the Gosforth Park route to trolleybuses in 1948. Thereafter, in 1948 and 1949, the tram routes in the Heaton, Byker, Benton, Forest Hall and West Moor areas were converted to (mainly) trolleybus and motorbus operation. Finally, on 4 March 1950, the last Newcastle trams participating in the Saltwell and Wrekenton joint services with Gateshead were withdrawn in favour of motorbuses, and a once great tramway undertaking was no more.

The motorbuses

Though, as we have seen, Newcastle relied on trams for its main form of street passenger transport for many years, it was also a pioneer operator of motorbuses. In 1912, the transport undertaking needed to serve the then newly developing Westerhope area and the nearby North Walbottle Colliery. After considering various forms of transport, they eventually decided on petrol engined motorbuses. These ran from Westerhope via Cowgate to the junction of Barrack Road and Hunter's Road, Spital Tongues. Here they connected with the Fenham trams, and passengers completed their journey to the City by the trunk service tramcar. These early buses were open-top double-deckers, with solid tyres. On the rough roads of the period they must have given a bumpy ride to their passengers!

During the Great War petrol could not be obtained in the required quantities and some buses were converted to run on gas! A large inflatable gasbag was fixed onto the open top-deck and refilled at the Barracks terminus. In 1919, a steam bus and trailer were used on a route from Four Lane Ends to

Stagecoach

A tram replacement diesel bus turns from Raby Street on to Walker Road in 1948.

A motorbus and a trolleybus specially decorated for the 1953 Coronation celebrations.

Burradon. At the weekends it was used to remove horse manure from Corporation stables, but was thoroughly 'cleansed' afterwards!

In the 1920s, motorbuses were used by Newcastle Transport to act as feeders to the trams from such outlying places as Seaton Sluice and Branch End. More modern single-deck buses were used for these routes, but some London General-type double-deckers were purchased too. The 1930 Road Traffic Act changed bus route licensing, and Newcastle began to build up a network of suburban routes in the City, many of which are the basis of present-day bus routes. These filled gaps in the built-up area not served by trams, and served new estates beyond the existing tram termini. For instance, the No. 2 route ran from Denton to the City, and the No. 12 route from Milvain Avenue, Fenham, to the Haymarket.

Even in the Twenties, the Corporation promoted their motorbus services under the fleet name 'Blue Bus Services', and motorbuses continued to be painted this colour until 1949, when they changed to yellow. Most were double-deck 56-seaters, with a half-width cab and an open rear platform – the standard motorbus format for many years. Many Newcastle buses at this period had bodies built by Northern Coachbuilders of Spital Tongues.

The outbreak of World War Two in 1939 led to great shortages of both diesel fuel and rubber for tyres, and Newcastle Transport was forced to greatly curtail its motorbus services, the burden falling on the trams and the trolleybuses. After peace was declared in 1945, the economic circumstances had altered in favour of the diesel bus, rather than the trolleybus or the electric tramcar and Newcastle Transport converted a good proportion of of its ailing tram routes to motorbus operation. About £1.25million (1949 values) was spent on new vehicles: this was in spite of great difficulties in obtaining supplies of both motorbuses and trolleybuses in the immediate postwar period. Many of the new buses were built by Northern Coachbuilders. This enabled most of the prewar motorbuses to be withdrawn in the period 1945-1950.

About 150 new motorbuses served such expanding suburban areas as Westerhope, Blakelaw, Kenton and Longbenton, as well as being used for the Gateshead joint routes, and the long Haymarket to Tynemouth service via the Coast Road. In the 1950s, the diesel bus provided the cheapest urban passenger transport in the country.

In 1960, the Leyland Atlantean rear-engined, front-entrance motorbus made its debut with Newcastle Transport, and this type of bus became widely used throughout the country. Atlanteans were used to replace all the City's trolleybuses between 1963 and 1966. From the early 1950s declining passenger numbers were experienced, and growing traffic congestion affected the punctuality of services. The increasing number of private cars was a major contributory factor.

On 1 January 1970, the whole of Newcastle Transport was handed over to the newly formed Tyneside Passenger Transport Executive, and municipal operation of the City's bus services ceased. In 1974, the Tyneside PTE became the Tyne & Wear PTE. The formation of these bodies was intended to assist the coordination of road passenger transport in the area. However, there were still large numbers of National Bus Company (as it was then) buses running into, and through the City. Gradually, a common route numbering sequence was introduced and a visible sign of coordination was the painting of company-owned buses in PTE yellow.

The opening of the Tyne & Wear Metro rail rapid transit service in 1980 led the PTE to begin the integration of bus services with the Metro. In this scheme, bus services were reorganised to act as feeders to the Metro, which then became the main carrier on trunk routes in the area it served. Virtually all cross-Tyne bus services ceased, and services south of the river terminated at the Gateshead Metro Interchange. Congestion on the bridges over the river was thus reduced. This plan was still underway when Bus Deregulation was introduced in 1986. From that date, any operator could be granted a licence for bus services, and attempts at a rationally coordinated public transport service ceased. Now the Metro and bus services operated by Busways (who took over former PTE vehicles and assets) were in competition for passengers. Since 1986, passenger numbers have declined overall, for both modes of transport. Additionally, road congestion has increased greatly, further disrupting bus punctuality.

The Trolleybuses

In the 1930s, the electric trolleybus (a bus with a powerful electric motor and twin trolley booms on the roof) was rapidly replacing trams in many cities and towns in Great Britain. The decision of London Transport to replace its vast tramway system with trolleybuses gave a lead to other transport operators throughout the country.

The trolleybus made its appearance in Newcastle in 1935 when the Westgate Road to Wallsend (via Walker Road) tram route was converted to trolleybus operation. The route was greatly extended at its western end by means of a loop through West Benwell and Denton.

Trolleybuses were seen as introducing a form of transport which was fumeless, silent and which continued to justify the heavy investment which the City had made for the trams in the electrical power generation and distribution network. Also, the trolleybuses would use electricity generated by coal-fired power stations, thus giving employment to local miners. Trolleybuses were ideal for climbing the steep gradients of Newcastle, such as Denton Bank and Westgate Hill, being superior to contemporary motorbuses in this respect. They also had a greater seating capacity than equivalent motorbuses, as all Newcastle's prewar trolleybuses were 60-seat, front-exit, 3-axle vehicles.

The trolleybus route opened with a civic ceremony on 1 October 1935, and within a few months, was carrying 26 per cent more passengers than the trams had done. Encouraged by the success of their new trolleybuses, councillors decided to convert more tram routes to the new form of transport. So, in September 1937, the Stanhope Street-Welbeck Road trolleybus service opened. Trolleybuses were now stabled in two of Newcastle Transport's depots, Wingrove and Byker.

In 1938, more routes followed: the Fenham, Wallsend Boundary, and Osborne Road services to Central Station. Trolleybuses now penetrated all three depots, the Osborne Road vehicles operating from Haymarket Depot. The centre of Newcastle was a colourful, bustling mixture of public transport, as trams, trolleybuses and motorbuses threaded the central area, the first two in yellow, maroon and cream, and the latter in blue and cream. Trolleybuses were now established on the main trunk services in the city, carrying office, factory and shipyard workers, shoppers, and cinemagoers about their business. The swift acceleration and high passenger capacity of the electric vehicles were to be invaluable to the transport undertaking during the coming world conflict. Such was the regard with which the trolleybus was held at this period, that the then General Manager of Newcastle Transport drew up an ambitious plan to convert virtually all the tram routes to trolleybus operation, at a cost of nearly £400,000 (1939 values). By this year, Newcastle had over 100 trolleybuses running under 22.5 miles of overhead wiring.

However, World War II broke out in September 1939, and this brought a halt to the expansion of the City's network. Fortunately, Newcastle did not suffer greatly from German air-raids, but disruption to trolleybus (and tram) services was caused by the bombing of New Bridge Street Goods Station (the present day site of the Warner cinema) in 1941. Shortages of raw materials and personnel affected the transport undertaking, at a time of greatly increased passenger numbers from factories and shipyards working full out for the war effort. Newcastle Transport, experiencing a shortage of trolleybuses due to this traffic upsurge, was forced to hire trolleybuses, initially from Brighton in 1942, and later from Bournemouth.

The only tram route to be converted to trolleybuses during World War II was the City centre to Benwell (via Elswick Road) service in 1944. This was opened using wartime utility vehicles, featuring spartan wooden seats. The only tram route left in the west end of the City was the long Scotswood Road to Throckley one, though trams were still conspicuous in the east end and on the joint routes to Gateshead. Immediately after the end of hostilities in 1945, a new scheme was initiated to replace the remaining trams. A vast trolleybus network was envisaged, which included projected extensions to such

A trolleybus in the rain at the Haymarket around 1949.

places as Westerhope and Wideopen, conversion of the Gosforth Park Light Railway and the running of trolleybuses into all areas of Gateshead.

However, great difficulties were experienced in obtaining supplies of new trolleybuses after the war, and not all the intended routes were served by the electric vehicles. In contrast to prewar days, when they had built only one trolleybus body for Newcastle, Northern Coachbuilders supplied large numbers of the bodies for the postwar fleet of 186 vehicles.

The first trolleybus route to be opened after the war ran from the Central Station to Gosforth Park in 1948, banishing the trams from Gosforth and the Great North Road. Twenty new 70-seat double-deck trolleybuses, of a London Transport body design, were delivered for the new conversion. They were described as 'the largest, most modern road passenger vehicles in the country' at the time. Further deliveries of new trolley vehicles over the next two years enabled several tram routes to be converted to trolleybus operation: two new services between Denton and Benton; circular services between the Central Railway Station and Benton Park Road, and Central Station and Heaton were opened in 1948 and 1949.

Eventually, however, the Gateshead & District Company decided to convert its tram services to diesel buses, so trolleybuses never ran across the Tyne and High Level Bridges. Also, some Newcastle tram routes for instance, were converted to motorbuses, not trolleybuses. Still, the City's trolleybus system was one of the largest in the country, and the swift, silent electric vehicles carried their passengers on the main trunk services throughout the 1950s. The last major extension to the system was in 1956, when trolleybus wiring was erected in Silver Lonnen, to connect the new Slatyford Depot to the routes in the Denton area. New services linking Denton, Fenham, the City centre and Jesmond were introduced. This brought the total route mileage up to 37.

As has been suggested earlier, the economic climate at this time was swinging more and more in favour of the diesel-engined bus, and against the electric trolleybus (and the tramcar). The cost of electricity was rising, most of the trolleybus infrastructure was becoming worn out, new vehicles were becoming difficult to obtain, and the trolleybus was 'out of fashion' in road transport circles.

The impending redevelopment of the City led to a decision in 1962 to abandon the whole trolleybus system by 1968. The first route to be converted to diesel buses was, ironically, the Denton Square to Wallsend service, in 1963. However, the conversion timetable was speeded up so that the last route, Denton Square-Stanhope Street-Welbeck Road, closed on 1 October 1966. So disappeared one of the finest trolleybus systems in the country

It's Quicker by Rail

In the early years of the 20th century, the railway system serving the City contributed greatly to its economic wellbeing. This economy was founded on coal mining, heavy engineering, and shipbuilding, all of which were ideally suited to being served by rail transport. It must not be forgotten that the early railways of the 1830s were built for freight traffic; passengers were often an afterthought. In the years before the Great War, the railways were the universal carrier: such was the volume of general merchandise carried (as well as coal, coke, steel, iron ore, heavy engineering products) that the North Eastern Railway had two major goods stations in the City. These were the Forth, just west of the Central Station, and New Bridge Street, near Manors Station. Forth dealt with freight traffic from the south and west, whilst New Bridge Street handled freight from the north and east. Such diverse items as coal, flowers, furniture, bicycles and foodstuffs passed through them.

After 1919 things began to change; large numbers of army surplus motor

Serious travellers on the new electric train between Manors and Benton, 1904.

lorries were available, and the railways lost traffic. The economic depression of the 1930s did not help, although World War Two temporarily created extra railway use. After 1945, the vast increase in the use of road vehicles, coupled with road improvements hastened the decline of the railway's share of freight. Both Forth and New Bridge Street goods stations were closed in the 1960s, and British Rail officially declared individual wagonloads undesirable, concentrating on bulk loads.

A train arrives at Jesmond Station – next stop Manors.

Being at the centre of one of the country's major conurbations, Newcastle became a focus for local passenger trains from the surrounding areas of Tyneside, Northumberland and Durham. The services between the Central Station and coast stations such as Tynemouth and South Shields were particularly intensive, but there were also good services to stations at Blaydon or Lemington, for example.

As we have seen, local tramways were electrified in the early years of the century, and the railways experienced heavy inroads into their steam-hauled passenger traffic. To counteract tram competition, the North Eastern took the bold step of electrifying its suburban services to Tynemouth and Whitley Bay in 1904; this move quickly recaptured many of the lost passengers. From 1917, a circular Central-Coast-Central service was worked. Right up to the 1960s, the Coast electric trains carried large numbers of commuters and holidaymakers. The South Shields line was electrified in 1938. A new station was opened in 1933 at West Monkseaton to serve a developing area: similarly Longbenton station was opened in 1947.

North Eastern Railway's electric trains of 1904 closely followed American designs of the period, and took their current from third rails. In 1937-38, the LNER introduced new articulated electric multiple-units on the North Tyneside services, to replace the older North Eastern stock. British Railways announced the withdrawal of electric trains on the South Tyneside line to South Shields from 1963; diesel multiple-units would be cheaper to run. In 1967, the North Tyneside loop electric services followed, again replaced by diesel trains.

The Metro

Whilst the diesel trains worked the lines, the newly formed Tyneside PTE was formulating plans to build a Metro rapid transit electric railway. They gained powers under the Tyneside Metropolitan Railway Act, 1973, to construct new underground railway sections beneath central Newcastle and Gateshead, together with a new bridge over the Tyne, convert the North Tyneside loop line to Metro,

The Metro under construction at the Central Station, 1977.

and (using some different alignments) also the South Tyneside line. New trains, formed of articulated twin units taking their power from overhead wires, would work the intensive services.

Conversion started in the early 1970s, and the centres of both Newcastle and Gateshead saw many working sites as the underground sections were bored. Many of the existing railway stations were rebuilt, some closed, and some new ones opened (such as Shiremoor). The first section, from Haymarket to Tynemouth, opened in August 1980, the line from South Gosforth to Bank Foot in May 1981, and the official opening by Her Majesty the Queen took place in November 1981. She named the bridge across the Tyne the Queen Elizabeth II Bridge. An integrated transport system was planned. Further Metro extensions took place, such as from Pelaw to South Shields and extra stations such as Kingston Park opened. A major development was the line extension from Bank Foot to Newcastle Airport in 1991 which carries more passengers than anticipated. A further new line is planned from Pelaw to Sunderland.

With the publication in 1998 of the Labour Government's paper on integrated transport, the Metro should once again play a major role in carrying people around Newcastle, thus fulfilling the City Council's vision of an 'accessible city', with less dependence on the private car, more reliance on good quality public transport, and less traffic congestion.

⤳ Noel Hanson is a retired librarian, and an expert on transport of all kinds. He is the co-author with T.P. Canneaux of *Trolleybuses of Newcastle upon Tyne*, 1985, and author of *Gone ... But Not Forgotten 3: Trams, Trains and Trolleys*, 1989, and *Wheels*, 1996, all published by Newcastle Libraries & Information Service.

Newcastle On Show
The North East Coast Exhibition, 1929

Ian Ayris

THERE WAS NO DOUBT IN THE MINDS of the editor, correspondents and advertisers of the *Newcastle Journal* that the 20th century dawned not in the year 1900 but on 1 January 1901. On the previous day, the last day of the 19th century, a day of heavy rain and glowering skies which saw the century out 'weeping and breathing hard', Lord Armstrong, perhaps, regionally, the old century's most representational figure, was laid to rest. This, however, was not seen as a portent of any great sea change in the continuing industrial vigour and prosperity of Tyneside in the new century. 'Our population is well off, our working class are busy, earning good wages, contented and loyal, the country is richer than it ever was ... emerging from a groping twilight, the masses have better cultivated tastes and manners are less

Newcastle Chronicle & Journal Ltd.

Visitors to the North East Coast Exhibition are dwarfed by the size of the Palace of Industry.

A magnificent entrance off Claremont Road welcomed the visitor.

gross' trumpeted the newspaper in its New Year's message. The *Journal* called for a 'less feverish century than the nineteenth' but could not have envisaged that only two decades later the region would reach the end of the era of economic and industrial prominence it had enjoyed since the high Victorian years. Nor that it would spend a large part of the rest of the century attempting to grapple with the crippling effects of economic decline and addressing the region's role and position in the changing country. The holding of the North East Coast Exhibition in 1929 exemplified that search for a future and an identity. As the biggest single 'event' which took place in Newcastle in the 20th century it holds a notable position in the history of the city. ' It remains in the folk memory as one of the greatest and most enjoyable events in its history', observed one writer, but it also had a considerable economic and social significance beyond the pleasure it gave to its four million visitors.

Born in the years of deepening recession, the North East Coast Exhibition was first and foremost an enormous trade fair which sought to return the industry of the area to the level it had enjoyed when the region had been known as 'Britain's anvil' – not sliding into depression as it was when the exhibition was planned and held, but bustling and innovative as it had been in the years immediately preceding World War I. In those years the North East was responsible for the construction of a third of the world's ships. Exports of coal from the Tyne were at an all-time high. The period was the last golden age of the industrial North. When, over half a century later, the North of England Open Air Museum was established at Beamish to celebrate the region's industrial heritage these were the years it chose to represent. After World War I, however, things would never be the same again. Hopes that the new century would bring the moral and spiritual improvement for which the Journal yearned at the opening of the century were left on the uncut wire of World War I battlefields. Tens of thousands of men from Newcastle and the region had volunteered for service. The Northumberland Fusiliers, the regiment of the men of Tyneside, raised 51 battalions, more than any other regiment in the Great War. The loss to the region from the war was correspondingly high. On the infamous first day of the Battle of the Somme, for example, 70 officers and 2,440 men of the Northumberland Fusiliers were killed. In the small mining village of Prudhoe 70 doom-laden telegrams were delivered on one single day. By the early 1920s severe economic hardship added to the miserable social and psychological legacy of the war. 'What a terrible disappointment the 20th century has been', observed Winston Churchill in 1922.

The origins of the economic depression which gripped the region following the short-lived post-war boom lay in pre-war industrial strategy. The economy which the 1929 Exhibition sought to bolster had in fact been precarious even in its years of high achievement. Tyneside's economic base had been narrowed during the period from about 1880 to the 1914-18 war. The massive concentration of industrial activity in mining, shipbuilding, heavy engineering and armaments led to an over-reliance on goods and trades which the country and overseas buyers, in the wake of the war, could no longer afford. The situation was further exacerbated by the development of alternative and rival suppliers both nationally and internationally. The post-war boom saw the export of coal from the Tyne reach its peak of 21.5 million tons in 1923, but demand soon collapsed. The situation was more acute in the shipbuilding industry – 238,000 tons of shipping had been launched from Tyne yards in 1913. This figure would slump to 7,000 tons by 1933. Unemployment rose quickly from 1923 onwards – in shipbuilding to over 40 per cent. The aim of the Exhibition, said the Prince of Wales in his opening speech to the 100,000 first day visitors, was to revitalise these industries.

The idea that huge trade expositions could generate great interest and, more significantly, numerous orders, had been illustrated by the Great Exhibition of 1851 (or the Great Exhibition of the Works of industry of All Nations to give it its full title) held at the purpose-built Crystal Palace in Hyde Park. Organised through a Royal Commission headed by Prince Albert and including the likes of Robert Stephenson and Isambard Kingdom Brunel, it had attracted six million visitors and was followed by a surge of orders for the products of the 'Workshop of the World'. Other internationally important exhibitions followed in its wake. The New York World Fair was staged in 1853, although its 'Crystal Palace' leaked, many exhibits were damaged, visitors were drenched and the event lost money. In France Napoleon III sponsored the Paris Exhibition of 1855 but this also could not match the success of the Great Exhibition. Until the Golden Jubilee of Queen Victoria in 1887 Newcastle's experience of exhibitions had been limited to two major displays of Arts, Manufacture and Practical Science held at the Academy of Arts in Blackett Street in the 1840s, and the first North East Coast Exhibition of 1882 which had actually been based at Tynemouth and had a specifically nautical flavour, concentrating as it did on naval architecture and marine engineering.

The Exhibition held to mark the Golden Jubilee of Queen Victoria in 1887 was designed to show that, like the Queen herself, the region was nationally and internationally blooming. Originally 31.5 acres of the Town Moor were given over to the 1887 exhibition – the origins of Exhibition Park (by the time of the 1929 event the exhibition area had expanded to 125 acres). For the Jubilee Exhibition an enormous grandstand was constructed. 'Upon a bleak Northumbrian Moor, Behold a Palace raised' began the ode specially written for the occasion. Within its four courts a huge range of exhibits were displayed, amongst which were reconstructed coal and lead mines. The coal mine consisted of a 500 ft long adit with 600 yards of galleries – the whole experience of mining was portrayed including men hewing coal, underground locos, ventilation fans and pit ponies. Transport around the Exhibition site was by an electric railway which conveyed people to a 1,500 seat theatre, a 300 ft long art gallery, machinery displays, a working dairy, gardens and verandahs, two licensed restaurants accommodating 300 people, a temperance restaurant, a cocoa palace provided by Mr Lockhart, an Indo-Chinese Café provided by Mr Lyons, shooting galleries, archery ranges, a model of Alnwick Castle, complete with guns, exact copies of Swiss chalets, a model hospital, a smoking pavilion, a Camera Obscura and a panorama of incidents in the ' recent Franco-German War', including a whole siege battery with guns. The site had its own gas and electric supplies, its own fire appliances, a complete Post Office and 30 policemen to keep order.

Dominating the northern part of the site was a model of the Tyne Bridge which had crossed the river from the 13th century until it was swept away in the flood of 1771. The bridge spanned the lake which had been formed for the event from the earlier reservoirs on the Moor. The 'model' was two-thirds of the bridge's actual size and based upon considerable historical research to recreate the bridge together with all its shops, houses and chapels. Inside the great grandstands were vast displays of ordnance, manufactured by Armstrong's, including a full sized model of a 110 ton gun, two of which had formed the armaments of HMS *Victoria*, and a whole range of products of a panoply of smaller companies, including displays of paint, iron, steel, coach-building, leather goods, printing, coke, gas lighting, lime and cement, tunnelling, horticulture, arboriculture – all representative of Tyneside at the time.

The content of the exhibition illustrated the serious intent of the trade fair but also the joyous celebrations which surrounded the Queen's Jubilee. Witnessing manifestations of the might of the empire and viewing the products of the workshop of the world were perhaps reasons in themselves for visiting the Great Exhibition of 1851. However, while more light-hearted amusements and entertainment had added a different dimension to Newcastle's Golden Jubilee exhibition, even these were a demonstration of the ingenuity and virtuosity of the exhibitors. Amongst other delights there was a gravitational railway and a toboggan where it was said 'young and old merrily desport themselves'.

When the North East Coast Exhibition was held in 1929, despite the urgent economic necessity which underpinned the event, amusement and entertainment were seen as a major part of the show. Large-scale communal events had been few and far between in the opening decades of the new century. Even the opening of the century had been a subdued affair. New Year's Day had been observed as a general holiday but the *Daily Chronicle* reported 'the difficulty with most people was to know what to do with themselves', whilst the events held to mark the end of the South African War, and in particular The Great War, combined sadness and relief with public celebration.

The North East Coast Exhibition was intended to be a great communal event which would educate, entertain and amuse its visitors but from the very beginning its main purpose was clear. 'Far seeing businessmen, captains of industry and commerce, leaders in civic life in the great centres of population from the Tees to the Tweed, eager only for the welfare of the District and therefore the nation, have pondered long over the problem of industrial depression and have deliberately arrived at the conclusion that an EXHIBITION is the best method of reviving and stimulating trade', announced an early prospectus for the event. The idea had first been floated in 1925 and in 1926 an Executive Committee had been set up under the patronage of King George V. The local patrons were the Duke of Northumberland, the Earl of Durham and Sir Hugh Bell, with Sir Charles Parsons as President. The appointment of Sir Arthur Lambert, Lord Mayor of Newcastle in both 1927 and 1929, as Chairman of the Committee was a catalyst to the process.

A party of schoolchildren visits the Palace of Engineering.

The event had been originally planned to take place in 1928 to coincide with the opening of the new Tyne Bridge but concern regarding the slow pace of donations to the guarantee fund and the spectre of the failure of the British Empire Exhibition at Wembley in 1924-25, where all the guarantees had to be called on, cast a shadow over the proposal. The introduction of a huge mock thermometer to the side of Grey's Monument showing the level by which the guarantee fund had increased day by day maintained public interest in the scheme but as time wore on the calls in the press, specifically the *North Mail*, to delay the event became almost feverish and the new slogan 'Newcastle upon Tyne in 1929' was taken up. The guarantee fund target was £150,000 and the impetus to reach the figure was accompanied by a number of 'big pushes'. As it turned out, the fund eventually exceeded this sum, reaching £173,755, and was not called upon as the exhibition made a small working profit of £6,785. The figure, however, had to be raised as a prerequisite of the Exhibition taking place. £32,750 was guaranteed by local authorities of which £25,000 came from Newcastle upon Tyne Corporation. Pledges to the fund came from 2,048 different sources, many from individuals with a pound or a guinea but the guarantors of four- and, in one case, five-figure sums reflected the growing financial clout of organisations involved in newer aspects of the economy – mass market media, electric power supply and retailing. The largest single commitment, £10,000, was made by Northcliffe Newspapers who had just launched the *Evening World* in the North East. £5,000 was guaranteed by the *North Mail* and *Newcastle Chronicle*, £4,200 by the Co-operative Wholesale Society and £3,000 by the Newcastle on Tyne Electric Supply Company. Whilst guaranteeing sizeable sums the industrial leviathans were not the main contributors to the fund, but it was hoped by many that they would be the major beneficiaries of the exhibition.

The buildings constructed to house the exhibits were on a heroic scale and, from the front at least, stylish – the architecture was contemporary fashionable art-deco. 'Architects and builders have brought into being a City Beautiful' crowed the programme. The effect was that of a set for an epic film (*Ben Hur* perhaps, which was showing in Newcastle as the buildings rose) – an impression further bolstered by the 12 Egyptian pylons which formed the main entrance off Claremont Road. The architect for the buildings, other than that of the Empire Marketing Board, was Stanley Milburn of Messrs. W. & T.R. Milburn of Sunderland. The style was the product of a number of influences – the discovery of Tutankhamun's tomb in 1922 which had had a tremendous effect on the decorative arts, the release of epic films, in particular Cecil B. DeMille's *The Ten Commandments* in 1923, the holding of the 'Exposition Internationale des Arts Decoratifs et Industriels Modernes' in Paris in 1925 which had been a catalyst for the art deco and Egyptian revival movements. As a style it represented the advent of architectural and artistic influences into everyday life, accessible to a wider public. As such, it was particularly appropriate for a huge public exhibition. The contract for the construction was won by Henry Kelly Ltd. of 26, St Mary's Place, Newcastle whose winning tender was for £114,071. In the end, £162,874 was spent on the construction of buildings, laying of roads and the earthworks which predominantly consisted of removing 50,000 tons of soil to enable foundations and floors to be laid, and using it to create the embankments of an open air stadium.

From the great gates, the 'Wembley of the North' spread out in front of the visitor. The Main Avenue, which led through the exhibition grounds, was flanked on the east side by the smaller pavilions which incorporated the Garden Club with its roof verandah, the Women's and Artisans' section, the Empire Marketing Board Pavilion, restaurants and horticultural exhibitions. Behind these, stretching to the Great North Road, were the gardens, tennis courts and bowling greens which survive to this day and the bandstand which had been built for the 1887 exhibition. On the western side of the Main Avenue were the huge sheds – palaces as they were grandly termed aping the Crystal Palace of the Great Exhibition (and perhaps even the City of Palaces which the centre of Newcastle, at the time still virtually unchanged since the death of Richard Grainger, had once been called). They were built of compressed asbestos sheeting on a steel girder framework with long concrete façades at the end of which were the great twin towers (echoes of Wembley) which dominated the site. Entrance to each of the two palaces was through two lofty doors flanked by flower gardens or through the Great Towers themselves. The Palace of Engineering had a floor space of 100,000 sq.ft. The Palace of Industry, originally planned to the same dimensions, was extended by 67,000sq.ft. to cater for the unprecedented demand for space. Even then 140 firms wishing to exhibit had to be turned away. At the head of the avenue lay the Palace of Arts, approached via an elegant bridge across the widened and deepened boating lake. Entertainment was provided in the Festival Hall, the 20,000 capacity stadium, the Evening Chronicle and Evening World Pavilions and in the extensive amusement park. The ensemble was completed by the administration, police, fire and postal buildings, a 23 ft high statue of a female figure representing Industry, and the motor park. The North East Coast Exhibition was perhaps the first event in the region's history to have a dedicated car park, in itself a sign of the changing economic and social backdrop against which the exhibition was held.

Tyneside's living but ailing industrial tradition was assembled in the Palace of Engineering. The belief that the region's future was tied to its heavy industries was typified in the speech by the Duke of Northumberland which accompanied his cutting of the first sod. Amid hearty cheers, having performed his duty with lusty vigour, he announced that the exhibition would be a great testimony to the North Easterners' determination that the prosperity, which the north of England had enjoyed in the past, would not be transferred permanently to the south. He was convinced 'that the great staple heavy industries of the north could never go south. The recovery might be slow but they would hasten it by their Exhibition.' The Palace of Engineering contained the displays of the heavy industrial firms desperately seeking orders. There were displays of steel arches from the Consett Iron Company, furnace linings by Henry Foster Refractory Bricks, stands of less well known firms such as Illingworth Carbonization Co. Ltd and Linkleters Patent Ship Fittings Company of North Shields, but also of the well known shipbuilding, bridge building, coal mining and locomotive engineering companies of the region – powerful coal cutting and rock drilling machines shared the 100,000 square feet of space with, amongst other exhibits, road surface materials, ship models, and cinema film of the construction of the new Tyne Bridge.

The exhibition sought to re-establish the past but did not set its face against change. The Prince of Wales had said in his opening remarks that the old industries needed to adapt and improve, that 'the march of time may have shown some branches of industry out-living their usefulness' and that 'encouraging the establishment of new works and new methods would provide further channels of labour.' Echoing his words, the spirit of modernisation filled the Palace of Industries. Display space was sold at 7s 6d (37.5p) per sq.ft., the smallest units being 400 sq ft (£150), the largest 1000 sq ft (£375) and the hall was full, extended and still oversubscribed. Much space was given

The Carrick's Café concession.

over to the application of electricity to modern living, to the introduction of new labour saving equipment and to the advantages that were to be had in owning them. The displays of the Singer sewing machine and the Hoover carpet cleaner encapsulated this. Singer encouraged people to 'Switch on and Stitch on', Hoover gave a demonstration of the use of 'positive agitation ... the new Hoover ... it beats ... as it sweeps ... as it cleans.' Cooking, cleaning, sewing, laundry and shopping were all simplified and improved by electricity. 'There is no end to the use of gas' retorted the Newcastle and Gateshead Gas Company, but it could not compete with the boasts of the electricity suppliers that 'The Well Lighted Store is Frequented More' 'The Hall of Light ... Preserves the Sight'.

The time saved in domestic drudgery could instead be applied to shopping. Retailers and specialist food and drink manufacturers competed for the attention of the exhibition goers. 'Particular People Prefer Powells' advised a lemon cheese manufacturer. Carrick's Café held a concession for the event, Smiths introduced their new product – potato crisps. Rington's tea, Pumphrey's coffee and J.C. Eno's Fruit Salts were all on display. A Temple of Health was erected by Scott & Turner Ltd of Gallowgate providing Andrew's Liver Salts. Newcastle Breweries produced Exhibition Ale especially for the event. Fashion, an increasingly important facet of the developing century, was also a key component of the attractions in the Palace. As local stores Bainbridge, Binns and Fenwicks were still the dominant names, but their dominance was beginning to be challenged by national chain stores, and in the years either side of the Exhibition, fourteen chain stores opened branches in Newcastle's main shopping streets, including C&A, Marks & Spencer and F.W. Woolworth & Co. Ltd.

Some perception of the developing role of women in the changing economic, social and cultural environment of the inter-war years was recognised by the Exhibition organisers. Important but separate, women were given their own pavilion – representing 'every branch of Women's Work, professional and otherwise.' Displays of Fine Arts, handicrafts, a potter's wheel, examples of many crafts and activities, lectures and demonstrations were presented by a Special Committee of Women who imparted 'an air of dignity and spaciousness to their exhibition.' The committee advertised for lectures and demonstrations reflecting the expanding interests of women in the 20th century – medicine, science, music, drama, literature, legal subjects, accountancy, insurance, sociology, psychology, electricity, engineering, and horticulture (suggestions, oddly, included goat-keeping). The organisers were rewarded with a wide range of subjects and speakers including 'The Liberty of the Individual', 'Architecture', 'Jane Austen', and 'The British Light Aeroplane around Africa'. Domestically orientated talks were relatively few – those presentations on Pastries (Rough, Puff, Cheese and Short Crust), Dainty Puddings and Sweets were the work of the Newcastle and Gateshead Gas Company keen to demonstrate the value and versatility of their gas cookers. The income generated from entry fees and commission on sale of goods from the Women's Section was low, but women nevertheless appear to have formed a large percentage of the visitors to the Exhibition. As the writer Cheryl Buckley has observed, images of young women at the Exhibition draw into sharp relief 'the contradictions of life in the North East between the Wars; the Exhibition was organised to revive and develop trade and industry in an area affected by high levels of male unemployment, yet at the same time young, working women, in particular, experienced the pleasures of independence and more modern lifestyles, especially in the region's towns and cities.'

Other parts of the Exhibition similarly demonstrated the modern age. Above the entrance to the *Evening World* Pavilion was 'an electric sign of an entirely new type which flashes out the latest news items … all important events are recorded here in letters of light. 'Inside amongst the changing displays were Malcolm Campbell's 'Bluebird', Sir Henry Seagrave's 'Golden

A tiny sideshow advertises the coal industry.

Arrow' and the S6 Seaplane. The largest telescope in Britain was also one of the exhibits, as was Eric, the country's most advanced robot. Outside, the buildings and the great fountain were illuminated. The fountain played nightly, reaching to three different levels, the highest being as high as the Exhibition buildings themselves. At the bottom of the basin was an ingenious arrangement of electric globes which enabled coloured and ever-changing lights to be thrown upwards and as they changed, the heights of the water jets were automatically altered. The buildings were topped by powerful searchlights which swept the skies when darkness fell. The Pavilions of both the *Newcastle Chronicle* group and the *Evening World* contained machinery demonstrating the processes by which the developing media reacted so quickly to local and national events. These types of displays exemplified how Newcastle and the North East was being influenced by national trends and adapting to the changing economic, social, technical and cultural environment of the time.

In the year of the Exhibition Newcastle Airport was founded, sound was being introduced into the city's most forward-looking cinemas, the motor car was being increasingly catered for in the city. Yet the basis of the region's economy was still largely embedded in its heavy industrial past. The new industries that were taking root in other parts of the country found no home here. The car industry, aeroplane manufacture, large-scale factory-based food processing were not part of the economic structure of the North East. Whilst companies such as Boots were building state of the art homages to new technology, typified by their Wet Processes building begun in Nottingham in 1930, the North East remained virtually untouched by these trends. Significantly and symbolically, one of the principal locations for the construction of new buildings with contemporary architectural influences in the North

East was the area's coal mines where the pit head baths building programme which followed the 1920 Mines Welfare Act produced a series of impressive modernistic buildings. Remarkably few prestigious buildings were added to the centre of Newcastle in this period; the Tyne Bridge, opened in 1928, and Carliol House (1924-28) a new headquarters for the North Eastern Electric Supply Company are notable exceptions. J.B. Priestley in his *English Journey*, published in 1934, observed that 'the centre of Newcastle has a certain sombre dignity … it is chiefly built of a stone that has turned almost a dead black. Newcastle is even blacker than Manchester, and might almost have been carved out of coal.' The sharp contrast between the blackness of Grainger's legacy and the gleaming white Portland Stone of the headquarters of the electricity supply company symbolised Newcastle's dilemma.

The mixture of modernity and tradition manifested itself further in the amusement park and the programme of entertainment. Traditional events such as the performances of Captain Harry Amers and his band, fresh from Eastbourne, the staging of Highland Games and a knockout football competition received a mixed response. The football challenge cup, surprisingly for this area, was not a great success. Newcastle United, Sunderland and Middlesbrough all withdrew from the event and crowds were consequently sparse. There was, however, huge interest in the spectacular new 'rides' – the 'Himalayan Railway' a 1.5 mile roller-coaster ride climbing to 80 ft from the ground, which the promoters claimed reached speeds of 80 to 100 mph, proved the biggest draw with over three-quarter of a million thrill-seekers. 'A particularly rollicking form of amusement is The Diabolic Whirl' claimed the programme, as was 'The Great Water Chute' which had run so successfully at the International Press Exhibition at Cologne in the previous year. Equally popular were the exotic exhibits – Chapman's Jungle with its 'elephants, tigers, lions and other denizens of the forest', the Monkey Paradise and The African Village. The organisers promised '100 natives from Senegal living in a replica of one of their homeland communities going about their daily lives as though their feet were upon their native heath'. Accompanying them was to be a tribe of Fullahs – 'practically savages'. In the best traditions of showmanship when the Governor of Senegal refused to allow the tribes-people to leave the country because of the French smallpox fear, a large number of Algerian Arabs, Bedouins and Dervishes were recruited, later bolstered by 28 Nubians and 2 Fakirs. The promoters noted that the life seen in the African village would be primitive but that visitors to the Amusement Park would have the opportunity of 'going even a step lower' by viewing a huge Chicken Incubator where 800 chickens a day issued from their shells. 'With so many chickens coming almost simultaneously into existence they find themselves in a position analogous to that of the great mass of human unemployed. The problem of what to do with them is a problem indeed,' declared an exhibition publication. An observation that was as tactless as it was portentous for, as popular as the exhibition proved to be, it did not achieve its main aim. As it closed, the western world spiralled deeper and deeper into depression and the problem of unemployment became even greater.

When the exhibition closed on 26 October, 4,373,138 visitors had passed through the great gates. The final day was the busiest, 119,940 patrons made sure that they did not miss the show. The weather had been kind to the event, a heat wave in July helping to buoy up the crowds. Whit Monday had also seen a 100,000 crowd. Only a handful of days were seriously marred by weather and even then between 12,000 and 15,000 visitors came to the moor. Approximately 40,000 season tickets had been sold (at a guinea each for adults), and 2.5m visitors had paid at the gate. Gatekeepers had been scrupulous in ensuring that season tickets were not misused – they were non-transferable, not even to a wife or husband. The organisers received a number of letters explaining the unfortunate circumstances in which a season ticket had come to be used by a friend or neighbour and pleading for their return. Some visitors, who presumably did not have to pay, received a considerable amount of attention – King Alphonso of Spain, Lady Baden Powell, numerous members of the local gentry who had loaned works of art for exhibition in the Palace of Arts, Sir Thomas Beecham. The most charismatic VIP was the 'smiling' Sultan of Zanzibar, who broadcast on the BBC, in Swahili, to the whole of the British Isles from the Exhibition.

The initial target of four million visitors had been exceeded. There had been few problems in the running of the exhibition. Only six cases of 'alcoholic over-excitement' required police intervention. Sadly one person had died after falling from the Himalayan Railway. Some problems had been encountered in the African Village – a number of Algerians were, not surprisingly, unhappy with the arrangements, in particular the climate. The ban on fires added to their discontent and a number found themselves escorted to Newcastle Central Station before returning home ahead of schedule. As early as 20 May, only a week into the exhibition, 'a row erupted between Fakirs and Algerians' to which the police were called but the disturbance was more voluble than vicious. Nevertheless, as *The Journal* reported, 'rumours spread that there had been blood-thirsty doings in the village.' An escaping monkey called Blossom, a minor mauling by a lion, a row over profiteering engineered by two squabbling newspapers, were a small tally of hiccups for such a large event. Damage to the exhibits was unknown until the penultimate day when students, either as part of a caper or perhaps in an attempt to provide some artistic criticism, poured runny black tar over the head of the statue of Industry. This action was sadly all too representative of the state of the region's indus-

Newcastle Chronicle & Journal Ltd.

The boating lake remains at Exhibition Park, but the bridge is long gone.

try. On 24 October, two days before the North East Coast Exhibition closed its gates, the Wall Street Crash signalled the headlong fall into the western world's longest and deepest economic depression. At the closing ceremony a message from the Prince of Wales was read expressing the hope that the Exhibition had done much to encourage local industries and to enhance the prosperity of the North East Coast. 'Our industries were badly bunkered', added another speaker 'but the Exhibition niblick has placed them safely on the green and each one must help to hole the putt.' The gains that the Exhibition made – and some firms did report orders which they could trace directly to the Exhibition, even in the faltering shipbuilding industry – were, however, brushed aside by wider economic forces.

The fate of the buildings typified that of the regional economy. A suggestion that the huge palaces could be adapted to a modern use and converted into film studios – to create an 'Elstree of the North' – came to nought. Instead with the exception of the bridge (eventually demolished in 1961) and the Palace of Arts (which had been built more robustly than the others in order to protect the valuable works of art inside it), the buildings were dismantled. Equally symbolically in 1934 the former Palace of Arts became a museum to the industrial and engineering tradition of the area, displaying many of the exhibits from the Exhibition.

It was not the Exhibition, but rearmament and World War II which finally revitalised the heavy industries. The period of post-war prosperity that followed World War II was longer lasting than that which followed the first. The long boom of the 1950s returned prosperity to the traditional industries and brought low unemployment to the region. These however were virtually the only years of vitality experienced by these industries since the early years of the century. But their terminal decline had not been arrested. The 60s, 70s and 80s saw the further collapse and final destruction of Tyneside's heavy industrial economy. Attempts in the 1960s to modernise Newcastle city centre represented a realisation that an era was ending and the area was adopting a new identity. The North East Coast Exhibition took place at a time when Newcastle and the North East first addressed this change. 'I think some favourable time was lost in looking back regretfully to the past and hoping the spacious Victorian days would return' said the Prince of Wales in his opening speech. There was still some vigour left in the old industries when the Exhibition took place, as was shown by the prosperity of the 1950s, but the life which was breathed back into them perhaps hindered the development of an alternative economic base for the area. By wishing to revive the traditional industries but embracing the modern world the Exhibition found the city looking both backwards and forwards. The North East Coast Exhibition demonstrates this central theme of the 20th century history of Newcastle and the North East.

⌇ Ian Ayris is the County Industrial Archaeologist within the Tyne & Wear Specialist Conservation Team and is author of *A City of Palaces: Richard Grainger and the Making of Newcastle upon Tyne*, 1997, and co-author with Patricia Sheldon of *On the Waterfront: An Historical Tour of Newcastle's Quayside*, 1995, both Newcastle Libraries & Information Service.

A Woman's Place

Dr Maureen Callcott

JANE AUSTEN'S HEROINE IN 'NORTHANGER ABBEY' COMPLAINED that she didn't care for history, where she found 'hardly any women at all – it is very tiresome'. Two hundred years later it still seems necessary to have a special chapter to bring women into view. It is true, of course, that women's lives have been affected by every other aspect of Newcastle's history explored in this book. But here, as elsewhere, the lives of half or more of the population often still remain 'hidden from history'. The end of this century is an appropriate time not only to observe the ways in which all women's lives have been altered, but also to highlight the experience of some particular individuals and some groups of women. This past hundred years has provided much both to celebrate and to mourn and neither should be ignored. Most of us do not live in the public eye and many of the women in my generalisations here are nameless. But a few outstanding public figures also have to appear. Certain themes demand inclusion. The dramas of the suffrage movement up to 1914 are important and it is interesting to question the significance of the role of women in political life since then, in the city and region.

Opportunities for education and employment have changed the lives of both sexes, but much more so for women. This, of course, is closely connected to the size of families and the state of the economy. It is also linked with the necessities of the home front in the two world wars which blighted the first half of our century. These are the themes which will be illustrated in this account. They represent but a fragment of the countless and complex experiences of Newcastle women over 100 years. Two further notions appeal to me. One is that

The rabbit skinners in this photograph were paid just 10 shillings for a 50 hour week at the turn of the century. The firm they worked for, Lee, Holme and Co. of City Road, made hats for the wealthy women of Newcastle.

we all can share women's experience of the whole century through what we learn, wittingly and unwittingly, from our mothers and grandmothers. They were born, as we were later, into a world quite different from the one we inhabit now. Nevertheless, we need to be alert to the continuity among the changes, the past in the present, the carrying from generation to generation of values and attitudes. And this experience provides each of us with our own history.

Looking first at our political history, the extent to which local women responded passionately, actively and sacrificially to the movement to obtain the right to vote for members of parliament is not always appreciated. Some Tyneside women had been active, even militant, in the 1830s struggle for parliamentary reform and in the Chartist movement of the 1830s and 1840s and also in advancing the Co-operative movement. The first Female Political Union in the North East was organised at Cookson's plate glass factory in Newcastle. They protested against the level of men's wages which forced the women to work outside their homes and led to child neglect. They denounced the new Poor Law and members of the FPU dealt only with shopkeepers who supported the Charter. So even though at the turn of the century fewer women were in employment outside the home than in any other area in England, largely because of the predominantly heavy industrial basis of the Tyneside economy, some had already shown themselves informed about, and involved in, political affairs. And in the examples given above we are not thinking only, or even mainly, of upper- and middle-class women. Political involvement for many women had been 'a bread and butter affair'. It probably continued so in the main but in the years before World War I women of all classes not only joined the major political parties – Conservative (often via its Primrose League), Liberal and Labour (a new party in 1900) – but also joined the various strands of the movement to acquire the parliamentary vote on equal terms with men. However, not all women considered this to be necessary or even desirable, deferring to the wisdom of the male, or perhaps regarding the vote as irrelevant.

Suffragettes advertise their journal, The Common Cause, *on Northumberland Street in 1912.*

Tyneside's role in the suffrage movement has only recently been researched (David Neville, *To Make Their Mark*, 1997). We learn that the Hon. Mrs Mona Taylor of Chipchase Castle was involved in the suffrage movement from its beginnings in the 1870s. She was an activist at national and local levels, a prominent member of five national suffrage societies. In 1890, at a conference of workers at Newcastle, she introduced the moderate suffrage leader, Millicent Fawcett, and in 1900 helped to create the Newcastle and District Women's Suffrage Society. She addressed public meetings, some at factory gates where thousands of leaflets were distributed, and persuaded members to campaign for parliamentary candidates, whatever their political background, who supported votes for women. Soon four other women joined the local suffrage campaign, all of whom

West Newcastle Local Studies

A suffragette addresses a quayside crowd, mostly men, around 1912.

made an impact nationally. Two were doctors, among the earliest women to have challenged the massive prejudice in their chosen profession in order to become qualified. Ethel Williams and Ethel Bentham shared a practice in Jesmond, and their special concern with women's health issues stirred their concern for the social and economic conditions of working-class women's lives. Both became active politically, Williams as a prominent Liberal, and Bentham, later on, as a Labour MP. The other two women activists came from the labour movement. Florence Harrison Bell was a schoolmistress, married to Joseph Nicholas Bell, secretary of the National Amalgamated Union of Labour which was based in Newcastle. Lisbeth Simm was the wife of the North East organiser of the Independent Labour Party. One of the regular venues for suffrage meetings was the Drawing Room Café in Fenwick's department store on Monday nights. It was here in July 1908 that the local group split between the supporters of Emmeline Pankhurst's militant group the WSPU (Women's Social and Political Union) and the more moderate group led by Millicent Fawcett the NUWSS (National Union of Women's Suffrage Societies). However, in Newcastle, unlike most other places, the two groups often campaigned together.

In June, just before this split, Florence Bell, amongst a group of North East women in a 10,000-strong NUWSS procession in London, related how they gained another recruit in a Geordie exile: 'A woman remarked in our own Doric way, "Them's nivvor from Newcastle" when she saw the banner. The banner carrier retorted "Wey, hinny hoo de ye knaa?".' One example of lively public suffrage activity in Newcastle can be taken from the 1908 parliamentary by-election. The NUWSS held over 120 outdoor and indoor meetings, but were overshadowed by the more dramatic events staged by the WSPU. Slides showing incidents from their campaign used in a magic lantern show in rooms on Shields Road were projected onto a sheet in the shop window and brought such crowds that police stopped repeat performances. The climax was a demonstration on the Town Moor attended by some 3,000

The caption to this newspaper photograph of Winston Churchill with Sir W.H. Stephenson, Chairman of the Tyne Improvement Commission, by the Tyne c1913 reads: 'Mr Churchill is raising his hat to Miss New, a suffragette, who shouted at him: "Remember the women in prison".'

people, followed by a march led by Emmeline Pankhurst to the Central Station to meet three suffragettes just released from prison. These women addressed a crowd of about 8,000 and were escorted to a decorated carriage and drawn to their hotel by a team of girls wearing the WSPU purple, green and white.

Particularly because of the time commitment required for campaigning, it is not surprising that upper- and middle-class women predominated in both organisations. Titled activists included Lady Parsons, wife of the industrialist, and Lady Blake, wife of Sir Francis Blake. There were quite a lot of teachers from different backgrounds, including Connie Ellis (better known by her married name, Lewcock), later Councillor for Benwell Ward from 1960-1971. Margaret Brown and Jane Atkinson were married to an accountant and engineer respectively and the resources of these and other such women meant that the WSPU could pay a full-time organiser in Newcastle from 1908 to 1913 and take on permanent premises. Mona Taylor was reported as giving half her income to the WSPU. A plea to members at the time highlights another aspect of women's lives: 'Will ladies with large kitchens sometimes arrange a meeting for servants and their friends'.

The North East as a whole produced several suffragettes who felt so strongly about the issue that they engaged in militant, disruptive activity – including serious attacks on property – knowing that they risked life-threatening hardship in brutal prison sentences. They include Laura Ainsworth from South Shields, Jane Atkinson, Norah Balls, Janet Boyd (widow of the High Sheriff of County Durham), Kathleen Brown, Lizzie Crow, Lettice Floyd, Lena Lambert, Charlotte Marsh (from Alnmouth, one of the first women to become a sanitary inspector), and of course, best known of all martyrs to the cause, Emily Wilding Davison, from a Northumberland family (though born at Blackheath), who was fatally injured trying to rein down the King's horse at the Derby on 4 June 1913. She is buried in the family grave at Morpeth. Between 1908 and 1914 there was increasingly militant, often violent and dangerous suffrage activity in Tyneside as well as in the better known London streets and parliament itself. This should shatter our illusions, if any still remain, of a tranquil Edwardian age of 'upstairs downstairs' when all knew and accepted their station in life, women deferred to their menfolk's better judgement and all was changed only by the traumas of the Great War. It might be observed that the women's violent protests were not unlike other violent areas in society at the same time. There was widespread trade union disruption and a highly dangerous Irish situation, where army officers threatened mutiny. Even the House of Lords found itself stripped of some of its powers because of its defiance of the democratic process. Thus, when women in Tyneside poured corrosive liquid into letter boxes (February 1913), cut telephone wires at Kenton, smashed windows at the Globe Theatre, Gosforth, burnt down the pavilion and bowls house in Heaton Park (March 1913), smashed the windows of the Northumberland Education Committee department at the Moot Hall and later set off incendiary devices there as well as at Barras Bridge Post Office, Gosforth Golf Club, Kenton railway station, Durham North railway station and provided a ceaseless threat to law and order, they were not markedly out of line with discontented males from all ranks in society.

Suffrage activity largely ceased with the outbreak of World War I and at the end of the war women were granted the vote, though not immediately on equal terms with men. Only women over thirty could vote until equality in that respect was granted in 1928. It is not argued here that it was militancy which produced the vote. There was continuous non-militant pressure at the same time and many Tyneside women were also dedicated workers in Millicent Fawcett's group. It became increasingly important for all the political parties to obtain the support of women and after women worked alongside men or took over men's jobs during the four years of war there was little opposition left.

So, have women been equal political partners with men since the vote, and with it the right also to become Members of Parliament, was won? Clearly not, if we examine the participation of women in the political life of our city both in the local council and parliament during the last 70 years of this century. So far Newcastle has never had a woman MP, and there have been only three candidates, one from each party, though more have sought nomination. However the North East region's political life was undoubtedly enhanced in the 1920s, 1930s and 1940s by a number of quite outstanding women (it seems that they had to be so) in parliamentary seats: Margaret Bondfield, the first woman Cabinet Minister, (Wallsend), Ruth Dalton (Bishop Auckland), Dr Marion Phillips (Sunderland), Mabel Phillipson (Berwick), Susan Lawrence (Stockton), Ellen Wilkinson (Middlesbrough and Jarrow), Grace Colman (Tynemouth) and Irene Ward (Tynemouth). A telling point about each of them, like the majority of parliamentary and other professional women until the last 30 years or so, is that all were unmarried women or widows and childless, except for Ruth Dalton who merely 'held' the seat at a by-election for her husband Hugh. This was a reflection of the prevailing ideology regarding 'a woman's place' as well as the economic and educationally privileged position of men, a condition only marginally shifted by women's contribution in both World Wars. Irene Ward was a Conservative and Mabel Phillipson Liberal, the rest were Labour women. Now, after a long gap, at the end of the century, we have a number of extremely talented women representing North East constituencies, Marjorie Mowlam (Redcar), Hilary Armstrong (North West Durham), and Joyce Quinn (Gateshead East) and all have government posts (and like their predecessors are all unmarried or without demanding family responsibilities). It has been very difficult to persuade constituency parties, often in the face of

Margaret Bondfield, the first woman cabinet minister, in 1929.

entrenched interest groups and prejudice, to accept the nomination of a woman candidate let alone to select one. Thus the Labour Party recently embarked upon the highly contentious policy of insisting on including at least one woman in every nomination list. At least one of these government members has attempted and failed to obtain selection for a Newcastle constituency, so we reach the millennium without ever yet sending a women to Parliament.

It is a good deal easier, and has been more acceptable socially, for women with families to participate in politics at a local level. The Municipal Corporations Act of 1869 granted the vote to women ratepayers and allowed them the relatively humble role of Parish Councillors. Other possibilities appeared around this time. The Education Act of 1870 allowed any woman to seek election to the new School Boards, and from 1888 women could be co-opted onto Council Committees. Many women had been involved in aspects of voluntary activity relating to the work of the poor law boards which ran the workhouses and, after much difficulty, they were allowed to stand for election as guardians from 1894. There was much prejudice against their election as they were feared to be over-generous with public money. There were three in Newcastle by 1907. Women were eligible for Municipal Council election from 1907 but Dr Ethel Bentham, the only woman candidate in Newcastle before 1919, was defeated. Only six women were co-opted onto any Council committee – all onto the Education Committee – before 1919. A trickle of women councillors began after World War I. It is impossible to evaluate the impact and contribution made since the first woman, Mrs Mary Laverick, entered the council chamber as a Labour member in January 1919, winning Westgate Ward at a by-election, but we can at least note their number and public roles. Mary Laverick, an ex-teacher, sat for five-and-a-half years for Westgate and then Walker Wards. She was a member of the Education, Finance, New Town Hall, Maternity and Child Welfare committees and within three months demonstrated her concern for the poorest of women when she introduced deputations from the National Federation of Women Workers and a Newcastle deputation of unemployed women complaining of being thrown out of work when the Armistice was signed. They 'wished to have work more than anything'.

Since Mary Laverick there have been 103 further women members of Newcastle City Council, though their arrival was initially very slow. There were only eight before 1939, but these included the first woman to become Sheriff and then Lord Mayor, Violet Graham, Conservative member for Fenham and Westgate Wards who served from 1937 until 1974. Often well-known in their wards they have been important in attending to the particular concerns of women as well as of all their constituents, chairing key committees, such as Education (Joan Lamb), serving for long stretches of their lives (Theresa Russell – almost 50 years by Autumn 1999). Even so, no woman councillor in any party has so far obtained the most powerful position – that of Council Leader. In 1998 there were 25 women on the Council of 75 members.

The theme of this chapter being 'A Woman's Place', even more significant than political life, has been the appearance and acceptance of women at work in just about every job, trade or profession. This is a feature of most modern western societies at the end of the 20th century and it has been accompanied, of course, by extended opportunities in education and training, choice about family size and the development of homes which are much easier to run. Let us see how this sociological change came about in Newcastle in the space of about three generations.

Traditionally, women in the North East, both single and married, were less likely to work outside their homes than in any other region. This can be explained partly by the predominance of heavy industries such as mining, engineering and ship-building, together with the custom of early marriage and consequent high birth rate. The expectations for girls before the war are exemplified in the aims of the new higher elementary school opened at Atkinson Road, Benwell in 1910:

'To a great extent distinctive instruction will be given to boys and girls, so that each may be the better fitted for the duties of adult life. For boys the special training will comprise handicraft, drawing, mathematics, and elementary science. Those who intend to enter the engineering and allied trades will receive a course of instruction in the elements of machine drawing, physics and mechanics; while for those intended for commercial life a course in book-keeping, shorthand and commercial practice will be given. The girls, as a rule, will receive a training in needlework, dressmaking, cookery and laundry, and be instructed in domestic science and hygiene; but the other courses will also be open to them should it be desired.' (From *Wor Lass: Sources for Women's History in the North East*, Tyne & Wear Archives, 1988)

Against such a background, obtaining the opportunity to work on any sort of equal terms with men has not been a story of steady advance for women. The first dramatic impulse was provided by World War I, with its tragic consequences affecting everyone. After conscription was introduced for unmarried men between the ages of 17 and 42, women were recruited, though not conscripted, into offices, shipyards, munitions work, public transport and numerous activities previously largely confined to men. Munitions work provides a prime example. By the end of the war in 1918, 90 per cent of its workers were women. The Armstrong Whitworth works at Elswick was one of the country's most important sources of munitions and from 1915 began to employ women from all backgrounds who competently learned and performed most of the tasks involved in gun and shell making, although they were dubbed 'dilutees' by trade union agreements and not paid men's wages. Ruth Dodds, of

Women at war: munitions workers at Armstrong's Elswick Works in 1916.

Gateshead, a middle-class woman of 25 who had never been employed before, described her work (a 'weekender') and companions in the shell-shop on the night-shift.

'... they don't seem to think their lives hard; they are full of talk and fun, and all sorts of silly school-girl-ish jokes run up and down the shops ... It isn't true to say that working women never smile; all these girls had pleasant open smiles to greet us with; perhaps it is true of older women – married women with big families, and the dinner and the washing always on their minds ... I was told there are 2,000 girls in shop 40, but then one hears many things; certainly there were a great many ... At the benches all sorts of filing, polishing, bur-nishing and fitting goes on by hand ... Behind me is a line of machines on benches, hard to work as the girls on them have to stay all the time and hold a lever in each hand ... All beyond on the right of me are more and more machines in great complication so that the men and girls threading up and down with the heavy trays of bodies are always making blocks ... one forgets colds and all else in the intense excitement of the work ... It was very exciting to get paid ... I hold my head much higher now I know I am worth something ...'

She left to take on men's work in her father's printing business on the Quayside and retained for the rest of her long life a sense of the dignity and worth of employment, mourning its loss when in 1926 she ceded her place in the firm to her brother.

Many issues were raised by women's work during World War I. They included those of equal pay, health and safety, morality, working hours, transport and child care. None were seriously tackled, above all because the majority of people regarded the work as temporary, and as servicemen were rap-idly demobilised so women had to leave their jobs with equal speed. Probably the majority of them at the time accepted this. But those who needed a wage had great difficulty in finding employment or enti-tlement to it, and most of those who wished to work for any reason were extremely limited in their choice, training and remuneration.

The notion that 'a woman's place is in the home' prevailed until well after World War II and even during the miners' struggles of the 1980s the abusive response to the women's support groups could be 'gan home and see to yer bairns'. In the 1920s, for example, even after the experience of a wide range of employment during World War I, the proportion of women employed on Tyneside was down to pre-war levels – just over 20 per cent of all occupied persons compared with about 30 per cent in England and Wales. Although many women needed to increase the family income, and also to live more fulfilling lives, the opportunities were limited and usually very poorly paid. Few married women went out to work and, indeed, were discouraged from doing so by the ideology of the time. Professional women, not paid equally for equal work, normally had to leave their employment on marriage, home and child care without modern electrical appliances were tiring and demanding and there was serious male unemployment. The opportunities women found are shown in these figures from 1921 for Tyneside as a whole. In that year 76,000 were officially out at work. About 17,000 of these were indoor domestic servants, and about another 10,000 were barmaids or laundrywomen. About 9,000 were clerks or typists, and some 11,000 shop assistants or saleswomen. Over 6,000 were dressmakers, tailoresses, or involved in clothing. About 5,000 were nurses or teachers. The 10,000 or so of industrial workers were in a number of industries no one of which employed a large number, e.g. food, printing and stationery, light metal-work and rope-work. Most of these were unmarried. We don't know how many married women needing to supplement the family income when the breadwinner was sick or unemployed, or with an impossibly low wage, found work, badly paid and unregulated, as washerwomen, taking in sewing, or cleaning.

In any case the home was very demanding. Housework, child-care, shopping and cooking were much more labour-intensive before the benefits of electrical appliances became generally available. On the whole, even alongside the depression of the inter-war years, living standards were improving and women were encouraged in the popular magazines to become model housewives and indeed many took great pride and pleasure in so doing. Working men also worked longer hours than today and had little time and energy for work in the home even when they found it acceptable to contribute in this way. And we know that even today, in these supposedly more liberated times, when almost 50 percent of mothers of babies under one year old go out to work, women perform a hefty proportion of the household tasks as well.

After only 20 years of peace came the outbreak

Nurses, c.1920.

Women learn to be bus conductresses in 1940.

of World War II. This time it was 'total war' and from 1939 to 1945 women were conscripted into the armed forces for the first time, though not as combatants, as well as into numerous areas of heavy industry and work on the land. Their experience was many-sided. Much war-work was arduous and exhausting and often hazardous. But sometimes there was a liberation from the restrictions of oppressive home life, and tedious and poorly rewarded work. There were new friends and challenges and more money than there were goods to spend it on. Newcastle mothers were often anxious particularly about the moral, i.e. sexual, risks their daughters might be exposed to if conscripted into the forces and some persuaded them to sign up quickly for factory work to avoid this. For example Betty Hutchinson and her sister, from Walker, registered at Vickers. Betty was 18 and had been employed at the Cremona sweet factory earning about (old money) 12s 6p per week (65 pence). At Vickers she earned between £2 10s and £3 10s, the latter for the night shift, though this was for a 12 hour day or night 7.30-7.30, five-and-a-half days with Saturday half day. Sometimes a bonus brought the wage to £4 – 'a fortune practically to us'. They judged that women learned their new jobs, in their cases operating the lathes, very rapidly, were more conscientious than the men, the men 'acting themselves' (getting worked up), not liking the women working harder. At the end of the war, as it had been in 1918, these two, like most others, ceded their jobs to men. If they continued to work they often found less skilled and more poorly paid employment, for example, in Betty's case, at the Domestos factory. Here she also did 'a man's job' for three or four years loading wagons, accepting the 'really heavy' work because she liked the open air.

Opportunities to continue working and earning did continue and expand in some areas. There was a severe post-war labour shortage and the career of Helen Walker who had qualified as a teacher at Armstrong College in 1916 illustrates a new opening for women created by the new Labour Government – pensions reform. She had soon moved from teaching to a Civil Service post at the Labour Exchange at The Windmill Hills, Gateshead, but had had to leave on marriage in 1921. She did not have another 'proper' job until recruited to the Ministry of Labour during the war. After the war she transferred, obtained permanent status and worked until retirement age, to the Ministry of Pensions, just opening at Longbenton in temporary buildings. She had many female colleagues there, the majority unmarried. It was a big employer of women of clerical grade, and these women, like teachers, regarded themselves as having 'proper jobs'. The Department of Health and Social Security has become one of the major employers in Newcastle.

One difficulty in following the history of women's employment and unemployment in Newcastle and the North East in general before the 1970s lies in an understandable preoccupation with the region's heavy industries and the (often erroneous) presumptions about women's domestic role. Statistics relating to employment and unemployment simply disregarded women's economic activity. Unemployed women have not been visible in the way that men have been portrayed – adrift, idle, deprived of their major function as bread-winners occupied in 'real work', that is, stereotypically, heavy industrial work. Moreover, until recently women have not always claimed for themselves a strong working identity. They have found positions which allowed precedence to be given to their household and family duties.

As Elaine Knox pointed out in *Geordies*, many women did not think of themselves as workers, even when they earned money through employment. She gives the example of the part-time barmaid, working within a traditionally 'womanly' occupation, not necessarily viewed as 'working' by her husband. Numerous such jobs have been accommodated but not counted. 'A nice little job for a woman', which now sounds so patronising, was accepted by husbands and wives until quite recently as indicating modest enterprise but a proper sense of priorities.

In this area many things have changed. As Knox argues, the growth of the female workforce became the 'most important dynamic in postwar Tyneside's economic development'. And married women working has been the most significant feature of this development. By 1956 the number of women over 18 officially employed overall in Britain was some 75 per cent higher than in 1938 and higher than at any time during the war. (*Growing up in Newcastle*, Miller, Court, Walton, Knox). The trend towards women working, and in many new fields, increased dramatically from the 1960s onwards and by the 1980s, the greatest growth in regional and national workforces was married women, including women with children. The two-job family and the working wife became socially acceptable. Moreover, Tyneside women, way below the average in the 1920s, have been employed in line with the national average since the 1980s.

Girls in a position to choose have clearly desired the opportunity to achieve in education and employment and to a striking extent are seizing the opportunities now available. In recent

Girls in the sewing class at Whickham View School, 1945.

89

University of Northumbria at Newcastle

Congregation, University of Northumbria.

years girls nationally, and in Tyneside, have achieved better qualifications at age 16 than their male peers. More women then men are entering previously male-dominated professions such as law and medicine (currently there are 1,523 women out of 2,566 medical and dentistry students at Newcastle University), and growing numbers studying business and accountancy. In 1995 women numbered 55 per cent of all students in Higher Education, though to date men spend on average more time in higher education than women and more men have higher degrees. For academic 'role-models' Newcastle University has only appointed seven per cent of women professors 16 out of a total of 222 – though at the newer University of Northumbria there are 14 women to 33 men in that position.

These figures have to be closely linked with opportunity, education, training, spending power, independence, freedom, tolerance, and an equality unknown to our mothers and grandmothers. These certainly should be celebrated and few would turn the clock back. But they have brought with them new social and emotional pressures. How can family life be balanced with advancement at work, with the requirement to work in shops, not only on Sundays, but for any of the 24 hours in the day, for example? If things have advanced so much for women, have men both shared the benefits and co-operated with the consequences? In all walks of life women now regard employment outside the home as 'normal' and periods caring for children or elderly relatives (and women most often are the carers) as temporary. Many women are home-centred for a hefty proportion of their prime years and their chief demands today therefore are for family-friendly attitudes and policies to enable them to accommodate richer lives. Women have always worked, though often in the past it was a regretful necessity, unrecognised, statistically submerged and poorly rewarded. What was hidden is now evident and accepted, associated with choices and liberation, an achievement of the 20th century. Women have gained in quality of life and in visibility, making an acceptable and enhancing impact in institutions of all kinds, from education, politics, the workplace, to the church, sport and the media. In our famous 'party city' many women can be seen most nights of the week publicly and confidently enjoying their spending power and their freedom to experiment with fashion, in restaurants, pubs and clubs down the Bigg Market and the Quayside.

∽ Dr Maureen Callcott is retired Senior Lecturer in History at the University of Northumbria and is editor of *Pilgrimage of Grace: the Diaries of Ruth Dodds 1904-1974*, 1995, Bewick Press.

Ambition and Harsh Reality
Local Politics … Local Politicians

Nigel Todd

AS A WORLD WAR RAGED IN 1942, the general commanding the military district at Newcastle upon Tyne found that he had a little local difficulty. Many of his soldiers were very bored at weekends. To solve the problem, the general had the bright idea of asking Newcastle's cinemas to open on Sundays. Newcastle, in common with many other towns and cities, maintained a prohibition on Sunday cinema, and application had to be made to the City Council to lift the ban. Little may the general have known that he was about to unleash a storm of controversy. Although the Council's Watch Committee, charged with regulating public entertainments, sympathised with the army's request, the majority of the Council's members saw matters quite differently. When the proposal was debated in the Council Chamber in July 1942, the general risked eternal damnation. Speech after speech invoked 'the Commandments given by God to Moses' to keep Sunday holy, denounced 'this Sabbath Day paganism' and asserted that 'the pictures had not helped the children of this City, but had been the means of bringing many of them before the Courts.' After all, this was a place where everything from running electric tramcars on Sundays to holding concerts and sports in public parks and opening theatres on Sunday afternoons and evenings had been vigorously opposed by religious factions. The cinemas fared no better and the long speeches led to a resounding rejection of Sunday opening.

This was by no means the end of the tale, of course. Following the war, the cinema owners sought to end the Sunday ban. They tried in 1947, only to be blocked by

Political theatre: the Town Hall, 1965, the stage for local politics until the move to the new Civic Centre.

councillors who were more inclined to listen to the Lord's Day Observance Society. The Council threw out the idea by a hefty majority again in 1949. But now the reformers wanted the decision placed in the hands of Newcastle's people through a plebiscite, as stipulated by the Sunday Entertainments Act, 1932. The notion impressed neither the Council members nor the Lord's Day Observance Society, which said that a referendum would merely leave Sunday to the mercy of 'the irresponsible members of the community.' Undaunted, cinema lovers made a further bid in 1950, but were rebuffed. Then in July 1952, the cinema owners forced another Council debate. By this time cinemas were open on Sundays in towns outside Newcastle's boundary, and the bus services were ferrying thousands of desperate filmgoers across the borders.

Pleas from local cinema owners and Associated British Cinemas, heavily emphasising the case for a referendum, introduced the debate. The Newcastle Council for United Christian Action restated their interpretation of the Commandants and opposition to the 'clamouring of the crowd.' Probably sensing that democratic sentiment was edging towards a referendum, the opponents of Sunday opening secured a postponement of the decision until the following September. Yet the tide had turned. Despite impassioned attacks upon the commercialisation of the Sabbath, the September meeting declared in favour of seeking Sunday cinema. The law required the Council to take the proposal to a public meeting and, if requested by one hundred electors, a referendum as well. Accordingly, the Council arranged a public meeting at the City Hall on 14 October. This well attended meeting spent two-and-three-quarter hours in 'forthright and pointed' argument, producing a vote of 693-513 against Sunday opening. Within two days, the supporters of Sunday cinema collected over 2000 signatures to requisition a Council-organised poll across the City. The consequent campaign was hotly contested. Nevertheless, when the votes were counted at the Laing Art Gallery it was confirmed that 28,673 people had polled in favour of being able to go to the cinema on Sundays, overwhelming the 14,323 who were against lifting the ban. Thereafter, Newcastle became slightly more interesting at weekends.

The cinema episode exposed several ingredients of Newcastle's local politics. For one thing, politics were not always about parties and election results. Many other items entered into an arena made 'political' by conflicting interests, such as the secular and the religious, and by the pervasive presence of the City Council. Newcastle has been animated by a rich variety of campaigns and movements. Occasionally, these enthusiasms have taken a cultural form. The People's Theatre, now in Heaton, began in 1911 as an adjunct of the British Socialist Party whose members wanted to stage Bernard Shaw's plays among other examples of 'committed' drama. It was a torch picked up by the Left Book Club Theatre Guild in 1937-39, with plays on the Spanish Civil War and trade unionism often performed in the Bigg Market and at factory gates. The Co-operative Arts Players continued the radical theatre tradition in some ways after World War II at the Newcastle Co-operative Society's theatre in Jesmond.

Women's suffrage produced animated agitation before World War I, and mass unemployment gave rise to local branches of the National Unemployed Workers' Movement in the 1920s and 1930s. The NUWM was given rent-free accommodation at Pilgrim Street by the City Council in 1926 for use in representing the unemployed and, during the 1930s, the Movement mustered Hunger Marches in the Bigg Market, a venue for open-air oratory. Until the 1960s the Bigg Market offered free entertainment during the evenings as the local Speakers' Corner. Religious and political advocates regularly set up their soapboxes to denounce each other, preach to the converted or recruit for their causes.

Newcastle's political 'street theatre' has been largely peaceful, with people making their

Street politics: a meeting in the Bigg Market for the 1910 local elections.

points sometimes noisily, occasionally colourfully but generally without violence or disorder. The principal exceptions to the rule have been Fascist movements. In 1933-34 Sir Oswald Mosley poured considerable sums of money into planting his British Union of Fascists (the 'Blackshirts') on Tyneside. BUF clubrooms were opened at Benwell's Adelaide Terrace and on Clayton Street in the City centre, and a good deal of violence was directed against Jewish people and the Blackshirts' opponents. As a high point of his efforts, Mosley called a rally to coincide with the Town Moor Festival in June 1934. The preparations involved his lieutenants staging open-air speaking at Cowen's Monument in Westgate Road and a meeting at Gateshead Town Hall on the evenings of 13-14 May 1934.

Newcastle's Anti-Fascist League had other ideas. When Mosley's men marched to Cowen's statue on 13 May their meeting was closed down within minutes by a large AFL crowd. Robust street fighting, barely controlled by mounted police, spread between Clayton and Blackett Streets, and ended with the Blackshirts either besieged in their clubroom or under arrest for assaulting plainclothes police officers. On the next evening, vast numbers of police prevented further conflict, especially when the crowd tried to throw the Blackshirts off the Tyne Bridge. Mosley rapidly postponed his appearance at the Town Moor by a month, and then he held a fairly lacklustre gathering. These events gave national prominence to Newcastle and all but finished the BUF locally. Apart from brief visits by Mosley's deputy, William Joyce (the 'Lord Haw Haw' of wartime Nazi radio), Blackshirt activity remained subdued over the rest of the 1930s. A limp revival of Mosley's movement was attempted in the late-1940s, but was exposed and ruined by Jewish ex-servicemen and their supporters.

It was not until 1976-78 that neo-Nazis, under the National Front label, again promoted racial ill feeling in an openly organised manner. The Anti-Nazi League opposed the NF in the 1970s, and a more distinctive local response developed from the 1980s. A Tyne and Wear Anti-Fascist Association was cre-

Newcastle Chronicle & Journal Ltd.

Deflated supermen: Oswald Mosley and supporters in the Haymarket following a rally on the Town Moor, July 1934.

ated in 1983 by trade unionists, students, church and community groups, councillors and other anti-racists. TWAFA scored a notable first by handing out leaflets to counter NF newspaper sellers outside Newcastle United's St James's Park on home match days over 1985-86. This was the first venture of its kind in Britain, and came at a time when bananas and racist taunts were hurled at black soccer players visiting the ground. The TWAFA presence started a successful process, eventually adopted at other football clubs, aimed at eliminating racial hooliganism from the game. Any hopes that the neo-Nazis may have entertained fell on stony ground in Newcastle where, by and large, the community ignored their appeal. The prevailing mood was underlined in 1990 when the City Council banned the NF and similar organisations from meeting on civic premises.

The failure of racist groups to cultivate sympathy in Newcastle owed something to the City's long liberal tradition. From the first half of the 19th century, Newcastle had welcomed European exiles, black American fugitive slaves, Jewish refugees and Irish immigrants. These foundations underpinned a distaste for discrimination that found expression in May 1933 when 130 political, religious and industrial groupings held a meeting in the City Hall to denounce anti-Semitism in Germany. The Hall was packed to overflowing. Similar meetings took place in the 1970s and 1980s to reject racial hostility towards Newcastle's Asian inhabitants who had arrived over the previous twenty years, and in some cases during the inter-war decades.

Not everything was rosy, of course, and not everybody shared the liberal principles by any means. Racial violence erupted in Westgate Road in 1959, and tensions rose again in 1968 in the wake of Enoch Powell's notorious speech predicting wholesale bloodletting as a consequence of immigration. These incidents generated confusion over the choice of appropriate responses, and some angry exchanges took place between councillors and anti-racism activists on the role of protest demonstrations. A fairly unhappy period ensued as the City's 'establishment' sought to minimise concerns about the extent of discrimination. Over the longer term, however, events moved in a more positive direction, signified in 1986 by Ahmed Kutub's election in the predominantly white Fenham ward as Newcastle's first councillor from an Asian background.

Inevitably, the City Council has acted as a focus for political interest, providing services that have touched lives in a multitude of ways. Housing, education, social services, libraries, swimming pools and public wash-houses, tram and bus services, policing and poor relief, parks and cemeteries, street cleaning and lighting, highway repairs and planning, food safety, and administration of a myriad of rules and regulations are only a selection of municipal responsibilities during the century.

There have been radical changes in the Council's powers over time. In 1902, for example, the City Council was put in charge of schools on the abolition of the directly elected School Boards. Until 1969, the Council's Watch Committee governed the City's police force. The Council then lost the policing role when the area's small forces were amalgamated into the Northumbria Police. A separately elected Board of Guardians took charge of financial aid to the unemployed and the poor until the provision was transferred to the City Council in 1930, and then removed to central government in 1948. But over the century the Council has assumed important powers as an agency for housing and planning.

Municipal politics have always been a minority taste. For much of the century, election turnouts of between 30 and 40 per cent of the voters have been typical. The level of participation depended upon various factors, but when the City Council raised a high proportion of its income from local rates, and was to a wide degree in mastery of its own affairs, elections could arouse a certain excitement. In contrast, the insistence of central government on fixing the scale of civic spending and removing powers from local authorities during the 1980s meant that there was less scope for choice and disagreement at elections. Voter turnout went into steep decline and a miserable 11 to 25 per cent was not unusual by the mid-1990s.

It is worth noting, too, that the geography of the 'City Council' has altered over time. The City was really the town centre and its adjacent suburbs before 1904 when the heavily populated urban districts of Benwell, Fenham, Walker and a segment of Kenton were incorporated into 'Newcastle'. Parts of Newburn, Denton and Longbenton were gained in 1935, and the City adopted its present boundaries with the acquisition of the Gosforth, Newburn and Longbenton urban districts as well as Woolsington, Hazelrigg, Dinnington and Brunswick in 1974. The City's enlargement was usually viewed with suspicion by neighbouring boroughs. A Labour Party proposal to create a 'City of Tyneside' in the 1930s was not completely supported by Labour opinion along the river. And Newcastle provoked further shock waves in 1963 by suggesting that there should be one borough for the whole of Tyneside. These ideas were advanced on the grounds that grim social and economic problems could be solved only by a big, well-resourced piece of local government in place of a multiplicity of small, poorly financed and insular councils.

The principal step towards a large sub-region came with the formation of the Tyne and Wear County Council in addition to enlarged district authorities in 1974. The County's legacies were the Metro light railway system and, until privatisation of bus operations, a cheap and integrated public transport network. At the same time, the County brought together an impressive Tyne and Wear Museums Service on a scale unobtainable by the separate borough councils. But the experiment was brought to an abrupt end in 1986 when Mrs Thatcher's government abolished Tyne and Wear in an exercise described by the Conservatives as 'money saving' and by Labour as 'vindictive'.

Annual elections were the battleground for supremacy on the City Council. Before 1918, the Council was really the province of Liberals and the Conservatives with a small Labour group (nine councillors by 1915). Political issues oscillated between Lib-Lab enthusiasm for municipal tramways, ratepayers' suspicion of civic corruption and mismanagement (grounded in local Town Hall scandals of the 1880s), Liberal hostility towards Socialism, Tory and Liberal concerns to keep the rates and spending at a low level, and Labour's urging of public works for the unemployed and improved housing conditions. After 1918, politics were fundamentally reshaped. Liberals and Conservatives mainly abandoned their party identities in the Town Hall and united to oppose Labour, which boasted 17 councillors by 1921.

The Labour representatives tended to be engineering workers, railwaymen and miners, though they also included Newcastle's first woman councillor, Mary Laverick, elected in 1919. Confirmation that Labour was capable of attracting broader support came with the election of the solicitor Moss Turner-Samuels in 1921 as well as the defection from the Liberals of Sir Charles Trevelyan, who became a Labour MP for Newcastle Central in 1922. The anti-Socialist councillors were usually business and professional people. This class divide decorated Council elections in the early 1920s. A Business Group, which controlled the City Council, fielded candidates in most wards, whereas Labour contested some seats but left others to either an 'Unemployed Committee' or a Tenants' Defence Association. On the other hand, the Council was loosely co-ordinated. Labour was allowed direction of the Housing Committee, since the Business Group took little interest in service provision, and this gave the Socialists scope to build the City's first significant Council housing, erected at Walker in 1919 with money borrowed from the boilermakers' trade union.

When the Business Group faded during the mid-1920s, the anti-Labour bloc divided between Moderates and Independents, momentarily offering Labour a slight chance to take control of the Council in 1930. Apparently, a couple of the Independents hinted that they might vote with Labour and provide the party with a majority. These promises did not materialise but Labour did hold all its Newcastle seats in 1930, defying a national trend. Polling in those days took place on Saturdays and the 1930 elections coincided with Newcastle United's 4-1 home win against Leeds. According to the local newspaper, *Evening World*, the victory encouraged many happy working men, assumed to be Labour-inclined, to vote on their way home from the match. Any likelihood of Labour gaining control was swept aside the following year in the wreckage of the collapse of the 1929-31 Labour government. The anti-Socialists, reborn as the Progressives in the mid-1930s, held Labour in opposition for the rest of the pre-war years.

Labour's left-wing rivals experienced mixed fortunes as well. The Communist Party had influence within the unemployed workers' movement, opened a Workers' Bookshop on Westgate Hill and ran a lively youth league. From 1936-39, the Spanish Civil War drew converts to the party and several Newcastle members heroically joined the International Brigade in Spain. Yet the party's vote in Newcastle was extremely small. Aside from the CP, the Independent Labour Party, a founder of the Newcastle Labour Representation Committee in 1901, quit Labour in 1932 to be a distinct left-wing party.

Council on show: Part of the Lord Mayor's procession to the cathedral in July 1929 to give thanks for the King's recovery from an illness. The posters are advertising the North East Coast Exhibition.

The ILP maintained a Socialist café and meeting room in Newcastle's East End, offered a Guild of Youth, displayed visiting MPs such as the Glasgow firebrand Jimmy Maxton, but was completely overshadowed by Labour at local and parliamentary elections.

Council elections were suspended during World War II, and their resumption in 1945 saw sweeping Labour gains. Three of the City's parliamentary constituencies were captured, and the party won control of the Town Hall. James Clydesdale, who had been blind since the age of eight, led the victorious Labour councillors. Elected to the Council in 1922, he now became Labour's first Lord Mayor. Under Labour, the City Council embarked on a modest slum clearance programme and placed renewed emphasis upon developing municipal services. But the Progressives fought back over the next four years, ousting Labour in 1949 at a set of elections remarkable for a 50 per cent turnout among the voters and evenly balanced support for both parties – the Progressives received 48,785 votes and Labour had 48,321.

Interest in politics remained high in the late-1940s, and was especially fractious when linked with the Cold War. Moreover, these influences could affect the details of Council decisions. The Libraries Committee, for example, banned the Communist *Daily Worker* from library newsrooms in 1949. Several Labour councillors alleged that a Catholic majority at a Committee meeting had pursued a Church crusade against the Left, and in retaliation they later managed to ban the *Catholic Universe* from the libraries. When the row surfaced in the Council Chamber it prompted a heated debate on freedom of the press. One Labour man, Edward Short (later Lord Glenamara), even invoked the spirit of Stalingrad in defence of the *Daily Worker*. The Council told the Libraries Committee to put both papers back on the shelves.

The Progressives kept the upper hand throughout most of the 1950s, holding Labour at bay to an extent not achieved in most other major cities. Local circumstances no doubt contributed. The City had a sizeable owner-occupier population anxious to prevent the rate increases associated with Labour. In addition, business people could claim a vote at the commercial premises on which they paid rates, and in one ward there were almost 1000 'business votes'. These points assisted the Progressives who were also astute at managing aldermanic appointments. The office of alderman allowed councillors to appoint worthy persons for six year terms as voting members of the City Council. For parties with insecure majorities, appointing the aldermen offered an insurance if things went badly at the ballot box. Labour gains at the 1952 elections, for instance, brought the party almost level pegging with the Progressives, but the Progressives then denied Labour additional aldermen by having three Labour nominees ruled ineligible because of minor errors in their nomination papers. This shrewd move meant that the Progressives remained in charge even when Labour briefly had a majority of one among the councillors in 1955.

A chief architect of Progressive power was a flamboyant character named William McKeag (1897-1972). Born in Co. Durham, McKeag had joined the army in 1914, quickly becoming a junior officer. The military life appealed, and in 1918 he volunteered to fight the Bolsheviks and spent two years with the White Russian armies. Returning to England, he took up a career as a solicitor and was a National Liberal MP for Durham City from 1931 until defeated in 1935. He was elected to Newcastle City Council in 1936 and stayed on the Council for 25 years, twice serving as Lord Mayor. Driving a Rolls Royce car and wearing a pince-nez, which he used as a stage-prop in public speaking, McKeag deployed considerable energies in pursuing civic interests, acting as a director of Newcastle United, and savaging the Labour Party.

McKeag was singularly effective in 1943-44 when he probed the strange case of the disappearing fire engine. An old fire engine had been sold for scrap in 1940 but the Chief Constable of the Newcastle police, Frederick Crawley, could not produce an account covering the sale. The Council's Watch Committee seemed uninterested and this raised McKeag's curiosity. He asked searching and detailed questions, inviting a Home Office inquiry. Although hampered by narrow terms of reference, the inquiry did uncover evidence of the misuse of petrol, improper use of emergency stores and serious shortcomings in the conduct of the police and fire services. Resignation of the Watch Committee and the retirement of the Chief Constable soon followed. These were no easy targets. Crawley was a strong personality, much given to riding the streets on a police horse in the style of a cavalry commander. As a London constable he had shadowed Lenin, and in the 1926 General Strike he had ordered baton charges against Newcastle trade unionists. McKeag had taken on a tough nut, and in winning he unintentionally delighted the Labour Movement.

The passing of Alderman McKeag was as intriguing as his life. It emerged after his death that a woman Tory county councillor had secretly spirited away his ashes from the Newcastle crematorium and hidden them under her bed for five years. The story hit the headlines. Deeply embarrassed, the City Council revealed that their records of the cremation were incomplete, and so the exact details of how the county councillor had obtained the ashes were shrouded in speculation.

In McKeag and his associates, Labour faced formidable opponents. But another clue to Progressive dominance in the 1950s lay in the moribund nature of the City's politics. It was not uncommon for wards to go uncontested at elections and the Labour Party, led by the ageing Clydesdale, appeared complacent. This was all to change with the arrival of a fresh generation of Labour people clustered around the charismatic personality of Thomas Daniel Smith (1915-1993).

T. Dan Smith was one of the most provocative figures ever to grace English local government. His period as leader of Newcastle City Council (1960-65) was unusual, as his style resembled that of an American elected mayor, and he was capable of visible contradictions. A strong advocate of municipal enterprise, he ran his own string of private businesses. Notwithstanding a fierce commitment to state education, he sent his children to private schools. The burning desire to win social justice for the poor was combined with a lavish personal lifestyle, represented by his Mark 10 Jaguar car with its DAN 68 number plate. Smith was an unashamed exhibitionist, enabling him to be widely regarded as

Mr Newcastle: T. Dan Smith in 1963.

'Mr Newcastle', the voice of the North East in a national setting. This status was also constructed by Smith's cocktail of personal vision, rare charm, and ruthless determination to shake Newcastle out of its post-war torpor. His aim was to sweep away the City's dingy image. Newcastle was to become the 'New Brasilia', symbolising modern architecture, or the 'Venice of the North', a renaissance city of education and public arts.

Immense changes were indeed accomplished, but the price was arguably too high. Architectural heritage was sometimes needlessly destroyed in the love affair with modernism, and not all new housing and buildings were of good quality. Above all, Smith was dubiously entangled with a Tory businessman, the architect John Poulson, and a committee-room bully, the powerful Durham county councillor Andrew Cunningham. All three were ultimately gaoled in the mid-1970s for corruption related to building contracts. Smith's downfall was widely publicised although disputes about his motives have continued. Was he a Socialist idealist who felt that his ends justified the means and got lost along the way? Was he an authoritarian town hall 'boss' advancing the interests of builders and planners, doing what they felt was good for everyone else? Or was he simply 'on the make'? The answer probably combines each of these elements, but the root of the enigma lies in what proportions.

Dan Smith was born at Wallsend into a mining family interested in the arts and Socialism. Moving

Going up: the Noble Street flats under construction, 1957.

to Newcastle in the 1930s, he worked as a painter and decorator, establishing his own business. Smith joined the Peace Pledge Union and the ILP, and as a revolutionary Socialist in 1944 he was immersed in an extensive apprentices' strike at the Tyneside shipyards. Through these endeavours, he acquired organising abilities and was a frequent Bigg Market orator. Joining the Labour Party in 1950, Smith was soon elected as a Labour councillor for Walker, and strove to revive the City Labour Party.

Organisation was improved and policies developed, especially on housing. The Progressives had built Council flats in the 1950s but these were austere so-called 'slums on the drawing boards' at Noble Street and Longbenton. Labour wanted to do better.

The 1958 elections brought Labour back to power in Newcastle with an overall majority of two councillors. This new administration promptly embarked on providing accommodation for the 10,000 people on the housing waiting list, hiring planners to remodel the commercial heart of the City, and introducing adventurous educational programmes. By 1960, the Cruddas Park tower blocks scheme ('homes in the sky') was unveiled in a blaze of publicity bearing the Dan Smith imprint. Redevelopment of the City centre was structured in futuristic terms, and encapsulated in the Civic Centre opened in 1963. The site for the Civic Centre had been identified in 1939, and designs undertaken in 1950, but the Progressives had lingered over the practicalities. Smith drove the project forward, insisting that modernist Scandinavian features were incorporated into the building.

The early 1960s also functioned as a forcing house for educational change, complementing Smith's ambition for an 'educational precinct' in the centre of Newcastle. He argued that world-class cities with a future were those built around education rather than those content to be surrounded by coalfields. The Council pressed for King's College, a branch of Durham University, to be upgraded to the University of Newcastle in 1963, further education was expanded, and the groundwork was prepared for the Newcastle Polytechnic (now the University of Northumbria). Labour councillors considered locating this 'critical mass' in the City centre vital, but they had to outmanoeuvre their opponents who wanted to site the University of Newcastle at Gosforth.

A ferocious battle was fought over the abolition of the 11-plus in schools. Educational thinking was moving against segregating the majority of children into secondary modern schools, stigmatising them with the badge of 'failure' at a young age. This meant changing from selection to a comprehensive system. and the idea was implemented in Newcastle by the Labour Council from 1958. Vested interests connected with the grammar schools loudly resisted, and at one stage the King's College representatives resigned from the City's education committee in disapproval of the comprehensive plan. But the Council pressed ahead, amalgamating two new secondary modern schools at Kenton into Newcastle's first comprehensive in 1959. The evidence of comprehensive education at Kenton bolstered the case for change, and eventually the new system was extended to the whole City.

With change came upheaval. New roads and buildings displaced people, and the expensive costs of development added to the rates burden. Not surprisingly, ratepayers' protest meetings began to be organised. Politically, this turbulence oiled the Conservatives' return to local politics. Some Tories had long felt that the Progressives had outlived their purpose and, in 1959, the Opposition was transformed into the Conservative Party. The Tory resurgence actually came close to unseating Labour in 1961. Conservative gains in the City elections brought them equal with Labour. Consequently, control of the Council hinged upon the appointment of aldermen at a crucial Council meeting. The issue was literally decided on the streets of Paris. Two councillors, one from each party, had separately gone on holiday to the French capital and neither had been aware of the importance of the meeting. Both parties urgently telephoned hotels in Paris to find their councillors and get them back for the vote. Dan Smith won the race, ensuring that the Labour man was flown back to Newcastle in time to vote, before resuming his holiday. The Conservative arrived just too late. Given a slim majority, Labour replaced seven Tory aldermen with their own nominees, securing a comfortable majority.

The Conservatives were unable to dislodge Labour until Harold Wilson's 1966-70 Labour government reached depths of unpopularity. In 1967 the Council finally changed hands when, strictly speaking, the first-ever official Conservative majority took over at the Civic Centre. Buttressed by their command of the aldermanic bench, the Conservatives retained Newcastle until local government reorganisation in 1974 when Labour took the new, enlarged City Council. A long period of Conservative decline followed, and by 1995 Newcastle had neither Conservative MPs nor councillors for the first

Coming down: the Noble Street flats bite the dust, 1978.

time in modern history.

So, where does this leave us? It is difficult to make an assessment of Newcastle's 20th century political history in a brief summary. Problems that were familiar at the beginning of the century, notably in housing and unemployment, persisted as headaches at the close, though in somewhat different ways. Opportunities available to Newcastle's residents expanded, partly in response to political pressures, yet poverty and hardship were never entirely eradicated. Voting at Council elections rarely roused the population, but sufficient people had cared passionately enough about changing or preserving one thing or another to engage with the campaigning, arguing and governing essential in making democracy work. That at least was an inheritance worth passing on to the new century.

⌁ Nigel Todd is an historian and City Councillor, and author of *The Militant Democracy: Joseph Cowen and Victorian Radicalism*, 1991, and *In Excited Times: The People Against the Blackshirts*, 1995.

Lynn Pearson

Clarion call: the men of the Northumberland Fusiliers, with accompanying families and angel on their snow-decked World War I memorial outside the Civic Centre.

Sublime Spirals and Concrete Geometry:
A personal view of Newcastle's late 20th century architecture

Dr Lynn F. Pearson

THE WORLD SPED UP IN THE 1960S AND 1970S, when place, space and time were transformed by the apotheosis of the car. Its speed compromised real time and distance, while sense of place was physically diminished by the view from the mobile cocoon. Driven by the spatial needs of the car and urged on by its connotations of freedom, romance and innovation, British cities were restructured. Planners, architects and engineers designed swathes of motorway, complex interchanges and the inclined planes, swirling spirals and Guggenheim-like towers of the multistorey car park. Once the triumph of the highway engineer was complete, office blocks and shopping developments followed, but many of these were banal, lacking the power and excitement of the early road-related structures.

These monuments to modernism are not cosy buildings, and are not much loved. Crass office blocks now dominate the view of Newcastle from the south bank of the Tyne. Here, the fabric of the city has been reduced to a concrete jigsaw, grey block piled upon dull grey tower, obscure piece locked into nameless fragment. During the 1970s the architectural gods moved from detail to retail, producing the grim flat roofline of Eldon Square and dulling the sensory experience of the city centre.

The best of Newcastle's late 20th century architecture is only revealed by the low light and long shadows of the winter sun, or when darkness falls and lighting brings out its pure geometry. Multistorey car parks are transformed by night as their ramps swoop and dive, twist and turn to display their inner structure. In the dark, even the City Library aspires to car park status, as light shines out from beneath its concrete fins. Look, too, at the perfect curve of the Quayside as it disappears into eastern darkness, or explore the labyrinthine passages beneath Swan House, and enjoy the deliciously profligate decoration of the Civic Centre. Perhaps, like the Tyne Bridge – now over 70 years old – these structures will have the happy attribute of always appearing modern. There is beauty and complexity in these buildings, more delight for the eye by far than in the glum, ponderous offices which have now colonised the Quayside. Truly successful riverside buildings take their cue from the water, using acres of glass to make full use of their scintillating sites. The rest is dull, dull.

Already the buildings of the 1960s and 1970s are once more becoming fashionable. Our concrete future is now in the past, but we may come to love its architectural strengths. Its powerful forms and clear functionality seem likely to ensure its survival far longer than the more anodyne structures of the 1980s and 1990s, where trivial decoration fails to mask lack of confidence in the entire architectural enterprise. If the buildings of the past are any guide to those of the future, then successful design needs art, science, good fortune and time. Given the latter, the banal and the boring will be swept away by the bulldozers.

*Looking back two centuries from Manors Car Park to All Saints Church.
This complex low-rise car park, designed by the City Engineer and
opened in 1971, was Newcastle's first civic multistorey carpark.*

*A three-dimensional conundrum of curving planes at
Manors Car Park, before the first vehicle arrives to destroy
the pure geometric pleasure of the structure seen in early
morning light.*

Within the precincts of Swan House is a curious network of passages, stairs and pathways centred on that worm in the bud, the dreadful reproduction of Dobson's Royal Arcade. Remove this travesty and Swan House, a fine structure in its own right, may yet live again.

Brutalism fails through lack of confidence. A little less than a century separates the Union Club on Westgate Road from its beastly predator, Westgate House, a popular favourite for the title of the city's worst building. Dead weight and dull, it has no redeeming features.

The Quayside at its best, when night and lights bring out its steely curve. Of the new waterside structures, only the glass façade of the Pitcher and Piano makes any attempt at response to the imperatives of the site.

Seeing double? Might be the result of a hard stint at the Pitcher and Piano. This elegant little pub won a 1998 Royal Institute of British Architects award for excellence in new architecture.

The red sandstone and towering columns of the Law Courts make a strong statement on the Quayside. Designed by the Napper Collerton Partnership in 1984-90, this is certainly the best of the recent large-scale Quayside buildings. Its interior is bland, perhaps necessarily, but the slightly overblown exterior is very much of its time.

The Copthorne Hotel, built in 1991 by Arup Associates on the Close, takes full advantage of its riverside site and ensuing displays of slightly imperfect symmetry.

Beneath the golden globe, part of the Quayside sculpture Swirle Pavilion, the viewer sees only the brightly-lit entrance to a car park. This marriage of art and mammon sees art coming out second, perhaps due to the unimpressive appearance of the sculpture's metal and stonework.

The Blacksmith's Needle is a popular piece of Quayside artwork, its detailed catalogue of objects evoking instant recognition. In the distance, an altogether simpler structural form does precisely the same job.

Clean curves above the courtyard of the Bioscience Centre, one of the colourful and innovative structures forming the International Centre for Life, which was built in 1998-9.

The Laing Art Gallery's new entrance leads the visitor into a blank wall. Although an inherently difficult site, this was surely not the right solution, although its curving glazing produces unexpectedly agreeable reflections.

Chasing shadows in the sieve-like stair tower of the Bioscience Centre.

Waiting for the last bus – Haymarket Bus Station, night.

One high-tech structure nestles comfortably beneath another: the train shed of Dobson's Central Station (1845-50) shelters the glass-walled travel centre, built in 1985. Latterly, commerce-driven alterations have diminished the beauty of this under-appreciated little structure.

The spaceship Council Chamber ready for take-off. The massive stone drum of the chamber is raised on piers above the ceremonial entrance, and well protected by its symbolic moat.

Underneath the arches of the Civic Centre – undoubtedly the city's best building – designed by the City Architect George Kenyon during the early 1950s and built 1956-1969. Materials matter, and here high quality sliding metal screens complement the dense brickwork soaring overhead along the Ceremonial Way.

Its uppermost spiral ramps lost to the dusk, the eerie corkscrew of Eldon Square Car Park prepares to expel one final car into outer darkness.

All the photographs in this chapter are copyright of Lynn Pearson.

Lynn Pearson is a Newcastle-based architectural historian specialising in the buildings of the brewing industry and British seaside. She has published 13 books, including *British Breweries: An Architectural History*, 1999, and *Northern City: an Architectural history of Newcastle upon Tyne*, 1996, Newcastle Libraries & Information Service. She is research fellow at the School of Art and Design, University of Wolverhampton where she is producing a national gazetteer of architectural ceramics.

Palaces of Pleasure

Frank Manders

IN THE YEARS AROUND THE TURN OF THE CENTURY, leisure time expanded for the middle and working classes, who were able to take advantage of this to patronise existing entertainment venues and to inspire the introduction of new forms. In addition, women were an increasingly important factor in the equation, especialiy young or unmarried women. Commercial interests were quick to step in to provide what was needed. The cinema industry was the first to attempt to appeal directly to women, but they had formed a large element of both theatre and music hall audiences after the latter had broken their early link with public houses. The new-style music halls were keen to demonstrate that their shows, in addition to being entertaining, were wholesome and would not offend. The provision of entertainment was a serious commercial business, with considerable profits to be made if its providers managed to retain public approval but considerable losses if they misjudged or fell behind public taste.

In 1900, Newcastle had two theatres, the Tyne and the Grand. There were also three variety theatres/music halls, the Palace, Empire, and Queens. On 24 November 1899, the auditorium of the Theatre Royal had been destroyed by fire, only five years after it had been brought up to contemporary standards by the London theatre architect Walter Emden. The Royal was rebuilt with increased capacity and reopened on 31 December 1901. It joined the new century as virtually a new theatre and was part of a prestige circuit run by Robert Arthur Theatres, Ltd., succeeded by Howard and Wyndham, Ltd. The Royal had the pick of the best touring companies of the day and a succession of pre- and post-London hit shows.

The Tyne theatre in Westgate Road was the Royal's traditional rival, specialising in drama, comic and light opera and magnificent pantomimes, and had been run since 1894 by Howard and Wyndham. The third theatre was the Grand at Byker. It was built by Weldon Watts and his business partner, James Bacon, and was admitted to be something of an experiment as a large (2,500 seat) suburban theatre, though its owners pointed out that Byker and Heaton had a population as large as many independent towns. The Grand opened on 27 July 1896 with Shakespeare's *The Taming of the Shrew*. After a few years as a 'legitimate' theatre, it closed, was redecorated, and reopened on 1 August 1904, managed by Sidney Bacon, as a variety theatre. It is no surprise that a similarly large theatre proposed by Weldon Watts in November 1899 for the west end of the city, at the junction of Elswick and Bentinck Roads, was abandoned at the planning stage.

This brings us to the music hall scene at the turn of the century. Music halls in their original definition as singing or supper rooms attached to public houses, had died out in Newcastle by the turn of the century. However, the popularity of this form of entertainment had led to the building of purpose-

Northumberland Road, 1910, with White City, the roller-skating rink, later dance hall, which was converted to the Hippodrome Theatre in 1912. To its right is the Olympia, Newcastle's first purpose-built picture hall, opened in 1909.

designed halls which were, in effect, theatres. The transition period is marked by the Empire Variety Theatre in Newgate Street, which was far larger than the public house of which it formed ostensibly a part, the Royal Scotch Arms. Opened on 1 December 1890, it was a riot of red plush and elaborate plaster decoration, while being at the same time intimate and almost 'cosy'. The Empire was run by H. E. Moss and Richard Thornton until becoming part of the Moss Empires circuit in December 1899, giving it access to the first rank of music hall stars. Such was its success that it closed for rebuilding on 23 August 1902; in the interim, shows were relocated to the Olympia in Northumberland Road, a building which, happily, was owned by Richard Thornton and advertised as 'Empire at Olympia'. The new Empire Palace which opened on 14 September 1903 was a testimony, in its size and opulence, to the popularity of the music hall. Seating almost 3,000 in stalls, dress circle, upper circle and gallery, it had a roof which slid open for ventilation; the stalls benches were now tip-up chairs and even the gallery seats were padded.

The oldest variety theatre was the Palace in the Haymarket at its junction with St Thomas' Street. It had opened as a circus in May 1878 and in 1888 it was converted to a theatre by the Livermore brothers. In 1895 it was entirely rebuilt with a 'classical' frontage by new owners, the Palace Company (Newcastle) Ltd. The company prospectus claimed that the theatre was in a location which had 'a dense population of "all sorts and conditions of men," whereby it is assured patronage for every part of the house.' In 1896 it was taken over by the Rowe family, who owned it until closure. Its programming was varied: in addition to variety shows it was home to travelling opera companies, straight plays and melodramas.

Trailing along a good way behind the Empire and the Palace was the Queen's Theatre on Scotswood Road, a wooden building faced with corrugated iron sheeting which opened as a circus in August 1900. This soon failed and the building reopened as the Queen's Theatre of Varieties on 12 November 1900; becoming the Elswick Theatre in August 1903, it struggled on until refused a licence as a dangerous structure in May 1907. It opened briefly as a picture hall and was demolished in December 1909.

The first major new theatre of the century was the Pavilion Theatre of Varieties, opened on 28 December 1903 almost next door to the Tyne Theatre. It was cheaply designed and built for Tom Barrasford's circuit and held less than 2,000 people. One further variety theatre opened in the city before World War I when a former skating rink, the White City in Northumberland Road, was converted into the Hippodrome, opening to the public on 25 November 1912. The owners were the national circuit Variety Theatres Controlling Co., and the Hippodrome had almost 2,500 seats on a single raked floor and a stage which could be rolled back to reveal a 30,000 gallon water tank, intended to be used for 'aquatic shows'.

These variety theatres truly offered variety: far from staging week after week of 'turns', they in fact were capable of housing grand opera, light opera, musical revues and even drama. With the latter they were directly opposing the two 'legitimate' theatres. Their managements would give a home to anything likely to fill the theatre and thus generate a profit.

There were also in the city several large halls, most of which staged theatre-type entertainment on occasion. The largest, opened in 1893, was Olympia in Northumberland Road, built of cast and wrought iron and timber-lined, and reckoned to hold 5-6,000 on a flat floor with side galleries. Although used for bazaars, carnivals, exhibitions and flower shows, it was provided with stage facilities and was owned by a consortium which included Moss and Thornton. As we have seen, it was used to replace the Empire Theatre while the latter was rebuilt. It opened on 1 August 1904 as a variety theatre, although this use was short-lived and until destroyed by fire on 2 December 1907 it was a venue for cinematograph shows.

The Exhibition Hall in St Mary's Place was a 200ft by 100ft building of galvanised sheet iron on a wood frame, which had opened late in 1904 and was intended to be the new Olympia, as the latter was now almost permanently taken up by cinematograph shows. Like Olympia, it was a very adaptable hall, initially used for trade exhibitions, ballroom dancing and brass band concerts, but in December 1906 it was fitted up as 'a place of amusement' by James Carnegie, a contractor and decorator, with a winter garden and free ballroom dancing.

Around 1908, two rivals appeared to challenge the theatres' near monopoly of indoor entertainment: roller skating (which was short lived) and the cinematograph (which wasn't). Roller skating, an entertainment imported from the United States, was hugely popular for short periods until the novel-

Roller-skating in the Exhibition Hall, St Mary's Place, in 1908. Flags and bunting cannot entirely cover the spartan interior.

ty wore off. Buildings to house it could be cheaply constructed (unlike theatres) as the only requirement was a roof over a large flat space which could be floored with maple planking. The first building in the city to be adapted for roller-skating was the Exhibition Hall, St Mary's Place, which opened as a rink on 9 March 1908. It offered 'high-class' skating with free tuition and afternoon teas, all accompanied by a military band, at three sessions daily: morning (admission free), afternoon and evening (admission 1 (5p.)). Hire of the 'Samuel Winslow 1908 Model Steel Ball-bearing Skates' was 1s (5p).

It was well over a year before a second rink opened in the city: the Grandstand Skating Rink on the Town Moor 'five minutes from Blue House' near the old racecourse grandstand. This was a corrugated iron multipurpose hall with a partially glazed roof which was said to be adaptable for concerts, exhibitions or even lawn tennis, but it opened in November 1909 as a rink, promoted by a company whose subscribers were all Scots. Tuition was being offered at the Tyneside Physical Culture Society's rooms in Handysides Arcade to skaters who were apprehensive about falling over in full view of their friends. To cater for beginners, small rinks were opened in December 1909 in Ward's Buildings, High Bridge (The Cosy) and in March 1910 at the Old Infirmary (The Central): the latter, which clearly could not run to the expense of live music, had 'military band records on Parson's Electric Auxetophone'.

The grandest rink in Newcastle opened in December 1909: the White City, Northumberland Road. This was promoted by George Parkinson, a Gosforth builder, who headed a company formed by solicitors and shipowners from Newcastle, Grimsby, Durham and London. While basically a tin shed like the others, it was larger (230 by 90 feet) and had an impressive stuccoed frontage to Northumberland Road surmounted by a white-painted dome. Aware that roller skating was peaking in popularity, the management offered additional inducements such as promenade concerts, skittle alleys, French bowls and a rifle range.

Although the managements of all the main rinks attempted to maintain public interest by staging carnivals, races and displays by professional skaters, their basic problem was that once the art of roller skating had been mastered, there was little variety for patrons. By the end of 1912 all the rinks had closed; as places for couples to meet their role had been entirely taken over by the growing number of picture halls in the city, which offered new entertainment each week, were semi-dark, and required no athletic skill at all.

The cinematograph had of course been familiar to Newcastle audiences since 1896, when the first shows had been given in the Palace and Empire theatres. These shows had been treated as novelties, with no indication that this was the beginning of a new form of mass entertainment. It survived its difficult first 10 years due to the persistence of the travelling showmen who visited the city to give shows in theatres and hired halls. In addition to the Palace, Empire, Vaudeville and Grand Theatres, cinematograph shows were held in the Town Hall, Grand Assembly Rooms, Barras Bridge and Ginnett's Circus, Northumberland Road. By far the most regular venue was Olympia in Northumberland Road, which had cinematograph shows regularly from 1898 and intensively from 1903 until its destruction by fire in December 1907.

The early films were short, rarely more than a minute in length, with the subjects limited to 'actualities', travel, and vaudeville 'turns'. As Newcastle audiences could see live variety acts at any of five or six theatres, they were not likely to be impressed with the latter offerings, but the former did give them a chance to see pictures of life in foreign lands and, for example, the funeral of Queen Victoria and the Coronation of Edward VII. What changed the future of the cinema was the gradual development of what would later be termed feature films, that is films which told a story with recognisable characters with whom the audience could identify. The average length of films grew to one reel (approximately 10 minutes), but this was time enough to tell a simple story. These were usually melodramatic and akin to familiar plays from the popular theatre. The emphasis on actualities continued alongside this development, with films (real or faked) of foreign wars, such as the Russo-Japanese conflict of 1904-05, proving popular.

By 1908, films had grown in popularity to such an extent that Audrey Appleby, who had run the last picture shows at Olympia, felt sufficiently confident to open a hall primarily for the showing of films. The Star Picture Hall, Prudhoe Street, a disused United Methodist chapel, opened on 13 April 1908. Miss Appleby's initiative was rapidly followed by others. All these halls were intended to be permanent picture halls, but none was purpose-built. Seven cinema openings in the eight months to the end of 1908 seemed to have brought saturation and there followed a 12-month hiatus while potential cinema entrepreneurs tried to assess whether the phenomenon was genuine or merely a passing fad.

The next phase, beginning with the new Olympia, Northumberland Road in December 1909, was the building of purpose-designed cinemas rather than converting churches or shops. The years 1910 and 1911 saw the addition of a further 12 cinemas, of which only four were conversions of existing buildings. New cinemas could be designed for their purpose with good sight-lines for the audience, raked floors and attractive, welcoming exteriors (an exception was the Brinkburn, Byker, which had no pretensions at all!). This is not to say that money was spent needlessly: most had bare wooden seats or benches except in the higher-priced balconies or circles. The ornately plastered frontages concealed cheap brick rectangular auditoriums, often with roof trusses on display.

What was the attraction of these early cinemas? Seat prices were reasonably cheap, usually from 2d to 6. (0.8p to 2.5p) compared with the variety theatre's 3d to 1s 6d. (1.25p to 7.5p). Usually built at the heart of working-class residential areas, they were local and did not involve a tram journey. They were homely and welcoming, rather like community centres. The fare on offer was easy to understand (sometimes 'lecturers' were on hand to explain complicated plot developments) and varied: in addition to the films, there were competitions and variety turns, which were also useful to cover the frequent reel changes. Most early cinemas opened in the evening only with a first house at 6 PM, when work for the day was over. According to a semi-official report of 1917: 'in the main the vast majority of picture house patrons were not in the habit of attending other places of entertainment. The cheapness of this form of amusement has created what is really a new type of audience …' In other words women and children, who had for the first time a type of entertainment specifically geared to them. The same report went on to say: 'The picture house is emphatically the poor man's theatre, and it must always be remembered, is the only organisation which systematically provides amusement for children.'

These early cinemas, usually (and politely) described by the trade as 'industrial', i.e. with working class patrons, were almost all located in the city's suburbs. The cinema business, which by 1912 was well organised, decided that there was a potentially more lucrative market to aim for, of picture goers who would be willing or could be persuaded to pay more for a cinema seat. This was the 'ton patron', the middle- or upper-class cinemagoer whom cinema managements tried to attract. Their efforts led to the next development in the cinema, large, elegant halls, usually in the city centre. The first of these, which opened on 12 February 1912, was the Picture House at the junction of Westgate Road and Clayton Street. It was followed by the Empire, Grainger Street West, the Queen's Hall, Northumberland Place, the Grainger, Grainger Street and finally the Newcastle Picture House, Grey Street (6 May 1914). In these cinemas, which opened in the afternoons as well as evenings, the films were new and well-projected, the surroundings were elegant and comfortable, the foyers of marble and expensive woods, the interior decoration of richly painted plasterwork. Tea and cakes were served in the cinema café and an orchestra, rather than a lone pianist, accompanied the films.

Their patrons need not fear that they would have to share these facilities with hoi polloi, who were likely to be deterred by the superior setting and product on offer. Cinemas carried over from theatres the simple class divisions based on seat prices, which in these middle-class halls were usually in the range of 6d (2.5p) to 1s 6d (7.5p). In addition, there was invariably a separate entrance and pay box (often down a side-alley) for patrons of the cheapest seats, a tradition which applied even in the cinemas built in the 1930s.

By 1913, it was possible for F.W. Morrison, Secretary of the Newcastle Branch of the Cinematograph Exhibitors' Association, to make the following calculation: 'We have already in the city four theatres, with holding capacity per performance 7,500; three music halls, with holding capacity per performance 6,500; 20 cinema halls, with holding capacity 15,700; total holding capacity per performance, 29,700. Twenty-five of these places have 13 performances, and two of them seven performances weekly, showing accommodation weekly for 362,000 persons. The population of the city is now estimated at 277,000 … Since compiling this statement, an additional hall has been opened, with a holding capacity per performance of 1,000, making an addi-

The auditorium of the Hippodrome Theatre, seen from the stage in 1926, when the hall held 2,703.

tion of 13,000 per week to the holding capacity of cinema halls in the city'. Despite the fact that this calculation does not attempt to assess the proportion of theatre and cinema seats actually occupied, it does give a fair indication of the phenomenal growth of commercial entertainment in the early part of the century.

By the 1920s, there had been a few changes to the popular entertainment scene in the city. The Pavilion, having struggled for more than a decade to remain viable as a variety theatre, closed, reopening as a cinema on 10 December 1917. Its near neighbour the Tyne Theatre, succumbed less easily, but with less booking power than the Theatre Royal and a less favourable location, the restricted availability during the war of touring shows became critical and the Tyne closed on 1 March 1919. The lease was acquired by Sir Oswald Stoll, who reopened the theatre as the Stoll cinema on 2 June 1919. Both the Pavilion and the Stoll became first-run cinemas throughout the 1920s. The Grand Theatre, Byker, became a picture and variety theatre under George Black in 1913. With some of their rivals thus removed from the scene, the Royal, Empire, Palace and Hippodrome continued as before.

With 30 cinemas in the city by 1914, a saturation point appeared to have been reached. To protect their investment, existing cinema owners were beginning to demand that the City Council should not allow any more cinemas to be built, but the Council allowed market forces to prevail. After the war, in the 1920s, only three were built, which all filled gaps in the geographical coverage of the city, and one rebuilt. The latter was the Westgate, formerly the Picture House, which reopened as the New Westgate 31 October 1927 and briefly became the city's largest purpose-built cinema. One new theatre, the Majestic, Condercum Road, was built with even less success than the previous attempt at a suburban theatre. Opening on 3 October 1927 with the Denville Players in repertory, it was a cinema within three years.

Meanwhile, another contender for the public's money had appeared – ballroom dancing. Dancing had a long history, but had hitherto been confined to private occasions. In the 1890s dancing classes were being offered by several tutors in the Lovaine Hall, St Mary's Place, the Old Assembly Rooms and elsewhere, but actual public dancing was restricted to church halls and similar venues. By 1904, a Professor Williams was offering to teach dances based on black American originals, such as the Cake Walk and Buck and Wing, which had hitherto been confined to variety acts on stage. Like roller-skating, public dancing was an American import, popularised by the Anglo-American couple, Vernon and Irene Castle, and introduced before World War I. Its requirements in terms of buildings were simple, and it is no surprise to find the earliest public dances taking place in 1906 in the Exhibition Hall, St Mary's Place. James Carnegie's Carnivals at the same venue in 1907 and 1908, offered free ballroom dancing with prizes for the best waltz.

The first public dance hall to be built as such seems to have been part of the Assembly Rooms entertainment complex near Heaton Station. It was completed by November 1910, with a 106 by 40ft patent 'Voltairespring' dance floor. Next was the Brighton Assembly Rooms, opened on 2 November 1911 adjacent to the Brighton cinema on Westgate Road. The White City Rink opened briefly as the 'Dreamland Ballroom de Luxe' from 10 February 1912 before being rebuilt as the Hippodrome Theatre.

It was not until the 1920s that ballroom dancing really became popular, stimulated by the flurry of new dance steps and the syncopated music which accompanied them. Newcastle's premier ballroom,

Couples in the Dreamland Ballroom de Luxe, the former White City in 1912.

which opened on 22 June 1925, was the Oxford Galleries, centrally located in New Bridge Street A cut-down version of an expensive earlier plan for a cinema-cum-dance hall, the Oxford was a newer version of the prewar shed, but built of brick, with an elaborate frontage in faience tiling; the 133 foot by 61ft hall could hold an estimated 2,000 dancers.

Even before the Oxford was built, Henry Armstrong, the city's Medical Officer of Health, was expressing concern about 'the prevailing desire for amusement among all classes and including new and young mothers. Maternal duties naturally performed are incompatible with both the cinematograph theatre and the dance hall.' He realised, however, that: ' with the housing question in its present condition, home life must be very unattractive for many. The mother who, with her husband and two or more young children, spends all her days in one room, may be pardoned if she seeks change and relaxation away from it on one or two evenings in the week. '

It is unlikely that young mothers were deterred by this warning (if they knew of it): certainly the opening of the Oxford was followed by others throughout the city: soon there were, in addition to those mentioned, the Grand Assembly Rooms, Barras Bridge, the Corporation's new Northumberland (Baths) Hall (as the Premier Ballroom) and the Milvain, opened on the West Road on 28 April 1933. Tea dances were held at Fenwick's, Binns and elsewhere, and dinner dances at the Old Assembly Rooms, the Royal Station Hotel, Tilley's, and Rinaldo's. As only the Oxford was a six-day operation, the dance halls had little effect on the popularity of the cinemas.

Ballroom dancing was immensely popular throughout the 1930s and 1940s. Unlike going to the cinema, it was an occasion for men and women to dress in their best. Many men wore dinner-jackets (often second- or third-hand) and the women's long evening dresses were usually home-made. Attachments could be formed by dancers and non-dancers alike. Unlike roller-skating, there was plenty of variety and dancing tuition again became popular in order to learn the steps of the new dances, the Charleston, the tango, the fox-trot and the modern waltz. The most popular bandleaders – Peter Fielding, George Evans, Jos. Q. Atkinson – became household names and were supplemented by visits by nationally-known dance bands who also appeared at variety theatres and at the major cinemas on Sundays. There were competitions with prizes, exhibition dancers and cabaret.

In 1930, roller-skating made a surprising, though brief, comeback. As all the halls used in 1908-12 had been demolished or were in other uses, venues were scarce. Two Newcastle haulage contractors, Loughton and Joynson, bought the Festival Hall from the 1929 North East Coast Exhibition, dismantled it and re-erected it on a site on the south side of Prudhoe Street, where it opened in August 1930. Roller-skating rinks had already opened in converted dance halls in the Royal Arcade (Arcadia Rink) and in the Northumberland Hall. The fare was much as before – exhibition skating (The St Moritz Skaters – The Wonders on Wheels), fancy dress carnivals, speed racing – but with new elements: rink hockey between ladies' and gentlemen's teams from Newcastle and other towns and cities and a race between a skater (Harry Sergeant) and a motorcycle speedway rider, which the skater won. By May 1931, fashion had moved on, leaving roller-skating behind. The Festival Hall alternated skating and dancing for a while, but by mid-1933 was reduced to 'go-as-you-please' nights and concert parties

These guests seem to be enjoying themselves at the Farmers Ball in the Grand Assembly Rooms, Barras Bridge about 1930.

(admission 2d). It closed in about February 1934 and offices for the Ministry of Labour were built on the site. The other rinks became dance halls.

The cinema, meanwhile, had virtually reinvented itself with the introduction of talking pictures. Initially disliked because of their poor sound quality, the American accents of their actors and the fact that they obstructed the gossiping and generally high audience noise levels of silent pictures, by the end of 1930 only one city cinema (the Sun, Byker Hill), had not been converted to sound. Such was their popularity that at the Queen's Hall the manager claimed in January 1930: 'We are doing phenomenal business and this week we are having four 'capacity' houses a day. With silent films of the most popular type the average was two and a half 'capacity houses' in four performances. So great is the demand that on Saturday we are going to give a morning performance commencing at 10.15. I have known nothing like it.' The result was a rush to build bigger and better cinemas both in the city centre and in the suburbs, beginning with the opening of the opulent Paramount in Pilgrim Street on 7 September 1931. A total of 13 new cinemas was built throughout the city in the next eight years.

Theatres, too, entered a boom period. The Royal continued its sequence of pre- and post-West End plays and musicals. Of the variety theatres, the Empire hosted musical comedy, ice shows, revues, variety from the London Palladium and dance band concerts. The Palace stayed down-market with variety, revues and seasons of popular plays. All three offered rival pantomimes, which were all well-supported, though many people thought the Theatre Royal 'too posh for the likes of us' and went to the Empire or the Palace. The only casualty of the period was the Hippodrome, which closed on 20 May 1933, inevitable once its owner, General Theatres Corporation, was merged with Moss Empires.

The popular entertainment scene in Newcastle remained virtually unchanged until the late 1950s, theatres, dance halls and cinemas all retaining their popularity. The reasons have to do with employment and the home. The initial growth of cinemas (and roller rinks) in 1908-09 coincided with a period of higher than usual unemployment in the city. The coincidence is even more marked in the 1930s, when high unemployment corresponded with the explosion in cinema building and the spread of dance halls. For an outlay of a shilling (5p), or possibly less, several hours of entertainment could be bought, free from the worries of daily life. The fact that the majority who were in work were earning higher wages than ever before gave them more to spend on leisure and entertainment. Thus, all types of cinemas, from the 'gaff' to the relatively expensive super-cinema, were well-supported, as were all kinds of dances from the dinner-dance to the hop in the local hall.

Many homes were poorly furnished, cold and unwelcoming. Thus, as Henry Armstrong realised, people were keen to get out of them whenever they could, to join with others in a place that was warm and comfortable. In 1939, Hugh le Mounier, manager of the Essoldo cinema, commented in his newsletter to patrons that: 'In Winter few homes can offer so comfortable a warmth, free from draughts and with an atmosphere that is hygienically treated. In the Summer the superiority of the Essoldo even over your own home is no less marked'. Such a remark would be greeted with disbelief today, but seems to have been recognised as likely to be true and was accepted without apparent complaint at the time.

The inter-war years was a period of massive house-building, both public and private, in the city. In this lay the seeds of the destruction of much of popular entertainment. World War II, when audiences had even more need to seek entertainment as a means of escape, held off nemesis for a while, but as soon as the home became sufficiently attractive to retain people's interest, traditional entertainment collapsed. This happened in the 1950s, with a new boom in house-building. The main factor which tied people to their homes was the growth of television, encouraged by the opening of the Pontop Pike transmitter in 1953 and the televised Coronation of the same year. The advance was consolidated by the opening of Tyne-Tees Television in January 1959. There were other factors, of course, in the equation: increasing car ownership, holidays abroad, and home improvements, all of which bit into the amount of money families allocated to leisure and entertainment.

First to feel the change were the suburban cinemas, with 19 closing between 1958 and 1961. When a local cinema closed, its patrons almost all gave up the habit rather than transfer to other cinemas. Many suburban cinemas were converted to bingo clubs, which at least had the virtue that the new type of patron was unlikely to vandalise the building. Since the war, very little money had been spent by cinema owners on keeping their buildings attractive for a more discriminating audience. The main first-run cinemas in the city centre lasted longer and usually closed for reasons other than audience decline. By 1984, when cinema attendances nationally were at three per cent of their 1947 levels, the only cinemas still operating in the city were the ABC (formerly Essoldo), the Odeon (formerly Paramount) and one suburban survival, the Jesmond.

Theatres, too, were affected. The Palace closed in 1959, after a sequence of tatty strip shows. The Empire held on until 1963 by booking stars made popular by television (an ironic reversal of feeding the hand that bites you). The Theatre Royal was offered for sale by Howard and Wyndham in May 1971 and was saved from closure by the City Council, who bought it and have subsidised it ever since (except the period 1974-86, when it was sustained by Tyne and Wear County Council). When the Stoll Cinema closed in March 1974, it was purchased and restored by local enthusiasts, opening as the New Tyne

Queues to see Johnny Ray at the Empire Theatre, Newgate Street, September 1955.

Theatre on 12 April 1977. But by the end of the century, it was increasingly clear that Newcastle was not a sufficiently populous city to support two large touring theatres.

Ballrooms were also affected: in the early 1960s all closed or became nightclubs (except the Milvain, which burned down in May 1962). Rather surprisingly, two dance halls opened: the Rank-owned Majestic on 26 February 1959 (converted from the Gaumont – ex-New Westgate – cinema) and the Mecca owned Mayfair (bingo in the afternoon, dancing at night) in 1962.

With the traditional family audiences deserting the cinemas and theatres for their firesides and television, the young, who abhorred this sedentary style, went out in search of entertainment. This age group therefore began to dominate commercial entertainment from the 1960s, when the club scene began.

In the last decade of the century, a building was erected in the city which was, in effect, a reversion to the multi-purpose entertainment halls of earlier years, though much larger and smarter. The Newcastle (Telewest) Arena opened in November 1995 to the west of the city centre. This 500 by 200 feet structure can hold up to 10,000 people and can host sports such as basketball and ice hockey, in addition to concerts, touring shows, conferences and exhibitions.

Throughout the century the commercial imperative was dominant, driven by a public which became increasingly fickle as the century progressed. Building use was changed to keep up with public fashion: theatres became cinemas; cinemas became ballrooms or bingo halls, ballrooms became skating rinks; skating rinks became ballrooms; ballrooms became clubs. Nothing is more certain than that the new century will bring more changes to the entertainment scene in the city.

~ Frank Manders is a retired librarian and local historian. His publications include *A History of Gateshead*, Gateshead Libraries, 1973; *Cinemas of Newcastle*, Newcastle City Libraries, 1991; *Cinemas of Gateshead*, Gateshead Libraries, 1995; *Newcastle: the Earliest Photographs*, 1995; *Bygone Central Newcastle I* and *II*, Newcastle Libraries & Information Service, 1995.

Swinging Newcastle: the Sixties

Dick Godfrey

To those of us who grew up in them, the Sixties were extraordinary. Only with hindsight, however, are we able to look back and discern just how special they were. It was a unique period which both marked a transition and yet at the same time established an unmistakable identity of its own. Design – especially in clothes – was distinctive. So was the music. So, too, were the changes in the way we lived. The resonance of the Sixties will be with us long into the new century. The only other era with which it can perhaps be compared is the Thirties – that decade, too, put its stamp on the artifacts of the century with its own definable style. It was also a decade of transition, moving from the neo-classicism which remained from the pre-Great War period to the modern era. It gave us Art Deco and saw profound social change, but it also gave us the Depression and finally World War II. These are the abiding memories in spite of social improvements. The Sixties, on the other hand, was the decade when, in

The Haymarket, 1960, before the demise of the trolleybus and the arrival of the Metro.

Harold MacMillan's memorable phrase, we 'never had it so good.' Neither image is totally accurate. Each, though, is enduring.

It was possible, as the Sixties began, for the young to look ahead with confidence to a life which would offer work and excitement. Everything was possible and everything was changing. The last vestiges of the Empire which had defined Britain were fading fast. Again, MacMillan summed it up when he spoke of the 'wind of change' blowing through Africa. He was right. Dissolution of the Empire which had started with the independence of India in 1947 gathered full pace in the Sixties. At the beginning of the decade, we still had ten African colonies. By the end, we had none. Yet, paradoxically, it was probably the last decade in which Britain had a clearly defined identity of its own. Europe still began on the other side of the Channel. We drove British-made cars. We watched British-made programmes on British-made televisions, wore British-designed and British-made clothes. We knew who we were. It was a decade of confidence.

Above all, it was the decade of the young. We were children who would inherit the world our parents' generation had fought and worked for. We were children of the Welfare State. We had been kept healthy by it and, above all, educated by it. For the brightest, the grammar schools gave a high standard of education even if they did divorce many from their working-class origins in a country which was still sharply divided by class. It offered us free university education. It offered us work. Above all, it offered us a place in society.

It was the decade that created teenagers. They had certainly existed in the Fifties, but nobody acknowledged them apart from blaming them for the excesses of the early rock and roll years when cinema seats were savaged during Bill Hailey's films and concerts. They were bad news and the adult world hoped they would go away. But in the Sixties, they came into their own. Identified as a reasonably cohesive group, they were targeted by the world of commerce which provided the clothes and entertainments which still further defined them.. The contraceptive pill, when it appeared, offered the young a sexual freedom earlier generations were denied.

The Beatles and the other groups which appeared

City Repro

Not quite Newcastle's answer to Carnaby Street, City Stylish on New Bridge Street was one shop that dedicated itself to the youth market.

The Bigg Market and the old Town Hall in 1966. The Town Hall, used for exhibitions by the mid-Sixties, was demolished in 1970.

at the same time gave the young a voice. Bob Dylan, and others, gave them a vision. Political awareness grew with knowledge that the young could, perhaps, influence events. Involvement in protest groups – most notably the Campaign for Nuclear Disarmament – grew. It was the decade of the demonstration. Students in Britain occupied universities. They were a minority, but they were the peer group leaders whose actions were admired by those not prepared to act themselves. For young women, the works of Germaine Greer and Betty Freidan made them aware that they need not be second-class citizens in a male-dominated world.

At another level, it was the decade of the planner. As the dark years of the Thirties, Forties and even the Fifties grew more distant, it was possible to look to the future. It would be better, we were confident, and we had to be equipped to face it.

There was a legacy from those earlier decades, however, which was to impinge heavily on the optimism with which we started the Sixties. As the old decade died, a major problem emerged which was to force a fundamental change on the North East of England in particular. In October 1959 it was announced that mining manpower was to be slashed in a massive rationalisation programme. Between 29,000 and 60,000 jobs were slated to go over the first five years of the Sixties. The North East's share was to be between 16,000 and 23,000. In the event, Durham Coalfield, which had been 14,000-strong in the post-Second World War period, nearly halved its workforce by 1963. Four years later, the combined workforce of Northumberland, Durham and neighbouring Cumberland was only 75,000. By that year, 1967, Alf Robens, the former labour MP for Blyth, had become chairman of the National Coal Board. He announced that there would be still more pit closures and job losses. It meant that the 75,000 of 1967 would be down to 48,000 by the end of the decade. Suddenly, for many middle-aged men, the future started to look bleak. The leader of Newcastle's Labour-controlled City Council, T. Dan Smith, summed up the impact on the region's economy with his usual gritty eloquence at a meeting of the northern Economic Planning Committee. 'Suddenly, a bloody great hole has opened up.'

Back at the start of the decade, all looked hopeful. It opened with the heightened expectations commonly, if illogically, present at the dawn of a new decade. There was no awareness, of course, of the tumultuous changes which were to lie ahead. Why should there be? Newcastle arrived in the Sixties as it had left the Fifties. The A1 was still the North Road and still Great, taking both local and through traffic slap through the middle of the city centre via Northumberland Street. By the end of the decade, someone had thought to throw a temporary footbridge across the road, but before that crossing between Fenwick's and Callers – then a major furniture store and not simply a travel agent – could be an exhilarating experience. Newcastle still had the Town Hall with which it had arrived in the 20th century, an age-blackened, colonnaded, neo-classical hulk at the divides of the Groat and Bigg Markets now unhappily occupied by a building from the Seventies – a decade which turned out to be as down as the Sixties was upbeat.

For Newcastle's young in 1960 – still barely recognised as teenagers – the centre of the swirl of social activity was the Oxford Ballrooms in New Bridge Street. Girls in flared frocks which reached demurely to mid-calf and lads flaunting the tight trousers, draped jackets and Brylcream starched quiffs of the London Teddy Boys whose styles they aped, rocked and rolled to a band which was really much happier playing the Thirties and Forties dance numbers of their mid-week repertoire.

In a world that seems now so wonderfully simple, there were no parking meters or betting shops to be seen. We spent pounds, shillings and pence, measured everything in feet and inches and weighed in stones, pounds and ounces. Upon these apparently solid foundations of a stable society, those determined to build a different future began their work. Some of their proposals were regional and would affect everybody in the North East. The biggest of these was the Hailsham Plan produced by Minister Lord Hailsham who endeared himself to the South and made himself a figure of some ridicule in the North East by arriving in Newcastle sporting a flat cap in 1963.

He left behind a massive £50 million grant which was to provide the region and its capital with roads without parallel in Britain, plans for increasing incentives to new industries and for increasing the number of advance factories and homes built. It meant we would have new towns in Washington, Cramlington and Killingworth to compare with Peterlee. Newcastle, not to be outdone, had plans of its own. Under its energetic planning boss Wilfred Burns, and prompted by politician T. Dan Smith's grandiose vision of creating a 'Brasilia of the North', there was £200m for redeveloping the city centre.

1966: the Civic Centre rises with the new Polytechnic in the background.

The process began in 1960 with the laying of the foundation stone for a new Civic Centre at Barras Bridge. The question of the location for a new headquarters for the City council had been hotly debated for decades. At last, it was settled. When the Civic Centre finally opened, the old Town Hall became the site for exhibitions and indoor markets before being demolished.

Taking the mood of its splendid new HQ, Newcastle City Council determined to be a market leader in local government. To this end, in 1965 it appointed Britain's first City Manager. Until then, the function of what we would now call the Chief Executive was undertaken by the Town Clerk with a background in law, but little experience of increasingly important planning functions. Newcastle's – or rather T. Dan Smith's – answer was to appoint an industrialist from the motor industry to the job of taking the region's capital into the second half of the century. Frank Harris was outspoken and determined, he trampled smartly on local government's corns as he cut red tape, as he had been hired to do and filled the new Civic Centre with like-minded souls. The age of the civic mandarin dawned. With T. Dan Smith to urge them on – and give Newcastle a national figurehead – they planned, bulldozed and built. Amongst the losses was the classic 19th century Royal Arcade. It was pulled down to make way for the Swan house development – there were plans to re-erect it somewhere else, but the component parts were somehow lost.

Most of the plans laid in the Sixties did not become a reality until the Seventies. The visible legacy of the Sixties includes Eldon Square, the City Library and the Central Motorway. T. Dan Smith himself barely lasted the decade he dominated. It had brought him success and honours. He became the *Architects' Journal*'s Man of the Year, was awarded an honorary degree from Newcastle University and was appointed chair of the Northern Economic Planning Council. In 1968 he was out of politics and

devoting himself full-time to his career as a public relations consultant. His friends and his own position in the corridors of power made him very popular with those businessmen intent on riding the development gravy train both in Newcastle and elsewhere.

In that year, he was interviewed by the police in connection with his involvement in the affairs of the Borough of Wandsworth in London. He was cleared of offering bribes, but it was the start of his decline. He subsequently faced a number of corruption charges because of his

1969: Old Eldon Square comes down to make way for the new shopping centre.

close involvement with Yorkshire architect John Poulson in one of the biggest political scandals of the post-War period. Smith – tired, he claimed, of the whole business – pleaded guilty and was jailed. Until his death, he explained that he had never been found guilty of the charges he faced. He did, however, leave a stain on the reputation of the City of Newcastle which still lingers. Ordinary people in the Sixties were only dimly aware of these political shennanigans. Their lives were changing in other, more important, ways. Most notably, women's self-perception was about to undergo the most dramatic shift.

As the Sixties opened, attitudes towards sex and the problems associated with it had changed little since Victorian times. Venereal disease was killing 500 Britons a year. In 1961, a leading Newcastle doctor spoke ominously of the mounting toll unless moral laxity ended. In the early Sixties around 20,000 babies were born to unmarried teenage girls in Britain. Newcastle regularly exceeded the national average for illegitimate births at 2.7 per cent and frequently posted figures in excess of 5 per cent. The overwhelming majority of the unwanted babies were put out for adoption. It was to be a long time before it became acceptable to be an 'unmarried mother'. In 1961, the birth control pill which US Professor Carl Djerass had developed in 1951 became available in the UK.

Until the 1960s men were in control of sexual activity. They were the ones who had access to contraception. However, Boots the Chemist, and male toilets, did not oblige by selling condoms as they do today. Surgical suppliers did sell them and so, for curious reasons, did barbers – 'And something for the weekend, sir?' was invariably the question asked at the end of a haircut. There was also a suitably furtive shop at the junction between High Bridge and the Cloth Market. Then came the Pill. This was to change everything, and gave women a sense of freedom they had not enjoyed before. The new attitude was summed up by a 19-year-old with the 'Cathy McGowan hairstyle' – shoulder-length with a fringe – interviewed by the *Evening Chronicle* a few years after the Pill had arrived in Newcastle. 'This makes me the boss,' she said, displaying the pill held in her hand. 'That's all I'm going to say about it to you or anybody else.'

Other more subtle changes were also in train which made the arrival of the Pill welcome. The benefits of the Welfare State meant that girls were reaching maturity earlier. The clothes they wore and the music they enjoyed encouraged them to become sexually active earlier. This was was the time when the rates of VD and illegitimacy began to climb and cause concern. Newcastle's VD clinic – like those in other parts of the country – had full surgeries. The 'Lady Chatterley's Lover' trial in 1961 edged the country closer to a new, more open sexual attitude. Penguin Books were found not guilty of obscenity for publishing D.H. Lawrence's frank novel. It described things which had never before been read in public print, and bookshops in Newcastle ran out in one day even though purchasers were rationed to just one copy each. Sex became something to be discussed. For teenage girls who read it, it was the first intimation that sex could be wonderful and not the barely mentioned, strictly marital art they had been led to believe.

When it first manifested itself, the sexual revolution was restricted to safely and conventionally married women. When the Pill finally appeared in Newcastle in 1962 courtesy of the Family Planning Association, only married women were allowed to have it. For them, though, it was truly extraordinary.

For the first time in their lives, they could decide the size of their families and relationships with their husbands would never be the same again. Above all, it allowed women to enjoy sex. They wondered how their mothers and grandmothers had ever managed. 'Mutual satisfaction is at last a possibility for every married couple,' said a Newcastle doctor enthusiastically. 'When the wife enjoys physical love, the husband then discovers that his own enjoyment is increased and the couple can reach heights of married bliss hitherto unknown to them … We are on the threshold of a social revolution emancipating marriage and I firmly believe that we should be doing all in our power to encourage it.'

Handysides Arcade, Percy Street, 1967. The Arcade housed unusual shops such as Ultima Thule, the radical bookshop run by Newcastle poet Tom Pickard. The Summer of Love of 1967 happened in the Arcade if it happened anywhere in Newcastle.

Marriage was the key to this new world of shared enjoyment.

For the young and the single there was, initially at least, no Pill. The lack of easy availability of effective contraception was reflected in the continuing high rates of illegitimacy. Nationally, it was reckoned that one in five teenage girls were pregnant on their wedding days. They were the products of the immediate post-War 'baby boom'. When the Sixties arrived, they were the first generation which 'had it all' – and they wanted more. 'Dolly birds' with their styled hair, short skirts and heavy mascara expected to do what they wanted to do with their own lives, and that included their bodies. But it was not until 1968 when the Pill became comparatively widely available on Tyneside that Newcastle women joined in the sexual revolution. By then something else had happened to provide another form of birth control.

1967 had seen abortion law reform. Until then, the backstreet abortionist was a figure to be feared as much as she was sometimes sought. Medical complications caused by 'operations' which went wrong became a serious health problem. The law changed all that, but also gave Newcastle a sometimes unwelcome reputation. By the closing years of the Sixties, Newcastle had become known as the 'abortion capital' of the United Kingdom. One doctor rejected the implied criticism and accepted the credit for this state of affairs. The late Dorothea Kerslake had been associated with the campaign for abortion reform for a large part of her working life and when the law changed, Dr Kerslake made sure that its provisions were comparatively readily available in Walker Park Hospital where she worked. In the first nine months of 1969, for example, 411 terminations were carried out – more than in any other hospital in the country. If Walker Park headed the abortion league, said Dr Kerslake happily, it was due to her efforts. 'I have 15 beds at the hospital. If I had more, there would he more abortions.' She explained that she would rather see abortions than to have unwanted children brought into the world.

As the Pill became more widely available, so the need for abortions was reduced. The Pill became an accepted part of life. The teenager with the trendy hairdo who had proclaimed her sexual independence so emphatically to the *Evening Chronicle* reporter was one of many who led the way on a path which soon led to the use of the term 'permissive society' – it wasn't a pejorative description then.

Another development in 1967 confirmed the reality of the new tag. The law decriminalised homosexual acts between consenting adults in private. A leading homosexual rights activist in Newcastle – and few then were prepared to be so recognised – welcomed the move as the start of a new era. 'Now that we can behave the way we want in private, it will not be long before we have public acceptance,' he said. 'In a few years time, people will not turn a hair when they see us holding hands and even kissing in public. By the middle of the next decade, we will be getting married just like heterosexuals.'

Another development in everyday life did make spectacular progress in the Sixties, and Newcastle shared in the excitement. The Sixties was the decade when British pop music came of age and went on to conquer the world. Rock and roll had appeared in the Fifties and produced its own youth culture but it did not embrace a whole generation.

One phenomenon which would sweep the nation arrived in Newcastle on January 28, 1963, in the shaggy-haired form of The Beatles who had established themselves as the group to see. Pre-gig excitement was considerable and enthusiastic teenagers queued from Friday afternoon until the tickets went on sale on Sunday for the concert at the Majestic Ballroom. The reaction to the band was extraordinary – Tyneside hadn't seen anything like the head-shaking, shrieking frenzy which greeted the smartly-dressed Liverpudlians as soon as they went on stage. Afterwards, fans trooped backstage to meet their idols and get their autographs. The innocent accessibility didn't last long before it became impossible to get close to the 'fab four'.

The group – nobody called them a band at the time – were back at The Majestic in June that year. And Newcastle found a place in Beatles mythology. While staying at the Imperial Hotel in Jesmond Road, they wrote *She Loves You* which went on to become the biggest selling disc in British recording history. John, Paul, George and Ringo were back later that year for the appearance which really marked their arrival at the top of the pop tree. Newcastle City Hall was one of the country's top venues. Four thousand fans queued in the December cold for 48 hours to get tickets and worried parents prompted the police to mount 'chastity patrols' of the queue to see that nothing untoward happened. 1963 and 1964 were The Beatles' glory years. The following year they were back at the City Hall for what was to be their final appearance in the North East, and in fact one of their last concerts. Once again the City Hall was packed. Beatlemania reigned supreme. It was hard to hear the music because of the wall of noise from the stalls. A steady succession of fainting girls were carried out of the auditorium.

Tyneside was also producing its own pop heroes. The action focussed on a sweaty little club in Percy Street called the Club A Go-Go. It consisted of two rooms above the canteen serving the adjoining bus station. It specialised in the earthier blues which the Rolling Stones had made a rival to the melodically engineered pop songs of the Merseyside beat groups. In 1963, self-taught pianist Alan Price transferred his Alan Price Combo from the rival Downbeat Club not far away from the A Go-Go. They were a bunch of working-class Tyneside youngsters who found that the blues admirably suited their style, especially the singer Eric Burden, a gravel-voiced, ruddy-faced electricity board draughtsman. After an early performance at the A Go-Go, a girl in the audience told Price that they looked and played like a pack of animals. He agreed and changed the group's name to The Animals.

The Animals became the house band of the A Go-Go. But in 1964, fame and the lights of London beckoned and The Animals moved south, signed a record deal with the legendary Micky Most and became famous. They took America by storm the same year, and, along with The Beatles, brought America's Black music to a much wider audience. 'Fab and getting fabber and fabber,' enthused one New York rock writer. The accent intrigued the Americans. Tyneside became nearly as famous as

CLUB A'GOGO
PERCY STREET

The Evening Chronicle:
3 January 1964

Newcastle's most famous rock band, The Animals: Alan Price, John Steel, Eric Burdon, Hilton Valentine and Chas Chandler, from the programme of a concert given at the City Hall in the late 1960s.

City Repro

Grey's Monument in 1969, marooned in the traffic.

Merseyside – The Animals' version of the blues classic *House of the Rising Sun* went global. For a brief spell in the Sixties, there was talk of the Geordie Sound. It didn't last long. When The Animals left, they were followed at the Club A-Go-Go by The Junco Partners who performed similar music in a different style, but while they were a success they never quite matched The Animals' fame and Tyneside did not produce the stream of groups which made Liverpool so distinctive.

The 'Swinging Sixties' marked the beginning of different attitudes, life styles, and even ways of thinking. For Newcastle and Tyneside, as in for Great Britain as a whole, things would never be quite the same again. The scene was set for the rest of the century.

∽ Dick Godfrey is Chief Feature Writer on *The Journal*, Newcastle, and a former broadcaster.

Newcastle on Page and Screen

Christopher Goulding

IT COULD PERHAPS BE SAID THAT THE TRADITIONAL ATTITUDE OF LITERARY ENGLAND towards Newcastle upon Tyne is crystallised by Jane Austen in *Pride and Prejudice* (1813). When Lydia Bennett's new husband, the dashing young militia officer George Wickham, has been posted to Newcastle, her mother's reaction is to cry; 'Oh, my dear Lydia … when shall we ever meet again?'

The sense that such a posting is seen as a form of banishment to some unknown and alien region is further underlined by Mrs Bennett when she tells her neighbours in Longbourn of her daughter's fate: 'They are gone down to Newcastle, a place quite northward, it seems, and they are to stay, I do not know how long.' Her use of the words 'gone down' (where one might have expected the more usual 'up', as far as any southerner's reference to the north is concerned), even suggests that the residents of Hertfordshire have an impression of Tyneside as a rather infernal sort of place. Lydia herself is slightly more hopeful that there will be some vestiges of civilisation to be found: 'We shall be at Newcastle all the winter … I dare say there will be some balls.'

That, sadly, is the sum total of references to Newcastle in the whole of what is generally regarded as the canon of great English Literature. Other mentions of the regional capital of the North East in novels that come anywhere near acknowledged 'classic' status are limited to passing references and brief cameo appearances. These include Oliver Goldsmith's *The Vicar of Wakefield* (1766); a rather unfavourable mention by the 18th-century Scots writer Tobias Smollett in his epistolary novel *The Expedition of Humphrey Clinker* (1771); and then again in his picaresque tale *The Adventures of Roderick Random* (1748), which exhibits the author's familiarity with the town by mentioning Pilgrim Street.

Indeed, it is only in the non-fictional travel writing of such figures as Celia Fiennes (1662-1741) and Daniel Defoe (1660-1731) that Newcastle is featured to any recognisable extent. Happily, in the case of these two visitors, the town was appreciated as being as impressive then as it is now.

Newcastle fared little better in the 19th century, and it is to the 100 years shortly to come to an end that we must look to see the city at last figure in any significant way in the world of literature, albeit to a limited extent.

Life in Newcastle during the first two decades of the 20th century is fascinatingly chronicled from opposite ends of the social spectrum by two writers from very different backgrounds. Jack Common wrote *Kiddar's Luck*, his account of life in Edwardian Heaton, and its sequel *The Ampersand* from the point of view of his own working class childhood there. Yevgeny Zamyatin's *Islanders* is a decidedly cynical look at the stifling atmosphere of the middle-class Newcastle suburb of Jesmond as seen through the eyes of a foreign visitor. Together, they form a revealing portrait of life in two suburbs only a mile or so apart geographically, but separated at that time by a social chasm.

Taking its title from the catch-phrase of Jimmy Learmouth, a northern music hall comedian, *Kiddar's Luck* (1951) is a vividly descriptive work, evoking a Newcastle that seems almost Dickensian compared to the city of today. Common's autobiographical novel leads us by the hand through a vanished world of gaslit cobbled alleyways, trams, fleapit cinemas showing silent films, and still largely horse-drawn traffic crowding the streets. But this book is much more than a nostalgic sightseeing trip around Tyneside as it was between 1903 and 1917. In a narrative oozing with period detail, a very strong sense of the social cohesion that existed amidst the poverty and hardship of daily life in those days is conveyed to us. The camaraderie of the workplace, the corner shop, the doorstep, the local pub, and – for the children – the back lane are all used to recall an inner city landscape and a way of life that survived well into the 1960s.

Kiddar's Luck also forms a literary monument to the old industrial north that made it one of the great workshops of the world. The giant engineering works of Heaton employed thousands, Armstrongs of Scotswood gave work to almost the entire male population of that part of the city, the railways (where Common's father worked) and shipyards were all busy, and further afield were the pits of Northumberland and Durham. In such a society with a deeply ingrained work ethic, the author points out that within the average working family as much engineering know-how might be passed from father to son over the supper table as could be via an apprenticeship.

In its sequel *The Ampersand* (1954) Common introduces us to the world of commerce, which he entered upon leaving school aged 14. Taking its title from the '&' that appeared in the names and on the letterheads of so many companies, this novel conducts us through the bustling streets of central Newcastle. The Edwardian office blocks of Dean Street and Mosley Street are hailed as 'the newest castles of the Tyne' and successors to the Keep, whilst Pudding Chare is a warren of small offices, shops, and warehouses. Here too, the period detail leaps out of the page, with bygone clerical paraphernalia such as carbon paper, mechanical adding machines, and half-gallon bottles of ink being the common currency of the office junior.

The city's status as a port meant that it was not without its occasional glimpses of exotica. Foreign seamen were a common sight in the town, as were the often equally exotic girls who frequented the quayside seeking their company. Rare fruits such as mangoes and papayas occasionally appeared on fruit stalls, whilst a pet shop in the Butcher Market could boast a live monkey in its window.

With a disarming honesty, Common goes to some lengths to dispel any illusion that this was an age of total innocence. Petty shoplifting in Woolworths is described as 'a pastime' for him and his friends, whilst in the wider world, he wryly notes that city councillors always seemed to be getting wined and dined by the directors of construction companies.

Both of Common's novels, as well as his collections of essays such as *The Freedom of the Streets*, remain sadly underrated on the national literary scene, and are unfairly dismissed as being too parochial in character. (Parochialism of location was no bar to national success for, say, *Cider with*

Rosie.) Common's talent was recognised by his contemporaries and friends such as George Orwell, and he undoubtedly warrants a greater status today than that of the minor regional talent which he has undeservedly been labelled.

Across what Common called the 'banked greenery' of Jesmond Dene from Heaton lies Jesmond – scene of the regimented po-faced gentility of Yevgeny Zamyatin's novella *Islanders* (1918). A Russian marine architect working on Tyneside during World War I, Zamyatin was perplexed by what he saw as the dull, blinkered and top hatted world of the middle-class inhabitants of Jesmond, where he lived in Sanderson Road. The houses of the suburb are described as being 'smoke-blackened' like the city centre, but here the doorsteps shone in white rows 'like a Sunday gentleman's false teeth'. Whilst his portrayal of an insular bourgeois parish presided over by the Rev. Dewley doubtlessly had some foundation in fact, one suspects that his view was somewhat moulded by the bolshevik politics of his youth. As contemporary civic directories show, and the presence of streets of Tyneside flats bear witness, Jesmond has long been a dwelling place for the artisans of Newcastle, as well as for what were once called the professional classes.

The north is still very much an industrial landscape in A. J. Cronin's *The Stars Look Down* (1935). The story opens in Sleescale, a fictitious colliery town on the North Sea coast, but the action very quickly moves to the city of Tynecastle – a very thinly disguised Newcastle: 'Tynecastle, that keen, bustling city of the North, full of movement and clamour and brisk grey colour, echoing to the clang of trams, the clatter of feet, the beat of ship-yard hammers … a place of possibilities and adventure.'

Throughout the novel, the author has the curious habit of alternating between using real and fictionalised names for his locations. Thus, we see references to tea rooms in Eldon Square, Grainger Street is referred to by name as 'a place of big plate-glassed drapery stores', and other places such as Plummer Street, Elswick, and the Duke of Cumberland pub are mentioned. However, the hero Joe goes to live in the Scottswood (sic) Road, and other scenes are set in 'Esmond Dene', 'Sluice Dene', and a Tyneside ship-building town called 'Yarrow'. One suspects that whilst most of these names are deliberate (if rather pointless) fictionalisations, some are imperfectly recalled from Cronin's own memories of visits to the region during the 1920s.

During the 1950s, a thinly disguised Newcastle became the setting for a murder mystery by Nancy Spain. Now almost completely forgotten, Nancy Spain was once a household name in Britain, due to her status as a national newspaper columnist and a regular guest on TV and radio panel games such as *What's My Line?* Born in Jesmond in 1917, her native Newcastle was to crop up in many of her stories and autobiographical works.

In her popular thriller *Cinderella Goes to the Morgue* a pantomime season at the Theatre Royal in 'Newchester on Tame' is the setting for a series of murders. Postwar Tyneside is easily recognisable in the form of such features as 'Atkins Street' in which the Theatre Royal of the novel stands: ' … a pleasant street that had curved graciously down towards the River Tame since it was built in 1815.'

Whereas Jack Common was a chronicler of the life and culture of urban Newcastle, Sid Chaplin was more of a Durham coalfield man, whose literature sang the praises of the beauty and the industry of his beloved native county. His writings do, however, contain numerous references to Newcastle, where he lived for much of his life. His essays and journalism in particular contain some of the most poetic and lyrical descriptions of the city ever written.

Describing the panorama of the quayside for BBC TV in 1964 as looking: '...like a conference waiting for its picture to be taken', with the city's smile '... all the better for a blackened stump or two – the Keep, the Black Gate' – he went on to hail the Tyne Bridge as 'a bright bow of promise', whilst one of its neighbours became 'Robbie's High Level', acknowledging its creator.

Though in his column in *The Journal* he compared Newcastle as a 'little apple' of a city to New York's 'Big Apple', and championed its status as regional capital and a possible seat for a regional government, Sid had little time for the 'vertical villages' and 'prisons in the sky' that were being constructed in the name of housing at the time. Nevertheless, he was always able to see the wonder of nature amidst the urban environment: 'despite all of the ugliness we have set up against it.'

Most recently, Newcastle has featured as the setting of Pat Barker's novel *Another World* (1998). Rather like Common and Zamyatin at the beginning of the century, here two very different sides of Newcastle are portrayed, but this time within a single novel. On one side of the city are Nick and Fran, a young couple who live in the well-to-do suburb of Lob's hill – an obvious parallel to Jesmond or Gosforth. On the other side lies the altogether bleaker and run-down area of Summerfield, where Nick's grandfather Geordie is dying. References to a huge factory that once stood in this area and employed thousands – a clear reference to Armstrongs – implies Elswick or Scotswood in this case. The community is rather disparagingly referred to as being nicknamed Beirut-on-Tyne.

Like Cronin, the author also includes real locations by name, such as the Bigg Market, where the uglier side of the weekend's revelries are highlighted with a description of the sight of 'tattooed arms looking for trouble'. This novel juxtaposes the passing of an old way of life with the emergence of new ways of living. However, the sordid aspects in the past of even the most genteel parts of suburbia are hinted at when Nick and Fran find obscene Edwardian drawings on the walls of their period home when they remove the wallpaper, echoing the hints given by Zamyatin in 1918 that the stiflingly prim atmosphere of such bourgeois areas could conceal suppressed emotions and dark secrets.

As the new century arrives, Newcastle is becoming a burgeoning centre for new writing, and the city looks set to enjoy a greatly increased profile in the world of literature. We might thus hope that the Jane Austens of the new millennium will be less likely to cite our city's name as the civic embodiment of the back of beyond.

And on Screen ...

Until relatively recently, the majority of film production resources, screen writers, and directors in Britain were based in London and the South East. Thus, seeing Newcastle and its people portrayed in film and television drama productions – still a relatively novel experience – can give an interesting insight into how we are perceived by the rest of the country and how we see ourselves.

Unlike literature, filmed drama has to be physically located somewhere or other. Thus, Newcastle's appearances in film and television might be divided into two broad categories. The most interesting to us would be those where Newcastle is the specifically identified location, and its regional culture and character feature strongly in the plot. The other category would be those films where the city is merely used as an interesting but non-particular scenic backdrop, and Newcastle's unique civic identity is accordingly less of a noticeable feature.

As well as the interest of seeing familiar landmarks, places, and people, part of the game in seeing one's home town on screen is spotting inconsistencies, both visually and in the script. You know the sort of thing: 'Hang on a minute – the 33 bus doesn't go anywhere near Byker!' Perhaps it is the realistic nature of films that makes such things leap out of the screen at us. Some of these apparent 'mistakes' are simply due to the practical imperatives and limitations of film-making, or the over-riding preference for getting the best shot over attention to local detail. But as we shall see, until films (and later television) started to be produced regularly in the North East by local producers and writers, it was all too often the case that the portrayal of Newcastle (and especially its people) was at best left to mere chance, and at its worst was based on sheer ignorance and a lack of attention to detail on the part of a film industry that was based in the so-called 'home counties'.

In the absence of any known surviving silent dramas, Newcastle's first appearance in a feature film was as the ostensible setting for a rather creaky British drama entitled *On the Night of the Fire* (1939). As most of the film's action takes place within studio-bound interior sets, the only appearance the city itself makes is in a handful of mute establishing shots, inserted to instil an idea of geographic location. Among them are an overhead view (probably taken from the Tyne Bridge) of a working commercial quayside bustling with ships being loaded and unloaded, and later a view of what looks like a rather run-down part of Scotswood or Elswick.

The story is a tame drama concerned with the world of a petty criminal who is blackmailed and gets out of his depth. Ralph Richardson's performance as a local barber is as unconvincing as his accent, which swings wildly between Leeds and Manchester within the space of a single sentence, and never gets anywhere near Tyneside. All in all it is an unremarkable film, whose setting in the North East is never more than incidental.

It was to be some 11 years before Newcastle was to grace the

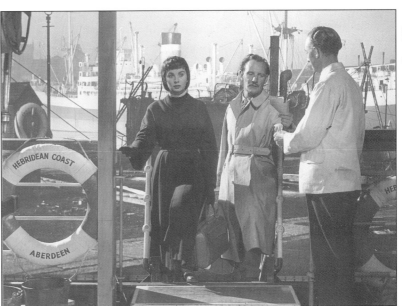

Trevor Howard and Jean Simmons in The Clouded Yellow, 1950.

Tony Hillman

silver screen again, this time as one of the destinations of a man on the run in *The Clouded Yellow* (1950). Taking its title from the name of a rare butterfly, this tale of espionage and intrigue follows maverick spy Trevor Howard and a young girl played by Jean Simmons throughout the north of England as they flee from the authorities.

With the police watching all ports for them, their sojourn at Newcastle is heralded by establishing shots of the Tyne Bridge and, once again, a bustling commercial quayside. We are also shown the interior of the Central Station, and even the old Haymarket Bus Station. Indeed, our local public transport features quite strongly in this movie, especially when the elusive duo board a Newcastle Transport number 3lB trolleybus at the foot of Westgate Road (with the Keep in the background) and Trevor Howard asks the conductor for 'Two to Jesmond, please.' After disembarking in Jesmond Road outside the towers of John Dobson's Victorian cemetery gates, they hasten to a rendez-vous at a house in what was then still largely a residential street.

At this house, which seems to be a sort of nerve centre for a community of East European emigrés, our hero is referred to one of their number who is a taxidermist, and can help him escape. A further clandestine meeting ensues at the shop in a nondescript dark alley where yet another meeting is arranged, to take place at: ' … the old steps, near the Surtees House.' This meeting subsequently takes place on a very gothic and shadowy looking Castle Stairs. In this scene, we are introduced to the taxidermist's daughter, who is the only character in the film purporting to be a native of Tyneside. Once again, the film-makers fail to go to the trouble of authenticity, and her accent has more to do with the Yorkshire-Lancashire borders than Tyneside, though at least – unlike Ralph Richardson earlier – she sticks consistently to the same voice throughout.

In *The Clouded Yellow*, the continuing importance of the river Tyne in the city's commercial life is perhaps surprisingly evident for a film of the 1950s. Much of the action in Newcastle takes place on or near the quayside, and the couple both arrive and depart from the city by water; initially by a steam packet from London, and finally by a rowing boat conveniently left moored near the Swing Bridge.

The frequent dark settings and black and white photography of this movie cast it almost in the *film noir* genre, and it is well worth seeing, not only for the local interest factor. However, one last small irritation is the reference in the film's end credits to the city's name as 'Newcastle-on-Tyne.'

During the swinging Sixties, Newcastle was visited only once by a feature film crew, to shoot the crime caper *Payroll* (1961). Actors such as Tom Bell and Billie Whitelaw make unconvincing geordies, but the plot is fairly action-packed, and the abundance of exterior photography provides a wealth of interesting footage of Newcastle as it was just before the ravaging developments of the mid-Sixties. Once again, however, the city is being used merely as a provincial setting that would be unfamiliar to a largely southern audience. Inevitably, the film's cultural relevance to its location is minimal.

With the now legendary *Get Carter* (1971), however, Newcastle was at last placed firmly on the cinematic map in its own right. Because of the fish-out-of-water aspect of the storyline of a cockney gangster coming to the north east, the character of the city and its people is very strongly emphasised and is an integral part of the plot. 'They're tough up north' is very much the message conveyed, and

Kenneth Griffith, Michael Craig and Barry Keagan in a scene from Payroll, 1962.

Tony Hillman

our regional character is repeatedly portrayed as being a stark, rough-and-ready contrast to the relatively sophisticated metropolis of Carter's London. This is particularly interesting, as the book on which the film was based, *Jack's Return Home* by Ted Lewis, did not specify the nondescript northern town of the plot. Newcastle was chosen by director Mike Hodges, who had been impressed by the city's lively atmosphere on a visit during his National Service.

Carter, played by Michael Caine, arrives in Newcastle by train, and his first encounter with local culture is a visit to the long bar of the Victoria & Comet pub, across the road from the Central Station. In a scene calculated to set the tone for the rest of the film, this bar – known locally as 'the spit & vomit' – is populated by dowdily dressed beer-swilling locals, and a portly chanteuse booms some club cabaret classic through a terrible PA system. Before long, two of the local females are rolling on the floor in a screaming cat-fight, until they are separated by a grinning barman.

This scene became famous to spotters of cinema trivia by the presence of Arthur Perkins, a local man recruited as an extra who had a thumb and five fingers on each hand. Caine was said to have commented off-screen: 'I bet he never drops his pint!'

His dead brother's house in the city's west end is Carter's next stop, and there are numerous shots of the huddled terraces and cobbled back lanes of the area which, whilst perhaps a predictable cliché, nevertheless provide a technicolour document of the housing in what was then still a largely unmod-

Tony Hillman

Michael Caine and Ian Hendry confer at Newcastle Race Course in Get Carter, 1970.

ernised area. More local colour is added by a march-past of one of the Juvenile Kazoo 'Jazz' Bands in full uniform, which were hugely popular in the north at the time.

The underworld attached to Newcastle's thriving clubland and gambling industry obviously features strongly – a disturbing reflection of the emerging reality of those days – and, in what was regarded as quite a violent film for its time, Carter uses a variety of local landmarks and features such as the Shields Ferry, the High Level Bridge (for some reason referred to as 'the iron bridge'), and Gateshead's multi-storey car park as venues for meeting and murdering his rivals and pursuers.

Director Mike Hodges resisted MGM's attempts to cast the film entirely with big name stars, going for British character actors instead. Unfortunately, very few were native Tynesiders or were capable of a convincing local accent, and once on film, Newcastle was seemingly populated largely by Yorkshiremen and Lancashire lasses. One notable exception to this was the superb performance by a young Alun Armstrong in the part of Keith.

Apparently Telly Savalas was seriously considered to play the character of Yorkshire businessman Cliff Brumby. Fortunately, the part went to Bryan Mosley (better known as *Coronation Street*'s Alf Roberts).

Mike Figgis

Tommy Lee Jones (Cosmo) and Sting (Finney) on the High Level Bridge in a scene from Stormy Monday.

Crime was yet again the underlying theme in Newcastle's next appearance on celluloid in *Stormy Monday* (1987), directed by the Oscar-nominated Mike Figgis, where the plot revolves around a property swindle and the seedy underworld of clubland. But despite the liberal use of local talent in the cast, there is a distinct lack of specific place in this film, which uses the local cityscape as a nameless backdrop. The setting of the action during a festival called 'American Week' removes us even further from the Newcastle we know, but accordingly makes interesting use of the architecture of the old quayside area, where the striking contrasts of level and the classical stone office buildings crouching beneath the towering steelwork of the Tyne Bridge are visually reminiscent of New York. The cosmopolitan atmosphere is enhanced by the presence in town of several European jazz musicians, who feature prominently in the film.

Mike Figgis's most recent film, *The Loss of Sexual Innocence*, was also partly filmed in Northumbria and Newcastle and features scenes set in the Central Station.

As far as representations of its local culture are concerned, Newcastle has fared rather better on television than it has on the cinema screen, probably thanks to the more regionalised structure of TV companies in this country. The formulaic nature of genres such as the detective drama also means that mass audiences are just as content to watch Spender policing the streets of Tyneside on a weekly basis as they are to see Taggart doing the same in Glasgow or Inspector Morse in Oxford.

Inevitably, parts of Newcastle have made more than their fair share of appearances as representatives of the 'cloth-cap-and-damp-cobblestones' image of the old industrial north. Dramas such as *The Stars Look Down* and *When the Boat Comes In* enjoyed a surge in popularity during the 1970s, and more

Tony Hillman

Mike Figgis films The Loss of Sexual Innocence in Newcastle's Central Station, 1997.

recently several of the novels of Catherine Cookson have been adapted for TV, making regular use of areas such as that around Hanover Square, which has retained much of its Victorian character.

However, television's appetite for regional variety has led to a number of series that portray a more upbeat image of the city. Building upon the success of *Spender*, actor and writer Jimmy Nail went on to produce two series of *Crocodile Shoes*, the rags-to riches tale of local lathe operator Jed Shepherd, who makes the journey from Newcastle to Nashville to become a country & western star. In the world of children's television, the Benwell-based *Byker Grove* has been running for over ten years as one of the most successful series of its kind.

But perhaps the most durably popular show for its endearingly dry humour in a Newcastle setting has been the 1960s sitcom *The Likely Lads*, and its 1970s sequel *Whatever Happened to The Likely Lads?* The almost forgotten original Sixties series was shot in black and white and introduced us to the antics of two young lads-about town, Terry Collier (James Bolam) and Bob Ferris (Rodney Bewes). Much more studio-bound than its successor, this series was largely based in the electrical workshop where the lads were employed, and in which their adventures the night before were usually discussed rather than seen.

The much more successful and still often repeated Seventies series followed Terry and Bob into adult life, with Terry remaining footloose and true to his working-class roots, whilst Bob married Thelma and aspired towards the middle classes. Indeed, the show subtly reflected many of the social changes then taking place in a Britain approaching the premiership of Margaret Thatcher. Terry's return to the North East after an absence of some years abroad with the army also provided an opportunity for regular commentary on the changing face of Newcastle, as the city of his youth transformed itself into the modern city of today.

The terraced streets in which the lads had grown up were demolished, and Terry went off to live in a high-rise flat. Bob and Thelma, of course, joined that generation of first time home buyers that sprang up in the Seventies, and moved into a semi on the 'Elm Lodge' estate, which typified the private housing estates then mushrooming in the outer suburbs around every large town and city. The passing of bars and clubs the two lads had once frequented was mourned by Terry with such memorable lines as; 'The Go-Go … gone!' The eponymous feature film spin-off from the TV series also made much of the passing of old Newcastle, and poignantly included footage of Bob and Terry watching their old local pub being demolished amidst large-scale redevelopment then taking place in the west end of the city.

Tony Hillman

Thelma (played by Brigit Forsyth) and Bob (Rodney Bewes) discuss a brick in The Likely Lads, 1976.

The credits sequence at the beginning and end of each episode formed a collage of shots of familiar locations, which included the Byker Road Bridge with the disused Cluny warehouse below it, the high-rise blocks of flats in Shieldfield, the All Saints office development near Swan House, and a demolition site in the west end.

As far as prominence in a serious drama is concerned, Newcastle's coming of age on the small screen was undoubtedly in Peter Flannery's epic series *Our Friends in the North*. Following the lives of four teenagers from the early 1960s through to adulthood in the present day, this landmark production also charted the shameful course of Newcastle's unwelcome foray onto the front pages of the national press when the Poulson scandal broke in the 1970s.

With the action swinging between the North East and Soho, this powerful political drama vividly captured the heady optimism of those times, and for once the north saw itself portrayed in a faithful and realistic way, free from caricature and patronisation. The way the four central characters' lives were seen to develop formed a microcosm of the part played by the North East in our nation's history through the past four decades.

On another level, the familiar game of location-spotting was enhanced for local viewers by trying to recognise characters depicting real-life figures whose names had been changed. Most prominent among these was Austin Donoghue, played by actor Alun Armstrong, who represented T. Dan Smith. Smith had been Chief Executive of the city council in the Sixties, and had dreamed of turning Newcastle into the 'Brasilia of the North'. Donoghue's office suite (filmed in Milburn House, Dean Street) looked out over the city's roofscape towards the quayside, the view dominated by a floodlit Tyne Bridge. Other locations included the high-rise blocks of flats (the ones used were in Shieldfield), which replaced the streets of terraced housing then being demolished by the acre. At one and the same time, these flats represented the solution to the national housing problem of the time, the social dissatisfaction and misery they caused among so many of their original residents, and the source of the bribery and corruption scandal resulting from the allocation of building contracts.

Though it documented an episode in Newcastle and the wider North East's history that many would rather forget, *Our Friends* remains a landmark in the television production of recent years, in which Newcastle might justly be proud to have featured from a purely artistic point of view.

It is to be hoped that the continuing expansion of the film and television industry in our region will lead to more home-produced representations of Newcastle, its people, and its culture finding their way onto our screens.

➢ Christopher Goulding is an actor (appearances in *Byker Grove*, *Crocodile Shoes*, Catherine Cookson dramas, *Our Friends in the North*), writer, and journalist. Previous publications include *The Story of the People's*, 1990; *Hidden Newcastle*, 1995; *Tinseltoon*, 1998; *Graingertoon* 1999; all published by Newcastle Libraries & Information Service.

Before TV: The wireless took pride of place in the sitting room.

The Cat's Whisker – and After
Radio and television broadcasting

Douglas Bond

IT WAS 23 DECEMBER, 1922 – only 36 hours to go until the magical time of Christmas. Shoppers thronged the city streets in the usual last-minute rush, and decorations festooned shops and houses. But another piece of magic – electronic magic – was just about to take place. On a fine but bitterly cold and frosty night, in a quiet stable yard behind the Co-operative warehouse in Blandford Street, three people stood beside a handcart waiting tensely for the minute hand to tick round to 8 pm. Then one of the trio, Tom Payne, moved close to an ordinary telephone microphone which rested on the cart. He spoke. 'Hello. Hello. This is 5NO, the Newcastle on Tyne station of the British Broadcasting Company'. One of Britain's earliest broadcasting stations had taken to the airwaves. For the hundred or so enthusiastic owners of crystal sets there followed a short programme of music, which must have been absolutely thrilling for those early listeners.

But why was the first broadcast from a stable yard, rather than a studio? This was the result of probably the first 'technical hitch'. A break in the cabling meant that the pioneer broadcasters were unable to perform in the studio at 24 Eldon Square. The engineer, Mr Thomas, told them that they would have to speak directly into the transmitter which was situated behind the Co-operative building, and it was he who requisitioned the cart for them. A dog barked throughout the performance, which had to be cut short as nobody could find the dog to shut it up! Of that memorable first broadcast, Tom Payne said. 'When we sang, played and spoke into that little mike, we were not at all sure that the broadcast would be a success. In a way, we felt rather foolish standing around that old cart and playing away seemingly for no audience at all. When we finished, I dashed home to my house in Morpeth, and on arrival, was told that the crystal set there had picked up our broadcast beautifully. That was when I really felt the thrill'. Amazingly, the broadcast reached much further than Morpeth. Contemporary reports indicate that sailors on board ship cruising in the Straits of Gibraltar also heard it! At this time the *Evening Chronicle* advertised a new wireless set costing £4 as 'nothing more acceptable could be purchased for the home'. The licence fee was 10 shillings per annum (50 pence in modern terms). Even though it was radio, all performers had to wear evening dress after 6 PM.

Before starting the radio station, and becoming its first director, Tom Payne had been one of the first cinema managers, and also a theatre orchestra leader. It was probably this latter occupation which led him into partnership with another orchestra leader, George Hornsby, who ran the orchestra at the Milvain Ballroom in Fenham. He opened an electrical shop in Gallowgate which was in business until 1978. Other regular broadcasters in the pioneering days were connected with the early days of the Jesmond Playhouse, and doubled for radio repertory.

Anthony Flowers

'The centre figure is Mr Bertram Fryer, the Director of 5NO, speaking into the microphone through which he has appealed to the affection of so many young persons. On either side of him is an "uncle" of 5NO'.

(From a Sunripe Cigarette card, Wireless Telephony Broadcasting Series.)

One of the most popular was actress Sal Sturgeon, who once remembered broadcasting from a studio where the microphone was hanging on a string and had to be 'chased around the room'! Many of the best known personalities were the 'uncles' and 'aunties' of Children's Hour. Newcastle had 'Aunty Kersty' (Mrs. K. Latham), 'Auntie Bridget' (Miss Agnes Strong), 'Uncle Nick' (Colonel Mill-ican) and, of course, 'Uncle Tom' – Tom Payne, who died in 1967 at the age of 84.

It was Tom Payne's considered opinion that 5NO was the first ever BBC station to open, as earlier stations were run by private companies. For the first four months of operation, Tom Payne was also 'paymaster'. There was no money forthcoming from the newly-formed BBC, and he paid bills and performers' fees from his own pocket. When Mr J.C.W. Reith (later Lord Reith) visited Newcastle and was informed of this fact, he arranged for the requisite funding to be made available on his return to London. On one occasion, Tom Payne recalled asking permission from the Co-operative Wholesale Society manager to broadcast from Blandford Street, and receiving the reply 'All right, as long as the caretaker has no objections.' Fortunately, the caretaker did not!

One of the early technicians, Mr Nicholson, recalled some details about the Eldon Square studio. It was a room 20 feet by 15 feet, its walls draped with heavy curtains, and the floor covered in a heavy carpet. When it was required to broadcast a choir and orchestra, the doors were left open, and the choir was grouped on the staircase outside.

Obviously, it was not long until it was realised that the first studio was much too small for the burgeoning service. Interest in the new medium was growing apace. On 21 February 1925, the Lord Mayor opened a Wireless Exhibition in St George's Drill Hall, and on 12 May the same year a local branch of The Wireless League was formed. The BBC began negotiations with Newcastle City Council to lease premises for new studios. On 29 September 1925, the old Maternity Hospital (the Lying-In Hospital) on New Bridge Street was leased to the British Broadcasting Company at an annual rent of £550. The new studios were officially opened by the Lord Mayor, Councillor Anthony Oates, on 23 December 1925, exactly three years after that first historic broadcast. Other guests at the opening ceremony included Dr Wild, the Bishop of Newcastle; Mr Reith, managing director of the BBC; Sir William Noble; Sir Thomas Oliver; Sir Theodore Morison, Principal of Armstrong College; and Lord Gainford, chairman of the BBC. Introducing Lord Gainford, Mr Reith who, alone of the officials and invited guests was clad in a light brown Harris tweed suit, made a humorous but sincere appeal to the lady who picked up his suitcase containing his dress suit in mistake for her own, to return his belongings. In his address, the Chairman defended programme policy against the charge that programming was overburdened by talks and educational matter. Alternative programmes were to be provided so that listeners could choose according to their mood or inclination. It was announced that for the benefit of those people unable to listen in the evenings, there was to be a short broadcast of a high standard every morning. The first such, to be broadcast the next morning, was to be a concert by the station's own symphony orchestra. The Lord Mayor was in the studios again on 14 April 1926, making an appeal for funds for the Children's Sanatorium at Stannington.

The first glimpse of television in the city was, surprisingly, as early as 1930, and, as might be expected, the far-seeing Tom Payne was involved. This demonstration took place at Payne and Hornsby's electrical shop in Gallowgate and featured a demonstration of the doomed mechanical system pioneered by John Logie Baird. The picture, just about the size of a cigarette packet, was broadcast from London, and, amazingly, picked up on an ordinary radio aerial. One of those present was William Henry Inness of Walker, who built his own equipment shortly afterwards, thus becoming one of the first amateurs in the country to build a successful television set. His set successfully received pictures transmitted from London to his home in Walker. Mr Inness was one of the most skilled radio and television engineers in the north, working for the General Electric Company at Magnet House in Newcastle until his retirement in 1960. Other witnesses to the historic demonstration were William Warburton Pope, secretary of the Newcastle Radio Society, Alex Hood, the ex-Lord Mayor of Newcastle Sir Arthur Lambert, Mrs W.R. Pape, and William Pape, the society's chairman.

Rediffusion began its service of cable-fed radio in Newcastle in 1931 from its premises in Grove Street, off Elswick Road. The company was established in Clacton some three years earlier. It was known then as The Northern Wireless Relay Company.

In 1936, Newcastle Broadcasting House recruited another star from the local amateur theatre, schoolmaster Cecil McGivern, who eventually moved to London and became Deputy Director of BBC Television. McGivern was responsible for the introduction of the most famous product of North East radio, *Wot Cheor Geordie*. Compared by Esther McCracken and featuring Tyneside songs and humour, the programme became a regional institution.

Tuesday 19 October, 1937, saw an important stage in North East broadcasting with the opening of the Stagshaw transmitter by the Duchess of Northumberland in company with Mr R.C. Norman, Chairman of the BBC. At night, a reminiscence feature entitled, *Stag-shaw Looks Back*, recalling past

The radio broadcast of Wot Cheor, Geordie *on 8 November 1949, recorded from Gosforth Central Hall.*

broadcasts, was presented from the Newcastle studios by Cecil McGivern, the new Programme Organiser for the North East. Although reception in Newcastle and district was greatly improved with the introduction of the new transmitter, the mast's closest neighbour, Thomas Southern at Beukley Farm, Great Whittington, had problems. He suffered from having absolutely perfect reception, which eliminated the signals from all other stations! 'Our set is rather old', he said, 'and it's impossible to get anything but Stagshaw. We turn the dial to any wavelength and the result is always the same – just Stagshaw!' In his address at the official opening ceremony, Mr Norman observed that Stagshaw marked another step on the way to the BBC's goal – a nationwide service of two alternative programmes for every listener owning a receiving set of moderate price. The old Newcastle transmitter at Blandford Street closed down ten minutes before Stagshaw was due to come into service at three o'clock, and during the interval there was silence, ended by the voice of the announcer introducing the speakers in the official party. Radio dealers in Newcastle reported that whilst they had no complaints as to the clarity of reception from the new transmitter, they had expected more volume in view of the greater power. The only area which suffered a loss in quality was that immediately surrounding the old transmitter.

The black year when the North East lost its own wavelength was 1945, and it began the period of what local MPs called 'subservience to Belfast'. Fade-outs of North East programmes to make way for those from Northern Ireland, and long dreary hours of Irish jigs and Ulster sports news brought a constant stream of protest. In 1954, the *Evening Chronicle* began a campaign to end the farce of the shared wavelength, under the banner 'North East radio programmes for North East listeners'. Local authorities were invited to a protest meeting and to support petitions to the BBC, the Postmaster General and the Prime Minister. The crux of the problem was that the 261-metre wavelength had been allocated to Northern Ireland, and North East programmes were only heard by consent of Broadcasting House, Belfast, in spite of the fact that Ulster had only one-third the number of licence-holders of the North East. The official 'North of England Home Service' wavelength on 434 metres was virtually inaudible in the North East. This unhappy situation continued for some considerable time, not being resolved until 1963.

Meanwhile, the North East also felt that it was being left out of the spread of the television service, and representations were being made to the BBC for the long-awaited North East

The control desk at Stagshaw from The North Mail, 19 October 1937.

transmitter. The enthusiasm for the North East shown by the BBC at the start of radio some 30 years earlier had certainly vanished by the start of the Fifties. In July 1951, a letter from the Postmaster General, Ness Edwards, to Mr C.F. Grey, MP for Durham, stated that 'when rearmament programme restrictions on new television stations are lifted the North East transmitter at Pontop Pike will probably be the first to be completed'. The previous week, Mr Grey had made a strong and sometimes bitter speech, focussing attention on the North East's plight. Mr Edwards' letter, however, made it quite clear that the Government would not yield to pressure over television coverage for the North East. The BBC plan was to have five high-powered and five low-powered stations in operation by the end of 1954. That plan had been revised early in 1951 when it had become apparent that the demand of rearmament required a reduction in civilian capital expenditure. This meant that the two existing stations at Alexandra Palace and Sutton Coldfield would only be joined by new transmitters at Holme Moss, Kirk O' Shotts and Wenvoe. The five low-powered stations including Pontop Pike had therefore been postponed indefinitely. In a reference to the shared radio wavelength, Mr Edwards regretted that he held out no hope of an early solution! However, all was not lost. Pressure continued to be put upon the Government by local MPs, local authorities, and members of the public, and eventually the decision to allow the construction at Pontop Pike to go ahead was made. When it was realised that the station was not going to be ready in time for the Queen's Coronation in June, 1953, more pressure was brought to bear on the BBC to come up with a solution. Beginning in the winter of 1952, BBC engineers and contractors worked long and hard for six hectic months to have the station ready for transmission before the great day – June 2nd. The BBC warned, however, that Pontop Pike would be merely a 'temporary' transmitter, in time for the coronation, so that the equipment would not be brand new, and the buildings erected would be little better than huts. The mast though, was permanent. A BBC official said, 'Even though the station is temporary, we are putting our best men on the job, and will build it as well as we can'. Following the Coronation, steps would be taken to erect a permanent station, as soon as the Government gave permission. In the build-up to the first transmissions, local dealers were concerned that there could be a shortage of receivers, and the public were advised to order early, even though transmissions had not even started! Another problem was the shortage of skilled aerial riggers. Mr T.A. Hood in an article in the *Evening Chronicle* in February 1953 said 'Cost of a television set – unlikely to be less than £70 for everything – may seem a lot, but not so much if present day values are compared with 30 years ago when the average price for a radio set was £25 to £30. For normal viewing the 12 inch screen is now accepted as standard. Most people will buy this type, and if it is a small table model, it will cost between £65 and £72, plus another £10 for aerial and installation'.

Shortly after came the announcement that Pontop Pike would be ready to transmit its first official programmes on 1 May, the day before the FA Cup Final. At this point, however, it is worth pointing out that some folks had already received television in the North East. With an aerial on an extremely long pole, it had been possible to receive very poor, grainy pictures from the Holme Moss transmitter, but May 1st 1953 was the first time good quality reception had been available.

Let us now look in detail at what the first day offered. The broadcasting day would have begun at 09.45, when viewers would have seen the 'art bars' (a black cross on a white background) accompanied by a tone; both used for 'warming up' the transmitter. At 09.59, the screen would have faded to a black screen and silence. At 10.00 the first 'real' picture came on – a view of the Thames and the Houses of Parliament, with the chimes of Big Ben, heralding the Demonstration Film. The Demfilm was not an advertised programme. It was the same every day, and was intended as a showcase for potential new viewers to see in shops, and encourage them to invest in television sets by showing them the sort of programmes available. It was introduced and compèred by popular announcer, Sylvia Peters, and was in 15 minute segments, lasting two hours. However, the transmission was also intended for the television trade, as engineers installing new sets needed sound and pictures to test the new equipment. For this reason, the film was broken every 15 minutes for a transmission of the now-famous Test Card 'C' and music. At the end of the Demfilm at 12.00, the screens would darken again for a couple of minutes

Steve Wood

The BBC Studios in New Bridge Street, 1960.

before an hour long transmission of Test Card 'C' and music. The records used at this time consisted of music by three orchestras. These were The Cedric Dumont Light Orchestra (from Switzerland) and included the tune *Serenade To Eileen*, which years later became a commercial hit for the Ray Martin Orchestra; a Latin-American band called The Cuban Caballeros, playing Latin standards like *Frenesi*; and The Sid Phillips Septet, playing modern dance music, including their later commercial hit, *Spanish Serenade*. At 13.00, screens would darken as the transmitter closed down until the start of afternoon programmes at 15.15. On this first day,

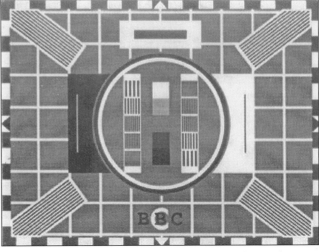

Test Card 'C', a familiar sight on the TV screen of the Fifties.

however, things were slightly different. At the end of the Demfilm, there was an outside broadcast of cricket until 13.30. Cricket again from 15.00 until 16.30. This was followed by some more of Test Card 'C' and recorded music until Children's Television at 17.00, which consisted of an episode of the American film series, *Hopalong Cassidy*. Evening programmes started half an hour earlier than usual at 19.30, with a visit to the Severn Wildfowl Trust, which was followed by the nightly Newsreel. There was another outside broadcast at 20.15 with a visit to the Royal Albert Hall for a display by the Boys Brigade. The magazine programme *Kaleidoscope* followed at 21.00, and then a political discussion, *In The News* rounded off the first evening's viewing. The last item of the night was the News, which, as usual for that time, was broadcast in sound only – the screen remained dark. On the following day, the FA Cup Final between Blackpool and Bolton Wanderers was televised in its entirety. Strangely, radio was only allowed to broadcast a commentary on the second half!

In a very perspicacious editorial, the *Newcastle Journal* observed that, 'Every citizen of North East England should feel a thrill of personal pride at the introduction of the television service from Pontop Pike. It matters little that it is a temporary service, rushed through so that people in this sometimes forgotten corner of the land may view the Coronation of their Queen. What is important is to remember that we have television today only because of the pressure of dynamic public opinion. But in the very novelty of the new entertainment form there is a possible danger of what may be termed over-indulgence. Soon, it is fairly certain, critics will begin deciding the influence of television on family life, on civilised conversation, and above all, on the susceptibilities of the children. These critics have a case. Their argument is never more pertinent than when applied to those who not only enjoy television, but who cannot resist its fascination. We suggest a television ration plan for children, so that they can be brought to regard viewing as an occasional delight instead of an after-tea institution'. The previous day, Aneurin Bevan had said that he 'sincerely hoped the British public would stand against sponsored television. Television itself is bad enough. I personally believe that people should have more time for reflection, or to read a good book, but I dare say I am getting old-fashioned'! Some weeks later, a film entitled *Kingdom In The North*, introduced by the Bishop of Durham, Dr Ramsey, was shown nationally. The first live transmissions from the area came in October 1955. Five programmes were broadcast: *Top Town* between teams from Sunderland and Blaydon; a Northumbrian Barn Dance; a public inquiry; a variety show; and a dialect play called *The Blue Suit*. The Gosforth Drill Hall was used as a temporary studio.

VHF radio transmissions were introduced from the Pontop Pike transmitter at the end of 1955, and eventually, North of England Home Service programmes were available to anyone with a set capable of picking up VHF transmissions.

On 14 December 1957, the Independent Television Authority announced the formation of a company to be programme contractors for their North East Station, with Sir Richard Pease as chairman. It was hoped to open the transmitting station to be built at Burnhope, near Consett, at the end of the following year, bringing Independent Television to another two-and-a-half million people. The original suggestion for the company name was 'North East Television' Burnhope's coverage would be from Alnwick to Northallerton and Hexham, with test transmissions scheduled to begin in August 1958. By October 1958, the company name was confirmed as Tyne Tees Television, with studios and offices in two converted warehouses in City Road, Newcastle.

The first official transmission from the new station was on 15 January 1959, and was watched by a quarter of a million people. Most rental companies had been rather slow in adding the tuning strips which were necessary to enable reception of the new service to receivers. The opening ceremony was performed by the Duke of Northumberland, in company with the Prime Minister, Harold Macmillan, and ITA chairman, Sir Ivone Kirkpatrick, who 'made no apology for the criticism levelled at ITV for giving the public what it wanted, rather than what they ought to have' – his criticism of 'Auntie' BBC! In an on-screen interview, the Prime Minister was of the opinion that 'men are rather like fish – the further north you go, the better they get'!

Locally produced programmes were a feature of the new service from the start. Highly popular was the daily lunchtime variety show, *The One O' Clock Show* which ran for five years from 1959 until 1964, notching up 1,098 editions. Introduced by all-round entertainer Terry O'Neill, the regular cast of Peggy Haig (Terry's wife) and her brother Jack, together with singers George Romaine and Chris Langford, and actor/writer Austin Steele soon became firm favourites in the area. Jack Haig was a fine comic actor who later achieved national popularity for his portrayal of the character Monsieur LeClerc in the television series *Allo Allo*. The weekly *North East Roundabout* magazine and news programme was introduced by announcer Tom Coyne, who later joined the BBC in Birmingham. Other early local programmes included George Taylor's *Sports Desk* and *The Bobby Thompson Show*, starring the region's best known and loved comedian.

Following criticism in the Pilkington Report, TTTV embarked upon a change of image in 1964, giving its local news programmes a more hard-hitting and professional style. It is probably fair to say that with the arrival of TTTV, the North East was given its own voice for the first time, thus giving us the chance to express our regional culture. The local programming was truly 'local content for local people'.

During the development of local television in the late Fifties, local shared radio continued, featuring programmes like *Wot Cheor, Geordie* and *Bob's Your Uncle*, starring popular local comedians like Bobby Thompson, Dick Irwin, Frankie Burns and Geoff Suggars. Local television news actually arrived ten days before TTTV's first broadcast. Canny as ever, the BBC broadcast its first news programme from Newcastle on January 5th 1959, read by George House, another presenter who was to become a household name over the ensuing years. This was a significant broadcast in that it was planned deliberately by the BBC to steal TTTV's thunder, and to win some of the publicity value by being first in the field. Another example occurred in 1964 when the BBC poached Mike Neville from TTTV just before he was due to launch the new flagship programme, *Newsview* – part of TTTV's new image.

Mike Neville stayed with the BBC for over 30 years, becoming probably the most well-known and popular regional presenter in the UK, until returning to TTTV in 1996. By 1961, the original BBC studios in New Bridge Street were too small to cope with the ever-increasing development of sound and TV broadcasting, so a two-storey extension containing many new and interesting features was added onto the rear of the old building. The ground floor consisted of workrooms, switchrooms and storerooms, whilst the first floor housed the main engineering store, dressing rooms, offices and boardroom. The second floor consisted of more offices and dressing rooms, plus a 36-seater staff restaurant.

7 January 1963 saw another landmark in local radio broadcasting. On that day, the hated shared 261 metre wavelength with Northern Ireland came to an end. Stagshaw was completely taken over by the North East, transmitting on the medium waveband, all the programmes that had been broadcast only on VHF from Pontop Pike. Consequently, programmes like the immensely popular *Voice Of The People*, a magazine programme for the North East, were available to everyone. The regional news, previously five minutes from Ulster followed by five minutes from Newcastle, was extended to a full ten minute bulletin. Four months earlier, on 17 September 1962, BBC Television began a nightly news and magazine programme entitled *North At Six*, with its catchy signature tune, *Lost Patrol* by the John Barry Seven and based on Tchaikovsky's *Capriccio Italien*. It was introduced by Frank Bough. When he moved to London, the anchorman chosen to replace him was Mike Neville. The rest is history!

An amusing incidence of pirate radio occurred in 1964. On 26 October, three Newcastle University students set sail intending to anchor three miles off the mouth of the Tyne to pull off the biggest Rag Week stunt on record – a pirate radio station. It was intended to broadcast Rag News, but only one mile offshore, the Radio Rag expedition was scuttled by thick fog and interference from the original pirate radio station, Radio Caroline. However, students in lodgings in Newcastle reported good reception in between bursts of Radio Caroline! Skipper George Straughan, secretary of the Newcastle Motor Boat Club commented, 'I've had some peculiar jobs, but this is the first time I've ever been a pirate!'

On Guy Fawkes night, 1966, a new television service, the long-awaited BBC2 opened officially in the North East. One of the first programmes to be seen was *As I Came Through Sandgate*, a half hour film comparing the region with the area around Newcastle, New South Wales. Tests during the previous fortnight had shown reception to be better than expected.

In September l969, a BBC spokesperson confirmed that Newcastle had been put forward as a likely site for one of 12 new local radio stations to be set up by September 1970. Radio Durham, one of the first of the BBC's experimental local radio stations, had been broadcasting experimentally since 1968. Radio Durham closed in August 1972. Premises for the new Radio Newcastle were chosen at Crestina House, Jesmond, at that time, the location of the various administrative departments of the BBC. The long-running *Voice Of The North* was the last feature programme from Newcastle on Radio 4 in early April 1970. In future such programmes would be broadcast by the new local station. By July 1970, however, there were serious doubts that Radio Newcastle would ever start. Christopher Chataway, the Minister for Posts and Telecommunications, announced that he was in favour of replacing it with a privately owned commercial station. Radio Newcastle survived this battle, and opened on 2 January 1971, broadcasting five or six hours of local programming daily, interspersed with selections from Radios 2 and 4. The station's first Director was Richard Kelly, already well known to North East listeners from his connections with *Wot Cheor, Geordie*.

Developments in commercial local radio commenced on 19 September 1973 when the winner of the contract for the local station was confirmed as The Metropolitan Broadcasting Company headed by Sir John Hunter. It was to cover an area between Alnwick, Hexham and Bishop Auckland, and chose a site for studios and offices at Swalwell. It began broadcasting on July 15th 1974 on 97MHz VHF and 261 metres medium wave, the old shared wavelength, thus maintaining an old broadcasting tradition. 6 April 1989 saw the start of Great North Radio, an offshoot of the Metro Radio group. Its stated purpose was to 'give more variety and an ease of listening approach – 40 years of hits, putting great music back in the North East'. Border Television of Carlisle gave backing to Century Radio, a speech-based station based in Gateshead. Covering the area between Alnwick and Ripon, its stated intention was to provide 55 per cent speech to 45 per cent music. It began broadcasting on 1 September 1994.

Meanwhile, the BBC was not sitting idly by. Broadcasting House in New Bridge Street had again become too small. After some sixty years, the old premises were finally vacated for the plush new Broadcasting Centre, the 'Pink Palace' on Newcastle's Barrack Road. BBC Radio and television finally came together in one purpose-built building in 1987, although the television news team did not relocate until January 1998, Radio Newcastle having moved there in May 1986.

And what of the future? Digital and cable broadcasting leave the way open for many more services. Indeed, one such, the Mirror Group's Live Television was rather short-lived, closing down in December 1998. It is doubtful whether the magic of the pioneering days will ever be recreated.

ᔕ Douglas Bond is a retired librarian, local historian, founder member of the Test Card Circle, and author of *Victorian and Edwardian Northumbria* with June Thompson, 1976, *Bygone Benwell Revisited*, 1994, and *Bygone Denton Burn*, 1997, Newcastle Libraries & Information Service.

The View From the Stands

Archie Potts

THE POPULARITY OF SPECTATOR SPORTS has been one of the major social themes of the 20th century and the foundations of this development were securely laid in the last quarter of the 19th century. Reductions in the working week, the introduction of bank holidays, and the establishment of the Saturday half-day for certain occupations, gave many workers more free time in which to watch or play sport. Increases in real wages from the 1850s also increased the purchasing power of people in the labour force and gave them the money to pay entrance charges to sporting events and cover their travel costs. Travel itself became easier as transport networks of trains and trams made it possible to carry large numbers of people to sporting venues. The various sporting activities had also become codified by the end of the 19th century with sets of rules and regulations administered by national organisations. Their governing bodies had organised league and knock-out cup competitions in most team sports. Local league and cup competitions grew up alongside the national sports bodies. Amateur teams attracted their own supporters. Newspapers and magazines covered sport in great detail and sports reports and comment were among the most popular items in many newspapers.

At the turn of the century football and horse racing were the most popular spectator sports on Tyneside, but while there were few race meetings in the course of a year, football was played by Newcastle United for nine months out of every 12. Throughout the 20th century Newcastle United has consistently drawn crowds of tens of thousands to its home matches. The support for Newcastle United FC has, over the years, matched that of any other football club in England. Through good times and bad the crowds have rolled up to see the players perform in their famous black and white strip, and this support was not to be measured only in terms of numbers: the fervour of the fans has rarely

Air Images

St James Park, 1995.

been equalled anywhere else in the country.

Initially there were two teams in Newcastle, East End and West End, each competing in the newly formed Northern League. When West End folded in 1892, East End took over their liabilities at an amalgamation meeting and soon after changed their name to Newcastle United. The new club was elected to Division Two of the Football league in the following year and took over the lease at St James's Park football ground. The stadium was very rudimentary with no big stands, no terracing and no dressing rooms. Facilities were gradually improved for both spectators and players, and when Newcastle was promoted to Division One more than twenty thousand people turned up at St James's for the season's first home game on 3 September 1898, to watch their team in action against Wolverhampton Wanderers.

Newcastle United FC quickly established itself as one of the top clubs in the First Division and the Scottish influence on the team's progress was considerable. It was a Scot, Frank Watt, who took over as club secretary (the equivalent of manager in modern terms) in 1895, and within ten years he had turned Newcastle into a major club playing in a modern stadium. Scotland was rich in football talent and Watt packed his teams with good players from north of the border. Few Newcastle fans complained about this policy because Watt only brought in the best. Newcastle United supporters have always had a love affair with the players who wore the number nine shirt in the team and Scottish international, Bob McColl, known as 'the prince of centre forwards' was the first in this long line.

Other outstanding personalities of the Edwardian years were Colin Veitch and Bill McCracken. Colin Veitch was a local lad who could play in several positions and he had a keen tactical brain. He won several international caps and once captained the England team. Veitch was a man of many parts: he performed on the stage at the Newcastle People's Theatre, helped to form the first players' union for

The Newcastle United team of 1906 pose on the stands with Leazes Terrace behind them.

professional footballers, and after his playing days were over he enjoyed a successful career in journalism. Bill McCracken was signed from Belfast Distillery in 1904 and was capped for Ireland several times. He was a master of the offside trap and is widely recognised as one of the greatest full backs of all time.

This was indeed a golden age for the club: Newcastle were First Division League champions 1904-5, 1906-7 and 1908-9 and were unsuccessful FA Cup finalists in 1905, 1906, 1908 and 1911. They lifted the Cup in 1910 although they never managed to win the elusive double.

The 1920s was another successful decade for Newcastle United in which they won the FA Cup in 1924 and the First Division League Championship in 1927. The same years saw the emergence of two football personalities whose names became inseparably linked with Newcastle United: Stan Seymour and Hughie Gallacher. Stan Seymour was born in a Durham mining village and he was playing for Greenock Morton when he was signed by Newcastle United. He played for the team for ten years and later returned to the club as an influential member of the board of directors. Hughie Gallacher was undoubtedly one of Scotland's finest centre forwards. He was only 5ft 5ins tall but he could get up to head high balls and he had wonderful ball control, above all he was a prolific goal scorer. He was signed from Aidrie to become the idol of the terraces at St James's Park.

Unfortunately, the successful team of the 1920s began to break up at the close of the decade and in the 1929-30 season Newcastle narrowly escaped relegation to the Second Division. Shortly afterwards Hughie Gallacher was transferred to Chelsea. In 1932 Newcastle won the FA Cup again, beating Arsenal in the final 2-1, with Newburn-born Jack Allen scoring both of Newcastle's goals. Two seasons later Newcastle were relegated to the Second Division and in the 1937-38 season they were saved from dropping into the Third Division North by one tenth of a goal. It was the lowest point in the club's proud history and the board of directors responded by inviting Stan Seymour, who now ran a sports shop in the city, to join the board. It proved to be a very shrewd appointment.

The outbreak of war in September 1939 meant that the normal football programme was suspended for the duration of hostilities, although matches continued to be played to provide the country with some sporting entertainment. Stan Seymour, who effectively ran the club during this period, kept his eyes open for fresh talent. Albert Stubbins wore the number nine shirt and rattled in the goals in wartime matches, while Seymour recruited Charlie Wayman, Tommy Walker, Ernie Taylor, Bobby Cowell, Jackie Milburn and Charlie Crowe. After the war Seymour brought out the cheque book and bought Joe Harvey, Len Shackleton, Roy Bentley and Frank Brennan. Unfortunately, Albert Stubbins moved on to Liverpool. Newcastle United's forward line of Milburn, Bentley, Wayman, Shackleton and Pearson was one of the most talented in the club's history. Perhaps this team relied too much on skill to secure Newcastle's escape from the rough and tumble of the Second Division. When George Martin took over as manager he transferred some of his star players and settled for a grittier side, with Jackie Milburn leading the forward line. This team won promotion in 1948.

Stan Seymour knew that United would need more quality players if they were to survive in the First Division and he brought in the Robledo brothers, Bobby Mitchell, George Hannah and Alf

Jackie Milburn, United's crack-shot.

McMichael. George Martin resigned as manager in December 1950. Stan Seymour took over from him as temporary manager and he led the club to FA Cup triumphs in 1951 and 1952.

These were the fabulous Milburn years. Jackie Milburn, a pit lad from Ashington, had signed for Newcastle in 1943. He started as a winger but had been persuaded to play centre forward, and this proved to be his best position. Jackie was fast with a cracking shot, and he was a scrupulously clean player. Moreover, he was extremely modest and never allowed his fame to go to his head. He always insisted that the great FA Cup victories of the 1950s were the result of team work and he was right. The 1951 and 1952 teams under the captaincy of Joe Harvey, and the 1955 one under Jimmy Scoular, were a good blend of skill and high work-rate but above all they had wonderful team spirit.

Duggie Livingstone, who had successfully coached the Belgian national team, was appointed manager of Newcastle United in December 1954 and he was in charge when they won the FA Cup in 1955. He wanted to drop Jackie Milburn from the FA Cup final team, but was overruled by the board led by Stan Seymour, and was eased out of his job shortly afterwards. Seymour took control once again until the appointment of Charlie Mitten as manager in June 1958. Mitten was a flamboyant character. He changed the Newcastle strip and brought in two outstanding players in Ivor Allchurch and George Eastham, who lined up with Len White to form a formidable attacking trio. Unfortunately the Mitten term ended the 1960-61 season in relegation followed by a faltering start in the Second Division. Norman Smith took over as caretaker manager in mid-season and ensured that Newcastle avoided the drop to the Third Division. This marked another low point in the club's history.

Newcastle also made history in a landmark court case. George Eastham was refused a transfer by the club's board of directors and he took them to court in a legal challenge to the maximum wage and transfer system. He won his case. Lord Justice Wilberforce ruled that the system operated by the League and Football Association was illegal. Footballers were henceforth free to negotiate their own contracts of service.

The Newcastle directors appointed Joe Harvey as manager in an attempt to restore the club's fortunes. United's former captain had been serving an apprenticeship in management at Barrow and Workington. He returned to his old club to find morale low and money tight, yet he succeeded in pulling the club round and going on to achieve some success on the field.

Joe was manager for 13 years and built three successful teams in that time. He got the best out of existing players such as Stan Anderson and John McGrath, brought in Dave Hilley, Jim Iley and Ron McGarry, and developed the talent of young players such as Bob Moncur and Alan Suddick. This team won promotion to the First Division in the 1964-65 season.

After a shaky start in the First Division, Newcastle United consolidated their position. With the purchase of Wyn Davies to wear the number nine shirt, and the emergence of Bryan Robson to play alongside him, and some shrewd buys, this team won the Inter-City Fairs Cup in 1969. After the break-up of the 'Fairs Cup team' Harvey built a third one. This time Harvey brought in the extrovert Malcolm Macdonald, a worthy wearer of the number nine shirt. This team took Newcastle to their eleventh FA Cup final in 1974 when their opponents were Liverpool. Newcastle, however, proved unable to raise their game against the Merseysiders and lost 3-0.

Joe Harvey resigned at the close of the 1974-75 season and was replaced by Gordon Lee, who steered the team to a League Cup Final in 1976, when Newcastle lost to Manchester City. In 1977 Lee moved to Everton and coach Richard Dinnis was appointed to succeed him. After five months of poor results Dinnis was sacked and replaced by Bill McGarry, but the change came too late for Newcastle to escape relegation to the Second Division.

McGarry had a clear-out of players at St James's Park and brought in some fresh faces, but after two seasons in charge he had failed to transform Newcastle into a promotion-winning side, and in September 1982 he was replaced by Arthur Cox.

Cox started cautiously, then in August 1982 startled everyone by signing Kevin Keegan from Southampton. Success did not follow overnight: Newcastle failed to win promotion in the 1982-83 season but in the following season, with Peter Beardsley and Chris Waddle playing alongside him, Keegan led the team back into the First Division. Having done so much to give Newcastle fans the success they craved, the 33-year-old Keegan announced his retirement from football.

Arthur Cox moved to Derby County in August 1983 and was replaced by Jack Charlton. Charlton successfully consolidated Newcastle's position in the First Division, then resigned at the start of the 1985-86 season after being barracked by the fans at St James's Park who had never warmed to his defensive approach to the game. Charlton was replaced by former goalkeeper Willie McFaul. Chris Waddle had left the club to be followed by Peter Beardsley and then by the hugely-talented Paul Gascoigne. McFaul brought in the Brazilian Mirandinha, who was not a success, and after a run of poor results McFaul was replaced by Jim Smith in December 1988.

Smith did some wheeling and dealing in the transfer market: Mirandinha left and was replaced by bustling Mick Quinn. Newcastle won a play-off position but were beaten by Sunderland over two games. Results were only mediocre in the following season and Smith resigned in March 1991 to be replaced by former Argentine international, Ossie Ardiles. Ardiles lasted only 11 months: he was sacked in February 1992 leaving Newcastle only one place from the bottom of the Second Division. Kevin Keegan was brought in as manager and Newcastle narrowly avoided relegation at the end of the 1991-92 season.

Sir John Hall had now taken over the Club and he saw the purchase of Newcastle United as the first step in an ambitious plan to create a Newcastle Sporting Club embracing a number of sports. Sir John financed the rebuilding of St James's and he gave Keegan the money to buy the players the team

Newcastle United, 1995.

needed. Keegan brought in John Beresford, Barry Ven-ison, Rob Lee, Scott Sellars, Pavel Srnicek and Andy Cole, and Newcastle were promoted to the Premier League in 1993. Peter Beardsley was lured back to St James's and Keegan added Ruel Fox, Darren Peacock and Phillipe Albert to his squad. United finished third in the Premiership, securing them a place in the Europe Cup. The Magpies made a good start to the 1994-95 season, but injuries halted their advance, and they were knocked out of the UEFA Cup by Athletico Bilbao. Kevin Keegan then sold Andy Cole, receiving Keith Gillespie in part exchange. Newcastle finished sixth in the Premier League and Keegan entered the summer of 1995 determined to strengthen his squad and make another bid for honours. Keegan chose players with style, including Les Ferdinand and David Ginola, but after the disappointments of failing to win the Premiership in the previous seasons some of his critics thought that results had been sacrificed to flair particularly when he brought in the notoriously erratic Faustino Asprilla. Kevin Keegan, however, was always his own man: he refused to change his approach to the game and most fans liked the exciting, attacking football he laid on for them. When he signed Alan Shearer for £15 million the fans were delighted. When it appeared that he had finally assembled the team of his heart Keegan announced in January 1997: 'I feel that I have taken the club as far as I can, and that it would be in the best interests of all concerned if I resigned'. Few fans would have agreed with Keegan and most would have preferred him to continue as manager, but Keegan, as always, knew his own mind and he was determined to leave.

Kenny Dalglish was chosen as Keegan's successor at St James's Park. Dalglish had an impressive record as a player and as a manager, and like Keegan he had his own approach to the game. He tightened up Newcastle's defence and shaped a team more difficult to beat but less attractive to watch. In his 20 months in the managerial chair at St James's he sold £24.6 million worth of players and spent £34.4 million on new ones. These changes meant that Dalglish never fielded a settled team. There were also some public relations disasters during his period of manager. He was accused of attempting to browbeat non-League club Stevenage before their FA Cup tie with United, and in March 1998 two of Newcastle's directors resigned from the board after revelations concerning their private lives. Dalglish was in no way to blame for the latter but the publicity was not good for the club. The decline was dramatic. Newcastle ended the 1996-97 season as runners-up in the Premiership and narrowly escaped relegation in the 1997-98 season. Dalglish steered the team to a FA Cup Final against Arsenal in May 1998 when Newcastle lost 2-0, leaving many Magpie fans critical of Dalglish's tactical approach to this important match. When Newcastle made a disappointing start to the 1998-99 season, Dalglish was replaced by former Dutch international, Ruud Gullit. Gullit promised the fans 'sexy football', but he had inherited a squad of over 50 professionals on top wages and first he had to slim down the existing playing staff before he could bring in new players. He asked the fans to allow him time to put together a team capable of winning the highest honours.

The 1998-99 season, therefore, was one of transition for Newcastle United, which ended with a middle of the table position in the Premier League. However Newcastle, once again, fought their way to an FA Cup final, where they faced Manchester United. Manchester United were already Premier League champions when they met Newcastle at Wembley, and they beat the Magpies 2 – 0. Manchester United then went on to complete the treble by winning the European Champions Cup. Ruud Gullit spent the summer break recruiting a number of fresh players, mainly from overseas, in readiness for the new season in August 1999. However, the season started badly for Newcastle United and after picking up only one point from their first six games, Ruud Gullit resigned, to be replaced by veteran manager Bobby Robson. The club enters the new millennium still struggling to fulfil its immense potential.

Women's football is one of the fastest growing sports around the world and in England the number of women players registered with the Football Association has tripled to 21,500 this decade. Women first took up the game during World War I when factory and shipyard workers formed teams to raise money for war-time charities. In 1921, however, the Football Association banned women from League grounds stating: 'The game of football is quite unsuited for females and should not be encouraged.' It was not until 1993 that the FA accepted women into the game, establishing a women's football committee and taking administrative control of the Women's Premier League and national squad. There are several women's teams in the Newcastle area playing in local leagues and there is no doubt that their number will increase over the next few years.

There has been horse-racing of one kind or another in Northumberland for the last 350 years. Races are known to have been held at Killingworth on a stretch of moor land in the early 17th century and ran there for over 100 years before being transferred to Newcastle's Town Moor in 1721 where they attracted huge crowds and became an occasion for heavy drinking and gambling. Facilities for spectators were very primitive, although a grandstand for 'the quality' was built in 1800. The first race for the Northumberland Plate was introduced in 1833, and for the next 30 years Newcastle race meetings attracted some of the finest horses in the country with jockey Tommy Lye winning the Plate six times between 1835 and 1844. In the absence of strict regulations, however, horse owners and gambling associates were suspected of fixing results and this led to the races being moved to a new site, purchased from the Brandling family, at Gosforth Park in 1881. Many people forecast that the move would bring about the end of the traditional races: the new course was a four mile walk from the city

A classic shot of Newcastle Race Course from Fred Halliday, photographer on The Evening World, 1912.

centre and spectators would have to pay an entrance charge. However, the pessimists were proved wrong: Newcastle Races – especially Northumberland Plate Day – still drew the crowds even if they no longer attracted the best horses.

The racecourse at Gosforth Park was taken over by the Army during World War I and the grandstand was badly damaged in a fire. Rebuilding and repairs were carried out after 1919 and in 1920 there was the highest ever attendance at a Plate meeting when 105,810 people watched Irish Lake storm past the winning post. In 1924 a tramline was extended from the city to Gosforth Park making it easier for spectators to reach the racecourse, and an increasing number of better-off patrons travelled to race meetings in their own cars. Although the facilities for spectators showed little improvement in the 1920s and 30s a growing number of women were accompanying their husbands to race meetings, and 'race week' became part of the North East's social calendar where women paraded in the latest fashions and expensive perfume mingled with the horsy smells of the racecourse.

As in World War I, Gosforth Park was taken over by the Army after the outbreak of hostilities in 1939. Nissen huts and mess halls were built in the grounds and racing facilities fell into disrepair. Although strenuous efforts were made to get things back to normal after 1945 the first post-war race for the Northumberland Plate had to be transferred to Liverpool. However, after this horse-racing entered a boom period with large crowds turning up to race meetings at Gosforth Park.

The course also attracted some of the finest horses ridden by the country's leading jockeys. Northumberland Plate winners in the 1950s included Joe Mercer (1953), Gordon Richards (1954), and Lester Piggot (1955).

In 1952 the running of the Northumberland Plate was moved from the traditional Wednesday to a Saturday and a crowd of 40,000 turned up to watch the race. Many miners who had previously been at work when the race for the Plate was run were able to attend on their week-end off, and they came with plenty of money in their pockets. The race had always been known as the Pitman's Derby and this was more true in the 1950s than it had ever been before.

The boom years, however, were coming to an end. The Betting and Gaming Act of 1960 legalised off-course betting and the betting shop became a familiar sight in Britain's towns and cities. This piece of legislation together with the showing of live racing on television caused a decline in the numbers attending race meetings in the 1960s and several racecourses had to close. The survival of Gosforth Park owed much to the stewardship of two post-war clerks of course: Randolph Gibson and A.C. Newton. Gibson was clerk of course for the 20 years after 1945 and he had the task of getting the course back into working order after the ravages of the war years and then leading it into the more prosperous 1950s. A.C. Newton joined the Gosforth Park staff in 1962 and served until 1988. He trebled the number of race meetings, increased sponsorship and developed the property held by Gosforth Park in order to bring in additional revenue. A fire in December 1962 severely damaged the grandstand at the course but with financial assistance from the Horse Betting Levy Board it was rebuilt and officially opened in April 1965. Newton carried on with the modernisation of the course as finance allowed, and Gosforth Park survived during a period when several other racecourses were sold off to property developers.

The sport of Kings is no less the sport of Queens. In 1962 the Queen Mother, whose ancestor Sir George Bowes had several of his horses entered for the Plate, attended Gosforth Park on the 100th anniversary of the Blaydon Races song, and she paid a second visit in 1973 when the Whitbread Gold Cup was run in Newcastle. In June 1993 the Queen, another lover of the turf, attended the Newcastle Races, the first reigning monarch to do so.

Another landmark in the history of the course was the emergence of female jockeys. The first Ladies' Race at Gosforth Park was held on 5th June 1970, when Jackie Ward riding St Remy romped to victory in the International Savanas' Stakes.

The 1980s saw the Gosforth Park course in financial difficulties. The costs of running the course were rising while revenue was falling and in 1982 the accounts of the High Gosforth Park Company, the owner of the course, moved into the red. In 1988 David Parmley became general manager of the company and clerk of the course, with the aim of running the company along more commercial lines. The new board of directors' solution was to build new housing and an exhibition centre on Gosforth Park land. The company's first planning application was rejected by Newcastle City Council, but a scaled down version was approved only to be rejected by the Secretary of State for the Environment with the words 'there is no special case to alter national policy which protects the green belt'.

The future of Gosforth Park looked bleak, when in July 1994 the Midlands millionaire, Stanley Clarke, through his company Northern Racing, bought the course for £3.5 million. Mr Clarke was a keen horse-racing fan and he put forward a five year plan of refurbishment and development. He was as good as his word and within three years had spent £3 million on updating facilities. An interest free loan of £900,000 was also obtained from the Horserace Betting Levy Board, sponsorship was substantially increased, and Mr Clarke negotiated a lucrative deal with Sky Sports TV. To crown these efforts, in 1998 Gosforth Park received the Regional Racecourse of the Year award from the Racegoers' Club. At the end of the 20th century, therefore, the future of horse-racing in Newcastle upon Tyne looks secure with a modern racecourse operating on a sound financial basis.

Cricket on Tyneside has never gained the support enjoyed by the game in Yorkshire and Lancashire. The Northumberland County team has been an undistinguished member of the Minor Counties since 1896 and has never had its hands on any silverware, although in 1960 the Northumberland County player, R. W. Smithson, was awarded the Wilfred Rhodes Trophy for scoring 563 runs with an average of 70.38, a feat that placed him top of the Minor Counties batting averages in the season. Northumberland is the only team in the Minor Counties to have its own ground, but this is a mixed blessing because the upkeep of the ground in Osborne Avenue, Jesmond, means that fewer resources are available to devote to strengthening the team. As the County team approaches the new century its hopes lie with the development of several young players of promise.

Cricket lovers would argue that all sporting activity – especially the playing of cricket – should not be measured in terms of trophies won and revenue taken at the gate. Playing the game for its own sake is still a powerful ethic. Several Newcastle-based cricket clubs have been in existence for over a century and their teams still play for enjoyment of the game before small but appreciative crowds. The long-established clubs of Benwell Hill, Benwell and Walbottle, County Club and South Northumberland play in the Priory League; and the newer clubs of DSS, Gosforth Park and Newcastle City play in the Three Counties Northumberland League. A feature of the local game in recent years had been the advent of players of Asian origin turning out for Newcastle-based teams, and the addition of their cricketing talents has been warmly received by cricket lovers on Tyneside.

Sponsorship, however, has touched cricket as it has affected most sports in the 20th century. In the 1970s several local firms came forward to sponsor County matches and local cricket leagues, and in 1981 Callers-Pegasus introduced the first of a decade of 'Cricket Festivals' in which leading cricketers were brought to Jesmond to play in specially arranged matches.

Few sports have undergone so many changes over the course of the 20th century as Rugby Union. In 1900 Rugby Union in Newcastle was a bastion of the amateur

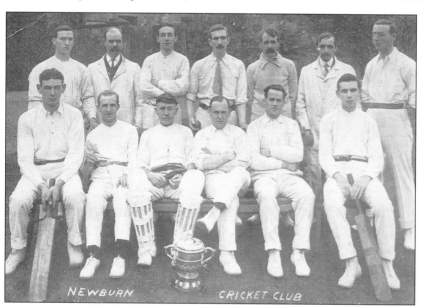

Newburn Cricket Club, 1911.

spirit in sport. Local clubs played other clubs purely for the love of the game, and often at some financial loss in terms of time spent away from work in order to train and travel to matches. The end of the century finds Rugby Union organised on professional lines with teams playing in leagues and challenge cup competitions. Sponsorship and television fees together with increased gate receipts have brought more money into the game and this has been used to pay players' wages and finance transfer deals, often involving overseas players. Some local clubs still consist of amateurs but the major Rugby Union club on Tyneside is Newcastle Falcons which has embraced the professional approach with considerable success.

The present Newcastle Falcons Club is descended from the Gosforth Rugby Club founded in 1877. The Gosforth Club had a nomadic existence, for many years it shared a ground with Northern Rugby Club in Gosforth, until it acquired its own ground in 1952. In 1990 the club moved to a new ground at Kingston Park, then played its first matches for the 1998-99 season at Gateshead International Stadium before reverting to Kingston Park. Gosforth won the John Player Cup in April 1976 when they defeated Rosslyn Park in the final at Twickenham, and retained the cup in the following year when they defeated Waterloo. These were halcyon days for the club.

The 1980s saw the creeping professionalisation of Rugby Union and in August 1995 the sport became openly professional. Sir John Hall took over the old Gosforth Club as part of his plans to create a Newcastle Sporting Club. Rob Andrew, who has won a record 71 caps for his country, was made director of rugby of the newly-named Newcastle Falcons and with plenty of money at his disposal he proceeded to recruit top coaching staff and several world-class players. The team was admitted to the Second Division of the Premier League in 1995 and won promotion to the First Division in 1996. The Falcons then went on to win the championship in 1998. In March 1999 Sir John Hall sold his majority share holding in the club to Ponteland millionaire, Dave Thompson, who promised to continue to provide the financial support needed to keep the Falcons among the country's top teams. The close of the 1998-99 season saw the Falcons in the final of the Tetley's Bitter Cup, when they lost to Wasps by 19 points to 29.

Boxing was well established in Newcastle at the turn of the century and there were regular promotions in local halls. Benwell-born Jack Palmer held the British heavyweight title 1903-6, and he fought Tommy Burns for the world heavyweight championship in 1909. In 1909 the North East's first purpose-built boxing stadium was opened in Newcastle's St James's Hall. This famous boxing venue was pulled down in 1930 and replaced by a larger stadium known as New St James's Hall. Boxing attracted many young men into its professional ranks in the depressed conditions of the 1920s and 30s, but without doubt the most famous Tynesider was Seaman Tommy Watson who won the British featherweight title in 1932 and went on to fight Kid Chocolate for the world featherweight title in New York. Boxing drew good crowds after World War II, but these tailed off in the 1950s and the Newcastle stadium was converted into a bingo hall in 1968. Boxing revived in the 1980s although Newcastle lacked a suitable venue in which to stage top class contests. Promoter Norman Fawcett put on shows at the Mayfair Ballroom in the 1990s which gave local up-and-coming boxers an opportunity of fighting

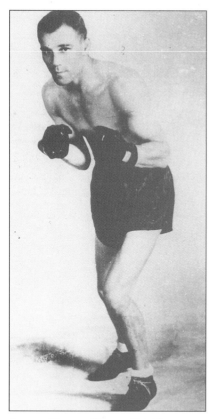

Archie Potts

Seaman Tommy Watson, British Featherweight Champion, 1932-34.

before a home crowd. Newcastle-born John Davison won the British featherweight title in 1992 and in the following year lost to Steve Robinson in a contest for the world title. As the 20th century draws to a close the Mayfair has been closed, meaning the loss of one venue, however in 1999 world title fights were successfully staged in Newcastle's Telewest arena.

Professional wrestling was first staged at New St James's Hall in 1930 and became a regular weekly feature after 1936 until the hall turned over to bingo sessions. Many famous wrestlers fought at the hall, including Bert Assirati the British heavyweight champion, who appeared regularly in the 1940s. After the closure of New St James's Hall a few wrestling matches were staged at Newcastle's City Hall when large crowds turned up to see Big Daddy and others in action, and in 1999 wrestling was staged for the first time in the Telewest Arena.

Swimming became a popular sport in the late 19th century and the Northumberland Road swimming baths were built at this time and replaced by the City Baths on the same site in 1928. Swimming baths were also built in other parts of Newcastle and have been refurbished over the years although the city still lacks a 50 metre Olympic-style pool. Local swimmers have had to travel to Leeds to complete their preparations for swimming competitions. In spite of this, Susan Rolph of Newcastle City Swimming Club won two gold, one silver and two bronze medals in the Commonwealth Games held at Kuala Lumpur in September 1998, and was awarded a gold medal for winning the European 100 metres freestyle title in July 1999. She is now looking forward to competing in the 2000 Olympics in Sydney. An Olympic-style pool would cost at least £5 million and the City Council is preparing an application for a Lottery grant to help towards the cost of providing a modern pool.

The City of Newcastle Golf Club was established in 1891, followed a year later by the Newcastle United Golf Club, making these two famous golf clubs the oldest in the City's boundaries. Over the years the two clubs have accumulated much silverware and they celebrated their centenaries with pride, although the going has not always been easy. The clubs have had to overcome financial crises and head off attempts to encroach on their land. The Northumberland Golf Club was founded in 1898. Gosforth Club was founded in 1906, Westerhope in 1941 and Gosforth Park in 1971. The older clubs began as male preserves but women have made their way into them, playing the game for pleasure and winning their share of trophies in various golf tournaments. In 1981 the prestigious Ladies British Open Championship was played at the Gosforth course of the Northumberland Golf Club.

Elswick Harriers is the oldest athletic club in Newcastle, founded in 1899. It was, by the turn of the century, a popular and well organised running club and one of its members, Frank Melville, won the Morpeth to Newcastle Road Race in 1908. The inter-war years was something of a golden age for the club in terms of the calibre of its runners, the facilities it provided, and the club's high reputation in the world of athletics. Club runner, Alex Burns, was a member of the British team at the Los Angeles Olympics in 1932 and at the Berlin Olympics in 1936. In 1952, another club runner, Alan Lillington, was in the British team at the Helsinki Olympics. The 1960s and 70s were relatively undistinguished years for Elswick Harriers, but there

Thomson of Newcastle United, driving off from the second tee, c.1930, in this Evening World photograph.

was an upturn in activity in the 1980s, and at the Los Angeles Olympics in 1984 club runner, Mike McLeod, won a silver medal in the 10,000 metres. Ladies sections were formed in the club in the 1930s and 50s but did not flourish. It was not until 1979 that a third attempt was made and this time it proved successful, with many young women taking up running in the 1980s and 90s.

There are several other athletic clubs in Newcastle: Claremont Road Runners, Gosforth Harriers, Heaton Harriers and Valli Harriers, who are all likely to benefit from National Lottery money trickling down to local clubs. Although Jonathan Edwards, the world triple jump champion, is a member of a Gateshead club he is resident in Newcastle and an influential role model for many young athletes in the area.

In addition to the races staged for club runners there is also the highly successful annual Great North Run from Claremont Road in Newcastle to South Shields. This charity run was first organised by Hebburn-born Olympic medallist, Brendan Foster, in 1991 and it is now firmly established as one of the region's main events.

One sport that has retained its purely amateur status throughout the 20th century is hockey. The oldest hockey club in Newcastle is St George's, which began in Benwell in 1896 and now plays in the North East League. For over a century the club

Newcastle Chronicle & Journal Ltd.

The Great North Runners, 1982: and still 13 miles to go.

An exciting incident in the game at Gosforth between Newcastle Ladies and Armstrong College c.1930, an Evening World photograph.

fielded only a male hockey team, but in 1997 it formed a women's team which plays in the Northumberland League as Newcastle Ladies, alongside other local women's teams from the DSS and the Universities of Newcastle and Northumbria. The officials who run the local hockey teams are hard-pressed to keep their clubs in existence. Playing hockey imposes considerable demands on an individual's time and energy, and teenagers now have a wide range of leisure activities open to them. The commitment of hockey-lovers, however, together with the provision of improved facilities should ensure the survival of the sport in the new century.

From The Journal.

Two new spectator sports emerged in the inter-war period: greyhound racing and speedway. Greyhound racing was introduced to Newcastle at Brough Park in 1928 and new tracks at Scotswood and Gosforth were opened in the 1930s. The 'dogs' attracted the punters in the post-war sports boom but attendances began to decline in the 1950s, and the city's greyhound stadiums began to look seedy and run-down. The Scotswood and Gosforth tracks were closed in the 1980s and the land sold to developers. Brough Park still survives and is being refurbished in an attempt to bring back the crowds.

Speedway has shared Brough Park with greyhound racing since 1928. The resident Newcastle Diamonds have had their ups and downs over the years, but they still survive in the Premier League. George Pepper was a great favourite with Newcastle's speedway fans in the 1930s and Ivan Mauger the New Zealand ace became world champion in 1968 while riding for the Diamonds, as did Ole Olesen of Denmark in the 1970s. The crowds may be smaller than they used to be but speedway fans are still passionately loyal to their team.

Ice hockey and basketball were brought to Newcastle by Sir

John Hall, as part of his abortive attempt to create a Newcastle Sporting Club embracing football, rugby and other sports. In 1996 Sir John bought the Durham Wasps, renamed them the Cobras, and after a spell in Sunderland the team arrived in Newcastle. Unfortunately, the fans of the old Wasps did not rally to the transplanted team and attendances fell to 2,500. In the summer of 1998 Sir John Hall surrendered his ice hockey franchise and it looked as though the team would die, written off as a failed venture. However, Superleague, the sports governing body, decided that an ice hockey team should continue to operate in the North East and it provided sufficient finance to ensure the team's survival for another season. The team was renamed the Riverkings and with Alex Dampier, a former Great Britain coach, and Canadian Mike O'Connor, as general manager in charge, the aim is to ensure survival by attracting larger crowds and developing local players. The other team purchased by Sir John Hall for his proposed Sporting Club was the basketball team the Eagles. The Eagles have successfully established themselves in the Budweiser League and built up a good local following.

At the end of the 19th century there were five tennis clubs in Newcastle and there are now twelve, including the Northumberland Lawn Tennis and Squash Rackets Club in Jesmond, which is sometimes used as a venue for international tennis tournaments. Bowling has become increasingly popular with retired people and there are now several bowling clubs in the City's boundaries. For younger and more energetic men and women there is an increasing number of squash clubs, a development closely linked with a growing demand for greater physical fitness. Cycling was immensely popular at the beginning of the century, both as an individual recreation and as a sport, but interest in it has declined steadily over the years.

An attempt to revive rowing on the Tyne, a mass spectator sport in Victorian times, took place in 1997 when Northumberland Water sponsored an inter-varsity boat race between the Universities of Durham and Newcastle. The trophies presented to the winning eights were named after two 19th century rowing heroes: the Clasper Trophy for the men and the Chambers Trophy for women. Crowds of over ten thousand lined the river banks to watch the races, and it was proposed to alternate the event between the Tyne and the Wear. After the completion of an environment improvement scheme at Newburn in the 1980s this stretch of the Tyne has been used to stage several regattas.

The fortunes of the various sports on Tyneside have fluctuated over the course of the 20th century, but the end of the century finds most of them in good shape. Sports facilities have been vastly improved for both spectators and

The Empire Rowing Club c.1900

Newcastle Chronicle & Journal Ltd.

Rowing from Scotswood to Newburn, 1978.

participants, and Newcastle has top teams and individuals represented in most of the country's major sports. In addition, efforts are being made to raise standards in sports that lag behind the others. The growing participation of women in sporting activities can be expected to continue, as can the development of special sporting events for disabled people. There is little sign that mass interest in sport is likely to diminish in the new century.

⌒ Archie Potts lectured at the University of Northumbria, and since retirement has been involved with Tyneside Open College local history courses. A member of the Association of Sports Historians, he is the author of three books on sports topics and is currently researching a history of professional wrestling on Tyneside.

Culture City

David Whetstone

THERE WAS A TIME, ACCORDING TO WELL-PLACED VISITORS FROM THE SOUTH, when Newcastle was a grand and glorious city, and Gateshead was where you held your nose and shielded your eyes before reaching the Tyne Bridge. Well, times change. But more of that a little later.

One way of reaching Newcastle while avoiding the place over the river was to come by train, which is what I did when I first ventured to the Geordie capital in 1979, although I had no motive other than the lack of a car. I clearly remember thinking, as I stepped out of Central Station beneath John Dobson's stunning portico, that here was a place worth devoting some time to. Admittedly I had been living in Doncaster, a mecca only for horse racing enthusiasts, but the immediate impact of Newcastle's architecture, combined with the buzz of early evening comings and goings and a bus driver's (then) barely penetrable accent, was intoxicating. It didn't take me long to discover that Newcastle had art galleries, theatres, an orchestra and as many small venues for entertainment as you could wish for. For a journalist interested in the arts, it was a little piece of paradise – and no disrespect to dear old Donny which had supplied many a memorable pie 'n' pea supper.

After 20 years, 17 of them actually resident in Newcastle, I still believe it is a great city; England's best provincial city, in fact. But in having affection for a person or a thing or a place, you must also feel ambitious on its behalf. It is not enough for me to think Newcastle is a great city; outsiders must also see it that way. In the light of that, I would like it to be taken that any criticism is intended to be constructive.

A foray into the archives takes us back to a report in *The Journal* of October 14, 1904, when the century was fresh and young. The previous day Lord Ridley had opened the Laing Art Gallery, a glorious confection designed – inevitably – more in the style of the century just gone

The Laing Art Gallery, c.1920, with the old Central Library alongside on New Bridge Street.

173

than with a nod to a brave new world. The Corporation of Newcastle, said the aristocrat, had 'accepted the somewhat responsible task of taking charge' of the gallery. It was generally understood, therefore, that the whole community of Newcastle had endorsed its action. Throughout the newspaper report, the word 'applause' appears frequently in brackets, as well it might since this was a gathering of the great and the good. In previous years, went on Lord Ridley, the city had 'not been wanting in its efforts towards exhibitions of art and the endeavour to make art wider known and more prosperous. These were the days of patronage by wealthy individuals, the men who had both created and done well out of the industry along the Tyne. Alex Laing, it was reported, had originally estimated that the gallery would cost him some £20,000; the final cost was probably nearer £30,000.

In the previous century it was men such as Alex Laing who had enabled the Pre-Raphaelite artists to stay off the breadline, as a memorable late 20th Century exhibition in the Laing Art Gallery would explain. There may have been no hint of it in 1904 but these men were a dying breed. Would their like ever be seen again? An appeal was made, during the opening of the gallery, to the 'munificence of private donors'. Newcastle had its gallery but had not yet amassed the art collection it would house. It was Sunderland, actually, which boasted the first municipal museum and art gallery in the country.

When, nearly 10 years after the Laing was opened, Gateshead put in a bid for the Shipley Bequest, there was derision in some quarters. The Bequest included a more than decent art collection and money towards building the gallery to house it. Newcastle didn't need it now but *The Journal*'s correspondence pages immortalise the braying sarcasm of those Newcastle folk who couldn't for the life of them understand why Gateshead did.

A downside, perhaps, of living in a regional capital, and particularly one so far from cities of comparable size and stature, is a tendency to high-minded snootiness; a dangerous attitude since it can curdle into complacency.

By the time I came to Newcastle it had been through the ravages of two world wars and an apparently mad municipal desire to bulldoze away the architectural legacy of the 19th Century in favour of concrete by the vertical and

Newcastle Chronicle & Journal Ltd.

The interior of the Theatre Royal in 1966 when the 130-year-old theatre was declared to be 'ailing and infirm'.

horizontal acre. The sad remains of Newcastle's old library can be seen stuck incongruously into a brick wall off Northumberland Street. If this was the brave new world I referred to earlier, then it was patently brave and stupid. Fortunately the hands of the demolition men were stayed in time to save much of Newcastle Quayside and what remained of the Dobson/Grainger-designed city centre. In 1979 the Laing Art Gallery and the Theatre Royal were still at the heart of the city's cultural life, although the latter, behind its glorious façade, was a grotty mess.

The new Central Library rises from the dust as John Dobson Street is blasted through to New Bridge Street in 1969.

This was pointed out in no uncertain terms by members of the Royal Shakespeare Company which had been wooed to the city two years previously after some admirable campaigning involving city councillors. On this occasion, they were sharp, far-sighted and united. Other cities, such as Glasgow and Manchester, would have paid a mighty sum to have provided the Stratford-based company the annual northern outpost it desired. Newcastle won, and whatever city-based theatre directors might say about the subsidy-rich southerners pinching their sponsors and their audience once a year, few could successfully argue that the annual RSC season hasn't done us proud. Many people will take to their grave the memory of Kenneth Branagh's Henry V or Anton Lesser's Richard III at Newcastle Theatre Royal. Dame Judi Dench was in the first company to take up residence in the city in 1977, among others whose names are now in the Olivier/Gielgud rank of familiarity.

There have been good seasons and average seasons since, and a few productions which have been mind-blowing. Successive RSC artistic directors have referred to Newcastle's discerning and intelligent theatre-going audiences. Not for actors in Newcastle the easy applause of the happy West End tourist, and the theatre scene is the healthier for it.

The more I learned about the arts in Newcastle, the more I realised how much was owed to certain inspirational individuals. Michael Hall, a 26-year-old from Whitley Bay, had just graduated from King's College, Durham (later to become Newcastle University), when he persuaded his father to part with £1,000 to help him set up a professional orchestra in the North-East. In 1998, when the orchestra was celebrating its 40th anniversary, he told me: 'It had to be a chamber orchestra rather than a big symphony orchestra. But I knew that we could rival the bigger orchestras in terms of quality and I always knew if I could get it started it would be around a long time.' He wasn't wrong. The first concert was in Newcastle City Hall on September 24, 1958, and the programme featured Mozart's Prague Symphony, Schumann's Cello Concerto in A Minor and Beethoven's Symphony No.2 in D. The hall was

The Northern Sinfonia at rehearsals in 1959.

half full but the applause was warm. The orchestra, the Northern Sinfonia, is still with us.

It was a similar love of poetry which inspired Neil Astley to set up Bloodaxe Books as a way of getting the words of brilliant but over-looked poets into the public domain. When major publish-ers in the capital were begin-ning to pay lip service to poet-ry, Astley, with his gritty-sounding northern imprint, was blowing the dust off it and making it sexy. Bloodaxe Books has moved out to Northumberland now but it has left its resonances in Newcastle, a city which throbs with literary achievement and endeavour. Bloodaxe has just celebrated 21 years.

Perhaps Tom Pickard should have been mentioned ahead of Neil Astley. He was the enterprising 18-year-old who, back in 1964, saw poetic potential in a little-loved yet historic corner of Newcastle. He offered Newcastle Corporation 10 bob a week for the use of the Morden Tower (ironically mis-printed in the Newcastle Evening Chronicle as the 'Modern' Tower), part of the ancient city walls – or, rather, it was his then wife, Connie, who, according to a *Journal* interviewer who met them in 1965, had the idea. 'Tom is a stylish mess with long hair and clothes which are part Bohemian, part work-man's,' wrote the interviewer. 'Connie is as neat and pretty as can be, and serves you with lemon tea.'

Many leading poets have read from their work in the comfort-free confines of the Morden Tower, including, famously, the American 'beat' poet Allen Ginsberg who cavorted with a tipsy-looking Basil Bunting. Bunting, who worked for many years in Newcastle – at *The Journal*, in fact – produced the epic poem *Briggflatts* while travelling home to Wylam on the train, and once favourably compared Tom with the young Auden.

Writers also helped to put Newcastle's theatre on the map. I never met C.P. Taylor but a produc-tion at Newcastle Playhouse of *Good*, his incredibly perceptive play about Nazism, leaves an indelible impression. His work has also been a staple of Live Theatre's output, where yet more inspiring indi-viduals – not the least Max Roberts, the artistic director – have striven for less than ample reward.

Live – dedicated to new writing – has given us a succession of good things. Tom Hadaway's plays, *Yesterday's Children* and *Long Shadows*, deserved to be seen and praised all over Britain, as did the tweaked version of *Close The Coalhouse Door* (words by Alan Plater, music by Alex Glasgow) with which it reopened after an extensive revamp. Others spring to mind: Janet Archer who runs Dance City and has had people dancing who once would have rather died; Mike Tilley who created Newcastle Arts Centre out of a collection of decaying historic buildings; Murray Martin and fellow members of Amber, one of the most talented film-making and photography groups in the country, and instrumental in saving Newcastle Quayside from destruction; Andy Balman and the group of youngsters who created the Riverside, Newcastle's influential independent music venue; Chas Chandler and Nigel Stanger who gave the city the Arena which ensured the big rock groups and sporting events kept coming to Newcastle.

But what of the 21st century? As I write this, there are interesting times ahead. If there ever was great rivalry between the local authorities of Gateshead and Newcastle, then the hatchet, at least as far as the arts are concerned, appears to have been buried.

It isn't an altruistic thing. Gateshead, long the poor relation, put its faith in the visual arts when to do so was unfashionable and courageous. Where Newcastle seemed complacent, its near neighbour seemed daring, commissioning artists to create artworks in the open air which would be vulnerable not only to public appreciation but public derision.

Gateshead's embracing of the visual arts was much in evidence at its National Garden Festival, which in turn was evidence of the fact that the town south of the Tyne, by dint of its comparatively disadvantaged state, could access large sums of public money.

When the National Lottery became a fact of British life in 1994, Northern Arts – based in Newcastle but serving the northern region – put a Case for Capital before the Government and the Arts Council, arguing that the North-East and Cumbria lacked major art venues. Gateshead, desperately in need of regeneration and having lacked the money-spinning attentions of the Tyne & Wear Development Corporation, was a prime candidate for whatever money might be winging our way. Importantly, the council had a track record in the arts. When the *Angel of the North* was erected in 1997, it could no longer be said that Gateshead was merely the featureless approach to Newcastle. Antony Gormley's sculpture may not be loved by all but I stand among its fans. Had I arrived in the North-East last week by car, the Angel would have done for me what John Dobson's Central Station portico did for me 20 years ago. Having

Steve Wood

Morden Tower in 1967. Tom and Connie Pickard created the Newcastle poetry revival of the late 1960s which still continues today.

The future: an artist's impression, Gateshead Millennium Bridge designed by Wilkinson Eyre Architects and Gifford & Partners, and the Baltic Centre for Contemporary Art.

had the pluck to back the Angel, built at a cost officially in the region of £800,000 (and not a penny of it from the pockets of Gateshead citizens), Gateshead was well-placed to win the millions required to convert the Baltic Flour Mills into a contemporary arts centre, due to open early in the 21st century. And when Newcastle prevaricated over the chance to build a regional music centre to house the Northern Sinfonia, Folkworks, a music school and two new concert halls, it was Gateshead who nipped in to claim the spoils.

All of a sudden Newcastle began to look hopelessly out-manoeuvred. Assuming the Lottery millions were forthcoming (a decision was expected in October 1999), the Northern Sinfonia, a feather in Newcastle's cap for 40 years, would be moving to Gateshead.

There were tales of division in the city council between those who saw value in the arts and those who regarded them as fripperies to suit the middle classes of Jesmond and Gosforth. Meanwhile Gateshead roared ahead. Criticism of the Angel sank without trace once it was up and motorists proved well up to the challenge of driving past it without crashing. Newcastle still has its Theatre Royal (now beautifully refurbished) and its Laing Art Gallery (ambitious expansion plans on the drawing board), and there is talk of a refurbished Dance City and a Centre for the Children's Book. Live Theatre has grave financial problems at the time of writing, though is producing brilliant work; the

Riverside has gone, as has the Mayfair, another much-loved music venue; the Hatton Gallery, saved by Dame Catherine Cookson, is enjoying a new lease of life; the future of the Tyne Theatre & Opera House, owned by businessman Karl Watkin, is uncertain.

So is Gateshead going to be the talking point of the 21st century, leaving its fuddy duddy neighbour to dwell on the glories of the past?

Well, a cynic said to me not so long ago that they would not have been building a Millennium Bridge across the Tyne if the Baltic contemporary art gallery and the Music Centre, Gateshead, were to be built on Newcastle Quayside. The powers-that-be in Newcastle and Gateshead know that the developments on either side of the river stand to benefit both of them. With this in mind, they are putting in a joint bid to be declared European Capital of Culture in 2008. That would be quite an accolade, and it would bring incalculable benefits to Tyneside as a whole. Newcastle, no longer the only – or even the biggest – city in the North East (Sunderland earned city status some years ago), nevertheless has the most beautiful centre. It draws an increasing number of students from all over the country and overseas and earns frequent accolades for being a party city or a good place to visit. Recently it has appointed, for the first time, a head of arts and culture to guide it into the 21st century.

My hunch – and I'm not being particularly clever in saying this – is that Newcastle will go from strength to strength, and that that strength will be built on a sense of partnership rather than of airy superiority. In this environment, if we are lucky, even more inspirational individuals will find the conditions right to give us the benefits of their talents. I'll raise a glass to them in anticipation. And here's one final thought, an answer perhaps to a question I asked near the start of this article.

At the opening of Anish Kapoor's sculpture, *Taratantara*, temporarily occupying the void in the part-demolished Baltic Flour Mills in 1999, the architect/entrepreneur Alan Smith, chair of the Baltic board, was talking in glowing terms about the artistic possibilities on both sides of the river. He was talking, in particular, of the gallery shortly to open in his renovation of the old Post Office opposite Newcastle Cathedral.

Not long after, I was talking to a rather more shy Newcastle businessman who is currently investing quite heavily in contemporary art, some of it to go on public display. Would we ever see the like of the 19th century businessmen who patronised the Pre-Raphaelites? Maybe these are they. And if they are, I'll raise my glass to them as well.

∼ David Whetstone is Arts and Entertainment Editor at *The Journal*, Newcastle.

BOOKS FROM NEWCASTLE LIBRARIES & INFORMATION SERVICE

Many of the photographs in *Water Under the Bridges* are from books published by Newcastle Libraries and Information Service.

The *Bygone Newcastle* booklets look at the suburbs of Newcastle through old photographs. Other photographic booklets: *Looking Back At, Gone … But Not Forgotten, Newcastle Revisited*.

LARGER TITLES

Northern City: An Architectural History of Newcastle upon Tyne, Lynn F. Pearson, £5.99

Newcastle upon Tyne: a Selection of the Earliest Photographs, Frank Manders, £4.99

Cinemas of Newcastle, Frank Manders, £4.99

What's in a Name: Some Newcastle Street Names Explained, £2.99

Hidden Newcastle, Christopher Goulding, £5.99

A City of Palaces: Richard Grainger and the Making of Newcastle upon Tyne, Ian Ayris, £6.99

A History of Newcastle's Public Houses: vol 1 Heady Days, the Central Area, Brian Bennison, £4.99

A History of Newcastle's Public Houses: vol 2 Heavy Nights, the North & East, Brian Bennison, £4.99

A History of Newcastle's Public Houses: vol 3 Lost Weekends, the West, Brian Bennison, £4.99

Brewers and Bottlers of Newcastle upon Tyne, Brian Bennison, £4.99

Our Bairns: Glimpses of Tyneside's Children c.1850-c.1950, Joan Foster, £4.99

Those Were the Days, Tom Callaghan, £4.95

Wanderlust, Tom Callaghan, £4.99

The Catherine Cookson Companion, Cliff Goodwin, £13.99

Basil Bunting: a Northern Life, Richard Caddel and Anthony Flowers, £7.99

Diary of a Doctor: Surgeon's Assistant in Newcastle upon Tyne, Edited by Alastair Johnson, £6.99

A Soldier's Life: the Story of Newcastle Barracks, Thomas L. Hewitson, £6.99

On the Waterfront: an Historical Tour of Newcastle's Quayside, Ian Ayris & Trish Sheldon, £6.99

Black Diamonds by Sea: North East Sailing Colliers, Dick Keys & Ken Smith, £5.99

Spanning the Tyne: the Building of the Tyne Bridge, Stafford Linsley, £5.99

Swans of the Tyne: Swan Hunter Ships 1861-1985, Ian Rae & Ken Smith, £3.95

Built With Pride: Tyne Ships 1969-1994, Ian Rae & Ken Smith, £4.99

Tyne to Titanic: the Story of Rescue Ship Carpathia, Ken Smith, £4.99

Down Elswick Slipways: Armstrong's Ships and People, 1884-1918, Dick Keys & Ken Smith, £4.99

From Walker to the World: Charles Mitchell's Low Walker Shipyard, Dick Keys & Ken Smith, £4.99

Turbinia: the Story of Charles Parsons and His Ocean Greyhound, Ken Smith, £4.99

Mauretania: Pride of the Tyne, Ken Smith, £4.99

Tinseltoon: or One Night In Newcastle, a story for children, Christopher Goulding, £4.99

Graingertoon: a Newcastle Adventure, a story for children, Christopher Goulding, £4.99

A free catalogue featuring all our titles in detail is available from Publications, City Library, Princess Square, Newcastle upon Tyne NE99 1DX; tel: 0191 2610691; fax: 0191 2611435.